HUMAN RIGHTS IN THE
MIDDLE EAST

Human Rights in the Middle East

Frameworks, Goals, and Strategies

Edited by
Mahmood Monshipouri

First published in 2011 by
PALGRAVE MACMILLAN® in the United States – a division of
St. Martin's Press LLC, 175 Fifth Avenue, New York, NY 10010.

Where this book is distributed in the UK, Europe and the rest of
the world, this is by Palgrave Macmillan, a division of Macmillan Publishers Limited, registered in England, company number 785998, of
Houndmills, Basingstoke, Hampshire RG21 6XS.

Palgrave Macmillan is the global academic imprint of
the above companies and has companies and representatives
throughout the world.

Palgrave® and Macmillan® are registered trademarks in the
United States, the United Kingdom, Europe and other countries.

ISBN 978–0–230–12061–7

Library of Congress Cataloging-in-Publication Data

Human rights in the Middle East : frameworks, goals, and strategies /
    edited by Mahmood Monshipouri.
      p. cm.
    ISBN 978–0–230–12061–7 (alk. paper)
  1. Human rights—Middle East.   2. Human rights—Religious
aspects—Islam.   3. Islam and politics—Middle East.   I. Monshipouri,
Mahmood, 1952–
    JC599.M53H85 2011
    323.0956—dc23

                                                           2011020954

A catalogue record of the book is available from the British Library.

Design by MPS Limited, A Macmillan Company

First edition: December 2011

10 9 8 7 6 5 4 3 2 1

Printed in the United States of America.

CONTENTS

TABLES

ACKNOWLEDGMENTS

This volume, which grew out of a conference on the Middle East and Islamic Studies, held on the campus of San Francisco State University, October 16–17, 2009, intends to enhance the global parameters of human rights by illustrating ways in which the protections against violence, torture, and discrimination, extrajudicial killings, as well as freedom from hunger in the region—and for that matter, the rest of the world—must be upheld in the name of human dignity, welfare, security, and social justice.

Of particular relevance to this project is the question of whether a commitment to the full range of human rights is even feasible given the cultural diversity, unequal economic circumstances, and socio-economic priorities of the expanding globalized world. It is equally important to ascertain the appropriateness and desirability of applying the international human rights framework in the Middle East. More-over, we hope the debates offered in this volume will shed light on the international human rights project originating from the Middle Eastern countries by helping to define political and human rights dis-courses in a way that transcends traditional and conventional thinking. Thus, in addition to inquiries about how international human rights norms have shaped the consciousness and behavior of actors in the region, we are interested in exploring the ways in which Muslim actors themselves have potentially contributed to the promotion of interna-tional human rights norms.

A culmination of many years of work on human rights in the Middle East and North Africa, this book represents a joint effort by many schol-ars from different disciplines—history, political science, international law, religious studies, public health, and international relations—and various parts of the world, including Australia, Egypt, Iran, Turkey, England, the Palestine, and the United States. I owe a debt of gratitude to all contributors to this volume who submitted several drafts of their proj-ects and endured through the lengthy process of review. Special thanks are also due to Jonathon Whooley and Ali Assareh whose assistance was an equally valuable part of completing this volume. Some of the most insightful remarks that we received were provided by anonymous external reviewers. We gratefully acknowledge their invaluable assistance and support at various stages of this book. Finally, we express our deep gratitude to the Middle East and Islamic Studies Center of the San Francisco State University that made it possible to bring about this human rights workshop.

INTRODUCTION

Mahmood Monshipouri

There is unfortunately little prospect of eliminating all obstacles to protecting human rights in the twenty-first century. Applying universal human rights standards across the globe is a difficult and daunting task. Many problems and challenges lie ahead. One of the most formidable tasks facing the international human rights community is to establish whether a commitment to the full range of human rights is even feasible given the cultural diversity, unequal economic circumstances, and socio-economic priorities of the expanding globalized world. A related focus of this volume will be on the extent to which the dynamics surrounding the human rights challenges in the Middle East conform to or diverge from such dynamics in other parts of the world. Since the protection of all human rights requires perfection regardless of region, two sensible questions to ask regarding the Middle East are: (a) To what extent progress or improvement can realistically be made on the status quo? and (b) To what extent are the apparent or real features of such uniqueness a function of contemporary manifestations of Orientalism and Islamophobia?

Another line of inquiry we would like to pursue in this volume is to ascertain the appropriateness and desirability of applying the international human rights framework in the Middle East. What does the international human rights framework offer Middle Eastern countries? In what ways does it foster local efforts to improve human rights in the Middle East and in what ways does its baggage of imperialism, neoimperialisms, power relations, and appropriations of human rights discourses by governments pursuing their own geopolitical interests damage such local and authentic efforts? This first inquiry inherently leads to a second: Is an Islamic social, political, and legal framework compatible with the notion of human rights? In addressing these two main questions, we hope to take on the task of examining the human rights project, proposing ways to apply universal norms across diverse nations and cultures in the region.

Additionally, we hope the debates offered in this volume will highlight potential contributions to the international human rights project origi- nating from the Middle Eastern countries. Thus, in addition to inqui- ries about how international human rights norms have impacted the consciousness and behavior of actors in the region, we are interested in learning about how Muslim actors—scholars, activists, lawyers, journal- ists, cultural elite, and policymakers—have, and potentially can contribute to the development of international human rights norms. There is a good deal of discussion about the barriers of transcending the application of Western human rights standards. They may have been Western in origin, but they have been globally endorsed, which suggests that human rights norms responded to dangers to human dignity found in all states and regions. We need to engage such discussions in order to substantiate or disprove the reasoning and rationale underlying it all.

Finally, given the state of contemporary international affairs, few discus- sions of human rights in the Middle East can transpire without at least some reference to the relationship between the Middle Eastern countries and the West, particularly the United States, its policies, geopolitical considerations, and human rights practices and discourses. We hope that contributors to this volume will help to illuminate the complexities of this relationship and the impact of its discourses and counterdiscourses on human rights, in a way that transcends traditional and conventional scholarship.

There can be no doubt that the increasing global attention to legal matters and human rights has fostered the idea of holding states to higher moral and legal standards, causing more dissonance than consensus among states on matters of interpretation and enforcement. With some exceptions, states have nevertheless cooperated with the International Criminal Tribunals for Rwanda and the former Yugoslavia, both of which have issued powerful indictments against war criminals. The International Criminal Court (ICC) has come closer to becoming an operational insti- tution. This is evident by the way in which the ICC's Prosecutor Luis Moreno Ocampo has pushed for the arrest of Sudanese President Omar Hassan al-Bashir, the most senior figure and the first sitting head of state, charged and pursued by the court. There are new developments in crimi- nal justice and international criminal law. While many obstacles remain en route to protecting human rights globally, it is important to continue efforts aimed at doing so. Human rights continue to figure in high-level foreign policy, as in the 2011 US-China summit. Similarly, human rights continue to figure in many regional and national developments, as can be seen in Ivory Coast, Honduras, and other cases.

These positive trends have marked a new era in defense of human rights, but the larger question of transnational norms development and transsovereign law enforcement still remain unanswered. Several issues typify practical and normative difficulties facing states, including sovereignty, military and humanitarian intervention, globalization, universal jurisdiction (national courts can prosecute serious human rights violations committed anywhere in the world), and international justice. It is in this context that we turn to the Middle East as a region that has been resistant to the enforcement of universal standards of human rights. It is imperative to explore the possibilities for compatibility—or their absence—between universal human rights norms and the tremendous diversity of cultural traditions, local and national identities, as well as socioeconomic and political conditions. Without taking into account the entire array of factors contributing to human rights violations or improvements, it is not possible to identify variables and policies that affect human rights practices in the region. The Middle Eastern region has no robust regional regime for real human rights protections, whereas some other regions, such as Latin America and Europe, do.

This book represents a joint effort by many scholars from different disciplines (history, political science, international law, religious studies, psychiatry and health sciences, and international relations) and various parts of the world (Australia, Egypt, Iran, Turkey, Palestine, England, and the United States) to explore the contemporary roots of human rights violations in the Middle East. The volume's main focus is to provide a systematic analysis of looking beyond the abuses of human rights in the Middle East with a view toward (1) problematizing traditional doctrinal thinking and concepts in the region; (2) ascertaining historical roots of human rights abuses in the Middle East, and (3) developing strategies for improving human rights conditions of the vast majority of people more generally and those of minorities and marginal communities more particularly. To constructively address and deal with human rights conditions, we will first attempt a thematic analysis to frame the debate by measuring and mapping out the nature of human rights and dignity. Here we will turn to the issues of group rights and localism that give meaning and value to human existence, diversity of perspectives, limits to the defamation of religion, and ways to reconcile Islam and the global normative consensus on human rights. Our analysis will also examine the difficulties as well as challenges one encounters in privileging Islam as either the savior of human rights or the main source of its violations.

In the second section, our focus will then shift to comparative historical studies to demonstrate the underlying human rights abuses in the region. In this section, we set out to examine the Kurdish question, sexual orientation and gender identity, the case study of Iran in the postrevolutionary period, and the extent to which women's rights have been incorporated into the programs of political parties in Turkey. These studies will scrutinize the status and acceptance of human rights conditions in the region. More broadly, this section attempts to illustrate that

Islam per se does not determine developments; that women's rights and political rights, inter alia, depend on more than just a nation's dominant religion; and that it does make a difference that Turkey is officially secular even with an Islamic party in power.

This volume's final section identifies strategies of promoting human rights through nongovernmental organizations (NGOs) and mechanisms to include minorities—both economically and politically—in national affairs. Also in this section, we argue that in the post-9/11 era, some Islamic movements have distanced themselves from condemning human rights and repositioned themselves toward embracing important parts of the internationally recognized human rights. Such a shift has enhanced the internal logical consistency and legitimacy of the human rights notion throughout the region. Human rights NGOs will need to work with states and civil society not only on whether their goals are desirable but chiefly on whether they are feasible and sustainable in the long run. To do so, it is necessary to engage Islamic networks, scholars, and activists, who—through study of and interaction with society—have gained a better understanding of local conditions, that is, the socioeconomic status of women, children, and the elderly. This cooperation toward achieving common goals is the key to finding the most effective strategies to obtain a wider acceptance of human rights standards in the region. To this end, both Islam, as a religion, and Islamic law (*Shari'a*), as a legal system, can be positively employed for the promotion of human rights in the Middle East. Thus a pragmatic version of Islam can affect developments if it is carefully related or adjusted to the facts of the region.

The findings and implications resulting from this volume will have theoretical as well as policy application. We hope to demonstrate the relevance of area studies to the study of contemporary international affairs. The similarities, differences, and interactions between Middle Eastern countries and the West must be fully explored to prevent potential conflicts in the future. Still, this volume, which grew out of a conference on the Middle East and Islamic Studies, held on the campus of San Francisco State University, October 16–17, 2009, intends to analyze the global parameters of human rights by illustrating ways in which the protections against violence, torture, and discrimination, extrajudicial killings, as well as freedom from hunger in the region—and for that matter, the rest of the world—must be upheld in the name of human dignity, welfare, security, and social justice.

Human Rights in the Middle East: An Overview

The spread of democratic values and fundamental freedoms across the globe in the past quarter century has turned the attention of experts to the Muslim world's internal struggles in achieving universal human rights standards. Whether impediments to observing modern notions of human rights in the Muslim world are inherent to Islam or linked to the social, structural, and cultural factors is an issue that has sparked intense debate over the nature of democratic change in these societies. More broadly, the struggle for human rights has revived an old rivalry within the Muslim world between secular rationalists and Islamists. In today's globalizing world, religious heterogeneity, emerging norms, and multiple loyalties have become so intricately entangled that it makes eminent sense, therefore, to talk about values and religious pluralism. Can embracing religious pluralism provide the best hope for effective adjustment to global change and the information age? Is value pluralism a necessary condition for making progress toward achieving social justice in the international community? What role does the human rights discourse play in nudging along the debate between Western and non-Western worlds, and who should be held to account for the persistence of human rights abuses in the Middle East? These are critical and complex issues that should be addressed.

In Iran, Barbara Ann Rieffer-Flanagan points out, there is some basis for hope in the future: There is limited progress on second generation rights (socioeconomic and cultural rights) and the political elites are increasingly using the language of international human rights. A pragmatic Islam that seeks a dynamic interpretation of Islamic law (*Shari'a*) can be an effective alternative to the sacred and textual rigidity of orthodox Islam. On balance, human rights prospects in the Middle East are uncertain if not entirely bleak. But beyond the Middle East, experiences of Muslims in Turkey, Indonesia, and India have been positively linked to human rights and democracy at least in certain periods.

Deciding between competing narratives regarding the relationship—or even the conversation—between religion and human rights has not been an easy affair. This can also be comparatively demonstrated, by examining the role of Catholicism and human rights both in the Western world and Latin America, Hinduism and human rights in India, Confucianism and Buddhism and human rights in East Asia—to cite a few examples. It is worth noting that some ostensibly Christian nations have produced admirable records of human rights and democracy, while others have produced fascism and other forms of totalitarianism. The same nation with the same religious heritage has sometimes produced both. Put very simply, the linkage between religion and human rights needs further nuanced and subtle analysis.

The Catholic Church has faced a myriad of criticisms regarding its complicity in corrupt regimes, gender bias in the nonordination of women and the regulation of reproductive freedom, unfair treatment of its own employees and members, and, perhaps most crucially, the exploitation of dependent and unemancipated persons receiving its services.[1] Over time, however, the influence of the Church's basic theological message and legal forms and policies has arguably helped account for the realization of human rights as a feature of Western legal institutions. The key point to note is that the richness and complexity of Catholicism's role in advancing human rights point to both successes and failures.[2] The Vatican has both identified with some human rights and also endorsed those violating rights, depending on which rights, eras, and issues one is addressing. One Pope was all for democracy in Poland, and another helped cover up child abuse in Ireland and elsewhere.

Similarly, it is important to understand the ways in which Hindu traditions both strengthen and weaken the struggle for human rights in South Asia today. Opposition to caste discrimination in the Hindu world has a long history. Yet many Indians tend to attribute the persisting discrimination against untouchables (*Dalits*) to Hinduism. As it is the case in Christianity, Islam, and Judaism, Hinduism has always contained both conservative and reformist, even radical variants.[3] In contemporary India, as Jack Donnelly notes, "Hinduism functions as both a support for and an impediment to the exercise and enjoyment of internationally recognized human rights."[4] The universalist elements of Hinduism—a single *dharma* governing an integrated, divinely infused reality and regulating a universal struggle toward liberation—have provided in both principle and practice an impetus toward shoring up local support for fundamental human rights.[5] Some experts on Islamic law have shown the competing trends in Islamic interpretation, similar to varieties of thought in Christianity, Southern Baptist and Congregationalist interpretations of Christianity.[6]

Likewise, Confucian tradition, with its strong communitarian strands and frameworks, has become a topic of much discussion in recent years. Many observers have argued that Confucianism can be properly interpreted to become compatible with modern human rights with respect to their content, if not legal regulation. Even though Confucianism has historically been based on a hierarchical foundation, especially in the context of patriarchal social and cultural traditions, classical Confucians took the view that all people have the capacity to become flourishing moral persons in the community, if not exemplary sages.[7] Like all traditions, Confucianism has been open to change and development in response to both internal social problems and external pressures. Currently, there exists a strong movement of New Confucians who tend to progressively reinterpret the tradition in robust engagement with the West.[8] As a dynamic tradition, Confucianism can be reinterpreted to provide a minimum of social guarantees for human rights in the form of supportive public policies and political reforms, including constitutionalism and democracy. Contemporary Japan and South Korea provide particularly apt examples for adjusting Confucian-influenced societies to modern human rights standards.[9]

ISLAM AND HUMAN RIGHTS

While focusing largely on the Muslim world, this book has examined both internal and external factors influencing the state and progress of human rights in the Middle East. The central theme underlying this volume's arguments is that religious factors seem extraneous to an understanding of human rights issues in the Muslim world. All religions have developed in patriarchal settings: They are largely expressed in patriarchal terms, and they are heavily influenced by patriarchal values. It is therefore wrong to examine the ambiguities and contradictions in Islamic sacred texts, instead of addressing social and structural causes of economic and political decay. The contributions by Manochehr Dorraj, Turan Kayaoglu, and Halim Rene have demonstrated that renewed emphasis on the relationship between religion and human rights has increasingly become an essential element of law, politics, and society in contemporary Muslim world. By way of contrast, the chapter by Lawrence Davidson has noted that, historically, all rights have local origins and have been shaped by local cultural traditions. Others, such as Anthony Chase, have argued that sexual and gender rights continue to challenge traditionally narrow notions of what constitutes a protected status against discrimination. Chase underscores the point that respect for rights based on a singular identity risks forgoing the emergence of fluid, multiple, and evolving identities of Muslims.

Although the issue of how to implement human rights remains unresolved, the gap between the Muslim and Western worlds over the issue of what constitutes human rights has been narrowed. The dispute between the two worlds over human rights is not a conflict in dialectics but one of perspective. In the post-9/11 era, Islamists and secular human rights forces have inherited overlapping priorities in areas such as the use of security prisons and courts, electoral rights, and freedom of expression, leading the way for bridging the religious-secular divide that had vexingly beleaguered human rights conditions in the Middle East.

Over the centuries, Muslim countries have been subject to political machinations and manipulation by great powers, driven both by rivalry and collusion. In the Middle East, for example, the Western world has gained more access to the region's oil resources by working with dictators rather than democratic regimes accountable to their people. The U.S. strategic ties with the governments of Egypt, Saudi Arabia, Turkey, and Pakistan have always been based on purely instrumental grounds, reflecting geopolitical impulses. The persistence of geopolitical concerns, especially in the aftermath of the U.S. occupation of Iraq, has rendered the work of human rights groups and organizations immensely difficult in countries such as Egypt.

Security considerations have dramatically narrowed the space for human rights claims and activities in the name of the global campaign dubbed the "war on terror." The chapter by Monshipouri and Mokhtari demonstrates the flaws of the so-called war on terror strategy undertaken by the Bush administration. Beyond the exigencies of "humanitarian intervention," and "the responsibility to protect," they point out, moral and ethical justifications for military intervention under the rubric of *security*, *stability*, and *nation-building* have fallen by the wayside. It may very well be the case that investing in nation-building and peace-building is an effective way to combat terrorism, but postconflict societies encounter a bewildering array of socioeconomic and political difficulties for which the military occupation cannot provide reliable panacea, and in fact may be the overt cause of many of these issues.

Exploring the root causes of human rights abuses in the Middle East and North Africa, Bahey eldin Hassan argues, the dominant role of the executive branch—and the security apparatuses at the heart of it—has led to a chronic failure to build a nation of rights and laws. Institutions and mechanisms that are meant to protect the individual and society from autocracy are used to legitimize and institutionalize a systematic assault on the liberties and rights of the individual and society, all the while methodically weakening civil society, which was created in some countries such as Egypt, Syria, and Iraq during the periods of relative liberalism in the first half of the twentieth century. In these countries, the constitution, legislative process, courts, parliament, and religious establishments have often been used as means of conferring legitimacy on methodical assaults on the rights of individuals and society.

The 2011 uprisings in Tunisia, Egypt, Libya, Yemen, and the rest of the Middle East and North Africa illustrate the fact that the spread of modernity and modernizing forces in a society is indeed a key contributing factor to the implementation of reform. These forces are likely to push a country toward a gradual democratic transition, a possibility that, as Hassan notes, seems more likely in Tunisia than Egypt given that Tunisia is the most modernized and urbanized country in the region. In Egypt, by contrast, modern forces are weak. The military establishment has been the main prop of the regime since 1952 and has vested interest in maintaining certain power relations and institutional arrangements.

THE INTERNAL FORCES OF CHANGE

Three groups have lately been the subjects of an intense human rights debate in the Muslim world: women, minorities, and migrant workers. Important segments of Muslim women have pushed for their rightful place in society and the polity, calling for more educational and employment opportunities. The rise of religious revivalism and extremism has provoked a backlash in the form of movements for women's legal rights, in particular, and women's rights to religious freedom, more generally.

Muslim Women: Gender Relations and Social Realities

The issues of women's role, status, and rights in modern societies of the Muslim world have generated highly emotive and divisive debates among Muslims of different ideological and political persuasions. Because of women's concrete struggles, political and business elites have come to realize that the issues of gender and development are interrelated. Many problems, however, stand in the way of improving women's rights. The Middle Eastern region has one of the lowest indicators of global educational standards of women. The Arab states of the Middle East have the least political participation by women of any region in the world.[10] Polygamy is practiced regularly, and women are not allowed to retain custody of their children if they separate from their husbands. Men have a unilateral right of divorce. Most Muslim women need a male relative's permission to get a passport.[11] In some contemporary Muslim societies, the status of women in matters relating to family rights such as marriage, divorce, child support, and child custody has improved considerably as a result of modernizing some aspects of the *shari'a*. This positive trend can be seen in countries as diverse as Indonesia, Iran, Malaysia, Morocco, Tunisia, and Turkey.

The great variation between Tunisia vs. Saudi Arabia in terms of women's rights is revealing. While Tunisian women have enjoyed modern constitutional rights since the 1950s, Saudi government has only recently—since the 1990s—accorded limited recognition to women's rights. In Indonesia, the women's movement and activism has been on the rise, albeit weak in relation to the state. The Indonesian women's rights and their unmet grievances are similar to those of their counterparts in the Middle East. As the economic crisis of 1998 intensified, dozens of women activists put pressure on the government to alleviate the negative consequences of the economic crisis for women and children. This development came to be known as the *Reformasi* movement, making many women cognizant of their collective power and voice.[12] This movement demolished the ideological façade of the old regime. Yet, the subsequent administrations of B. J. Habibie and Megawati Sukarnoputri failed to successfully address the main issues facing Indonesia women, such as female trafficking, the plight of women migrant workers, violence against women, and women's participation in politics. President Susilo Bambang Yudhoyono (2004–present) included four women in his 36-member cabinet. Many women's organizations argued that four women in the cabinet were not enough and that this showed that women's access to the political arena was routinely blocked.[13]

Iranian women participated in great numbers in the 2009 Green Movement—a movement that was homegrown but motivated by modern social movements and protest politics. What was perhaps most noteworthy was the increasing range of Iranian women who embraced human rights as an empowering tool. Many Iranian women felt vindicated and emboldened, even as the risks to them for staking their claims were not significantly reduced. This unique opportunity revitalized the Iranian civil society, posing new challenges to the control of the theological state—a dysfunctional state held together by coercive means and sheer intimidation. Many Iranian women, regardless of their ideological bent, saw a rare opportunity in the 2009 election to advance their struggles.

While acknowledging the significance of such movements throughout the Middle East, Zehra F. Kabasakal Arat's contribution in this volume has raised numerous questions about the actual status of women in Turkey. Her analysis is important and serves to caution us against the kind of naïve optimism that might lead one to believe that Turkey's leaders have solved the country's gender issues. Despite some improvements in the status of women in Turkey, as Zehra F. Kabasakal Arat has aptly observed, the country is far from granting equal rights to women and approaching gender equality. State agencies and major political actors continue to embrace traditional gender notions and women generally face all forms of discrimination and human rights violations.

The Muslim World's Minorities

The Muslim world's minorities—linguistic, religious, and ethnic—have been the subject of special inquiry by human rights groups and organizations. Likewise, the rights and the status of Muslim migrant minorities have received considerable attention. The citizenship laws of a number of European countries vis-à-vis Muslim migrant minorities would not pass the test of true pluralism.[14] For centuries, the Muslim world displayed as much or more tolerance and respect for religious minorities as did the Christian West. For example, the treatment of the Jewish minorities in Muslim societies stands as not only fair but also civilized when compared with the dreadful record of Christian European persecution of Jews over the centuries. Moreover, atrocities committed against Muslims in the early- to mid-1990s in Bosnia contrast sharply with the Muslim world's parallel experiences dealing with non-Muslims, especially in the context of the Ottoman policy of local tolerance and pluralism.

Jews, Christians, Zoroastrians, and Mandeans (Sabeans) have been allowed under Muslim rule to practice their faiths and be governed by their own laws under a contract of protection (*dhimma*), which guaranteed their life, property, freedom of movement, and religious practice. In fact, Muslim history is remarkably free from inquisitions, persecutions, witch-hunts, and holocausts that characterized the Western and other civilizations. Muslim communities protected their minorities from persecution by others; they protected Jews from Christians and Eastern Christians from Roman Catholics. In Spain under the Umayyads, and in Baghdad under the Abbasid Khalifahs, Christians and Jews enjoyed a freedom of religion that they themselves rarely allowed each other or anyone else.[15]

Known as the "People of the Book" (*ahl al-kitab*), non-Muslims enjoyed autonomy in the areas of personal-status law, worship, and education; they also had their own units with their own discreet religious, legal, social, educational, and charitable institutions. This autonomy was intended to compensate for the absence of equal status and the denial of political rights. Non-Muslims were also required to pay a special poll tax (*jizya*), although they were exempt from the *Zakat*, or alms tax levied on Muslims. Today, non-Muslims are politically integrated into the Muslim communities as active partners in the conduct of the states, despite contradictory evidence at times.[16] Muslims and non-Muslims are equals before criminal law.[17] Under civil law jurisdiction, *Shari'a* provides for some degree of *dhimmi* judicial autonomy. *Dhimmis* are allowed to resort to their own canon law, although they retain the right to access to Muslim courts. In certain cases, judges recognize *dhimmi* exceptions to the civil and criminal law.[18] Religious tolerance is mandated as non-Muslims have the right to choose one's religion and the right to practice one's religion.[19] Islamic law provides *dhimmis* with economic rights equal to those of Muslim citizens.[20] But, as with any legal system or theory, Islamic law may not necessarily be equated with Muslim practice. Tolerance of non-Muslims in practice depends on the interpretation and application of law, as well as respect for it. The impact of government policies as such on Islamic observances of non-Muslims' human rights cannot be underestimated.[21]

Dhimmis are not required any longer to pay any special tax. They are treated like other citizens, and most written constitutions in Muslim countries now guarantee the principle of equality for minorities. In Iran, Jordan, and Lebanon, non-Muslims are assured of a fixed share of seats in the parliament. This, however, does not apply to the Baha'i minority group in Iran. Although they are the largest non-Muslim minority (350,000) in Iran, Baha'is are not regarded as *ahl al-kitab*—that is, the protected people. The evidence in many Muslim countries points to a continued chasm between constitutional reforms and traditional precepts. Restrictions on minority groups, for example, are still taught and preached by religious institutions (madrasas) and scholars.

In some parts of the Muslim world, both the state and the people have shown intolerance toward religious minorities. In others, persecution of religious minorities has been sporadic and less marked. Ahmadiyas in Pakistan, Baha'is in Iran and Tunisia, Berbers in Algeria, Christians in Sudan, and some forced conversions of Jews are the most notable examples of the mistreatment of religious minorities. In Sudan, a new dress code has been imposed on women since January 1999, requiring them to wear Islamic attire and a headscarf, regardless of their faith. Even prior to this law, one study finds "Christian women and others had been detained and whipped for not dressing according to Islamic custom."[22] Since 1984, Pakistan's blasphemy laws have placed additional legal restrictions on the Ahmadiya community. Some of these restrictions are in clear violations of Article 2 of the Universal Declaration of Human Rights, which prohibits any discrimination based on race, color, creed, or language.

As Mahmood Monshipouri and Jonathan Whooley have demonstrated, in the cases of Egypt, Turkey, Lebanon, and Iraq, to the extent that minorities remain marginal, many policymakers wrongly construct their grievances, activities, and identities as existential threats to the national security of the countries in which they reside. In virtually all cases, including the Kurds in Iraq and Turkey, the Druze in Lebanon, and the Copts in Egypt, participation in the political process may potentially create a sustainable platform for boosting the causes of these minorities. The Islamist bombing of a Coptic Christian church in Alexandria on January 1, 2011, sparked widespread protests in Cairo. Copts accused the Egyptian government of refusing to acknowledge religious motivations as a factor in attacks against them, often blaming such violent acts on other factors. For its part, one expert notes, the government fears any overture to Copts would anger Islamists, who it considers the greatest menace to its power. The growing Islamization of society, coupled with the perceived or actual discrimination against Copts, has caused many of them to seek refuge in the church. The result may be the deepening of fault lines in church-government ties in years to come—an ominous prospect for a regime that prepares itself for a new leader.[23]

The Kurds, living in Iran, Iraq, Syria, and Turkey, compose the largest linguistic minority in the Middle East region. They have, for a long time, challenged the modern nation-states in which they reside, seeking goals such as statehood and political autonomy. These goals were and still are seen as menacing to the region's stability, which accounts for why the Kurdish cause has received little or no support from external powers. The Kurdish armed forces have received military and security equipment from some members of the European Union and Russia, as well as the United States, despite frequent and well-documented reports of human rights violations perpetrated against Kurdish villages in clashes between Turkish security forces and secessionist guerrillas in southern Turkey. The Kurds have been relatively disfavored economically, both historically and in the modern period. As a Sunni minority, the Kurds have rarely suffered

from religious persecution; their legitimate economic and cultural grievances have nevertheless been too often glossed over by the region's countries as well as the international community.[24]

The geostrategic map of the Middle East has changed since the
U.S. invasion of Iraq and the overthrow of Saddam Hussein's regime.
The Iraqi Kurds have gained a measure of political freedom that had
eluded them for much of their recent history, and the Kurdish struggle
in the rest of the region has gained an unprecedented momentum. Yet
resolving human rights problems in an ethnically heterogeneous society
like Iraq is no mean feat. As Nader Entessar has cogently demonstrated,
the Kurdish case involves a set of complicated political, social, and historical variables that generate a circular trap, pitting one nationality against
another. These complexities have thus far carried negative consequences
for the human rights of the Kurds in the region.

Migrant Workers

Under the watchful eyes of human rights organizations and groups,
combating workplace discrimination has become not only necessary
but also possible in the age of globalization. The miserable working
conditions of migrant workers throughout the world, but more specifically in the Persian Gulf region—where tiny Arab countries have found
themselves in desperate need of imported labor to modernize as well as
generate growth and urban sprawl—has brought to forefront flagrant
violations of human rights. Migrant workers have lived in the Arabian
Peninsula for more than two centuries. Starting in the 1970s, however,
the dynamics of migration flows to the Persian Gulf region took a new
twist with the rise in oil prices and the development boom in the region's
newly independent countries. These changing dynamics were most notable in the United Arab Emirates (UAE).[25] In 1968, the population of
the UAE was 180,000, of which two-thirds were nationals and one-third
migrants.[26] By 2005, the UAE's population had risen to 4.1 million,
of which about 80 percent were migrants.[27] The changing dynamics of
migration flows to the region have triggered a debate over labor conditions and practices that violate the rights of migrant workers and subject
them to modern day exploitation and abuse.

The recognition of a broader set of social, economic, political, and civil
rights for migrant workers has been conspicuously lacking in the countries of the Gulf Cooperation Council—GCC: Bahrain, Kuwait, Oman,
Qatar, Saudi Arabia, and the UAE. This is evidenced by the fact that only
Syria in the Arabian Peninsula has ratified the International Convention
for the Protection of the Rights of All Migrant Workers and Members of
their Families (the "CMW").[28] As the number of foreign workers in the
region has increased, so has their vulnerability to abuse at the hands of

employers and the nationals. The 2008 global food price hikes raised the specter of potential future food crises in the GCC countries, an ominous warning that migrant workers, who are most vulnerable to food price increases and shortages, will be likely to foment social unrest.

Migrant workers face wide-ranging problems, including poor workplace and living conditions, gender-related discrimination, and restrictions on their ability to organize and demand the protection of their rights. In the UAE, workers are *not* allowed to protest, and those who do are typically punished in a harsh manner.[29] The UAE government has not allowed for trade unions to form despite its promise to do so in the past.[30] These problems are further compounded by global migration trends, which contain paradoxes and ambiguities related to underenforcement of laws and vagaries of the global market.

The plight of migrant workers in the UAE is further complicated by nationalist and xenophobic sentiments. Today, some UAE nationals clearly view expatriates or migrant workers as threats to their cultural integrity and national identity, despite the fact that there is long-term and structural need for migrant workers—skilled as well as nonskilled—in the region.[31] Ironically, from the point of view of the countries from which these migrant labors originate, any halt in the flow of labor to destination countries will seriously disrupt their domestic economy.[32] In response to the widespread abuse of migrant workers' rights in the UAE, the international human rights community has put forth ways of constraining the range of possibilities for abuse while at the same time strengthening protections afforded to migrant workers in defense of their rights.

Despite recent improvements, deep structural and enforcement problems perpetuate the abuse of migrant workers' rights in the UAE. As a structural matter, the existing networks of employment and recruitment networks for migrant workers are organized in a way that facilitates the abuse of the fundamental rights of migrant workers, not only in the period before they leave their country of origin and while in transit, but also during the entire period of their stay. As an enforcement matter, quite simply there exists no powerful executive agency in the UAE to monitor or secure the rights of workers, as the existing agencies lack the necessary personnel and resources to perform the executive branch's supervisory or oversight functions. These independent but certainly interrelated problems have, unsurprisingly, allowed the private sector to step into the regulatory void and conduct business as it wishes. The private sector's free hand in managing its relationship with migrant workers has been facilitated by its prime position in the UAE's export-driven economy. The chapter by Mahmood Monshipouri and Ali Assareh underscores the importance of the UAE government assuming a more active role in addressing a variety of serious structural and enforcement problems that often produce substandard and undignified living conditions for migrant workers.

LIVING UNDER OCCUPATION
AND REPRESSION

In the Middle East as globally, there is a wide gap between the endorsement and the practice of human rights. For governments of Muslim countries, the real question is how to adopt democratic measures without jeopardizing their political longevity. It may not be possible for authoritarian governments to prolong their existence while endorsing genuine democracy; they can transition, but they cannot last. The challenge facing the Muslim world's ruling, cultural elite, scholars, and lawyers, if they wish to be cosmopolitan and act consistently with internationally recognized human rights, is to interpret Islamic law consistent with the human dignity found in emerging and modern standards. Many Muslims, however, have lost their confidence in the international system as a neutral problem-solver after the experiences of the post–Cold War era and the persistence of geopolitics of exclusion and double standards.[33] The current crisis in the occupied territories of Palestine has caused enormous damage to the Palestinians, as the bitterness and conflict between Israelis and Palestinians has festered and grown. Across the West Bank and Gaza Strip, one expert reminds us, the majority of the Palestinians are now living in poverty—that is, on less than $2 per day.[34]

The increasing deterioration of basic health conditions in the occupied territories of Palestine points to flagrant violations of basic rights of a people living under occupation. The contribution by Jess Ghannam best captures this tragedy, especially since the siege and invasion of Gaza and its aftermath. What is more troubling, Ghannam writes, is the continuing Israeli impunity and the failure of international entities—nation-states, NGOs, international judicial bodies—to hold Israel accountable. The Western world must treat Muslim masses as partners in the struggle against human rights abuses, while empowering reformist voices and civil society by giving them hope. Thus far, geopolitical considerations have dictated the policies of the West to the detriment of protecting and promoting human rights.

The initial U.S. reactions to civil disturbances and insurrections in Tunisia, which erupted on December 17, 2010, were typical. Unlike other situations, such as those in Iran, Burma, Serbia, and Ukraine, where the United States and other Western countries provided either moral support or limited amounts of economic assistance to prodemocracy groups, Secretary of State Hillary Rodham Clinton prior to the regime's overthrow expressed her concern over the impact of the "unrest and instability" on the "very positive aspects of our relationship with Tunisia," insisting that the United States would not take side in this uprising and would wait before even communicating directly with the country's rulers, Zine al-Abidine Ben Ali or his ministers. Rather than calling for a more politically open climate and an accountable government Clinton initially called for more open and free economy as the panacea for the country's unemployment, poverty, and general recession.[35]

However, on January 14, 2011, when Ben Ali fled the country and took refuge in Saudi Arabia, Secretary Clinton felt emboldened to push the U.S. Arab allies like Yemen toward economic and political reform. Many experts on North Africa have in the past—especially since the post-9/11 period—warned that the persistence of authoritarianism in the northern littoral states of Africa (collectively known as the Maghreb) must be seen as a source of radicalization in the region. More specifically, in the context of the global war on terror, some observers have drawn our attention to the problematic nature of the Western world's tolerance of and support for these illiberal regimes in the face of emerging democratic and popular challenges. Consider, for example, the recent uprisings in Egypt. They have reminded us that a growing sense of injustice and disappointment, in connection with the use and the abuse of state power, continues to shape political mobilization and radicalization not only in North Africa but also among North Africans living and working in Europe.[36] Even from a security perspective, Lise Storm posits, it is of paramount significance that the West put pressure on heads of states to embark on democratization processes and be prepared to invest money, political capital, and hard graft over the longer term.[37] In this regard, the Obama administration's support for easing Hosni Mubarak out of power in Egypt sent an encouraging signal. Yet it is not clear whether the U.S. government will keep pushing for reform consistently across the Middle East.

Unlike Tunisia and Egypt, which are ethnically homogenous, modern nation-states, Libya represents a difficult and highly complex case given the country's tribal texture, rentier state, vast landmass, and deserts. How far to go, and what means must be employed to end the violence in Libya and depose Col. Muammar Qaddafi's repressive regime pose daunting challenges to the international community. Perhaps even more problematic is the question of why NATO has rushed to the aid of the Libyan opposition movements while the brutal suppression of opposition groups in Bahrain are either marginalized or tacitly approved in the name of national security. To this end, the Obama administration's foreign policy risks degenerating into a state of debilitating inconsistency if urgent action is not taken to achieve mission clarity. If one engages to protect civilians, one risks becoming embroiled in what may turn out to be a lasting, violent, and ultimately uncertain civil war; however, to not act is to invite violent repression from leaders the region over. A complex vortex of tribal affiliation, identities, ties, and interests accounts for almost all major social and power relationships within the regime, the military, and what passes for political society. A quick overthrow of Qaddafi might not necessarily guarantee stability and may in fact ensure continued bloodletting.[38]

A relatively persuasive case can be made that Libya has forfeited its claim to sovereignty given the use of foreign mercenaries to attack prodemocracy supporters and shed the blood of innocents even at funerals for the recently fallen.[39] There is a strong urge on the part of the international community to invoke the "responsibility to protect" where a local government is unwilling or unable to help its own population. The emerging challenge of protecting civilians from mass atrocities requires developing new capacities—national as well as international—to intervene effectively and constructively.

It is vitally important not to lose sight of the fact that external pressures can play a very significant role in assisting prodemocracy and pro-human rights movements and groups. That said, the answer to the question of how best to enhance human rights and human dignity ultimately lies within the purview of internal domains. For human rights to be universal, they must be anchored in local cultures. Increasingly, a consensus has emerged that, in order to be effectively enforced, human rights principles must be locally justified and achieved.[40] The choices made by the leaders and people of the Muslim world will play a key role in shaping the politics and the practice of human rights in these societies.

SIGNIFICANCE OF THE BOOK

This volume's originality lies in our attempt to look beyond the abuses in the region, while admitting that there is no facile answer to the question of how to protect human rights in the Middle East. To meet more effectively moral challenges underpinning the struggle for human rights in the region, it is crucial to understand the limits as well as opportunities that local human rights movements encounter. Equally important is to understand competing interests and values that lead to alternative constructions of human rights and delivering human rights to all people and at all times. It is in this context that we underscore the need for promoting and protecting human rights through debate and dialogue. It is this possibility of engagement we intend to explore in this book.

We are cognizant of at least four prominent books on the subject: Abdullahi Ahmed An-Na'im, *Muslims and Global Justice* (University of Pennsylvania Press, 2011), Ann Elizabeth Mayer, *Islam and Human Rights: Tradition and Politics* (Westview Press, 2007); Anthony Chase and Amr Hamzawy, eds., *Human Rights in the Arab World* (University of Pennsylvania, 2006); and Kevin Dwyer, *The Arab Voices: The Human Rights Debate in the Middle East* (University of California Press, 1991). An-Na'im's work critically analyzes the role that Muslims must play in the development of pragmatic, right-based framework for global justice. His focus on a people-centered approach to rights aimed at empowering local actors as a way of accommodating a universal human rights paradigm is a valuable addition to the existing literature. Mayer's volume does an effective comparative/historical analysis of the cases of Iran, Pakistan, and Sudan. She is also very good in noting how illiberal circles have captured dominant interpretations in places like Iran and Saudi Arabia, while also noting that more liberal interpretations are possible in places like Turkey.

While Chase/Hamazwy's volume is a superb contribution to the literature, its focus remains confined to the Arab Middle East. This is also true of Dwyer's book. Our volume, in contrast, includes both discussions of problems with extant theoretical frameworks and the need for novel and local approaches. We also examine wide-ranging cases, including Iran, Turkey, Eurasia, as well as the Arab world, to advance our central arguments. Additionally, we provide strategies for protecting and promoting the causes of human rights in the region. We believe our volume will provide a comprehensive look beyond the abuses of the human rights in the region and will merit particular attention by students, scholars, lawyers, journalists, activists, and policymakers who work toward improving prospects for a pragmatic, measured process of protecting and advancing human rights in the Middle East.

STRUCTURE OF THE BOOK

This book is organized around three parts. The first part deals with the problems surrounding the current frameworks of universal and national movement of human rights and social justice. In the ensuing chapters, the importance of local conditions and cultural traditions in defining what human rights are is elaborated. It is also argued that Islam is not frozen in time and space. In the chapters that follow, details regarding an Islamically legitimate approach toward bolstering compatibility between modern standards of human rights and Islam's sacred text will give the reader a fresh perspective on the subject matter. And finally a case study in this part illustrates that protecting minority religions from defamation has positive consequences not only for freedom of expression and religion but also for the political participation of religious minorities.

Part II assesses common goals and case studies. Specific attention is given to the issue of human rights of the Kurdish people in the Middle East, underscoring the importance of safeguarding ethnic groups' rights by simply relying on the acceptability of broad universal human rights that avert pitting one group's rights claims vis-à-vis another group's claims. Turning to the state of progress on human rights in Iran since the 1979 Revolution, one contributor contends that given some of the limited progress on socioeconomic rights and the fact that the country's political elites are using the human rights vernacular there is some basis for hope for the future, despite the overt repressive methods used against the green movement proponents. The exploration of the issue of women's rights in Turkey raises some serious questions about the status of women's rights there. Although some improvements in the status of women in Turkey have transpired, the country is far from gender equality. State agencies and other major political actors still embrace traditional gender notions that discriminate against women.

To systematically examine ethnic and religious minorities, such as the Kurds, the Druze, and Copts, this section suggests that minority participation in the political process is likely to create a sustainable platform for promoting the causes of these minorities. In Chapter 9, Anthony Chase turns to the examination of sexual and gender rights and the way in which they have challenged traditionally narrow notions of what constitutes a protected status against discrimination, emphasizing that respect for rights based on a singular identity risks creating a straightjacket that denies the fluidity of identity.

The book's final section deals with strategies that Middle Eastern people can use to effectively improve their human rights conditions. While the debate over counterterrorism measures remains unsettled, it is evident that efforts aimed at promoting sustainable methods of peaceful, democratic change have received a great deal of attention in the face of the 2011 Arab awakening in the Middle East and North Africa. The departure of Tunisia's and Egypt's long-ruling authoritarian presidents has exposed the long-term costs associated with supporting repressive yet pro-West regimes. It is, however, still too early to proclaim the victory of democracy and human rights in the region, as the conflict continues between entrenched authoritarian forces in Tunisia and Egypt.

In the chapters that follow, the plight of migrant workers in the UAE takes the center stage. It is argued that today's Dubai, built over decades by migrant labors, stands out as the center of the Arabian Peninsula's finance and reexport business. Ironically, these same workers have been identified as the human collateral damage of the global financial and food crisis since 2008. The pervasive abuse of the rights of workers has led to mounting pressure for direct government involvement. There is no alternative to the UAE's intervention and prevention if workers' rights are to be ensured.

In Chapter 13 in the context of health and human rights in Palestine, the siege and invasion of Gaza and the role of the boycott, divestment, and sanctions (BDS) movement is examined. The occupation and colonization of Palestine stands out as a glaring example of how health rights are denied with dire consequences for the Palestinians. Given the centrality of addressing the humanitarian concerns of the Palestinians in Gaza to any possible resolution of the conflict between the Israelis and the Palestinians, the current stalemate over Gaza will complicate any serious efforts aimed at building peace and confidence between the two.

To remedy this situation, some suggest, among other things, the so-called BDS as one strategy for bringing justice to Palestine.

NOTES

1. William J. Wagner, "Catholicism," in *Encyclopedia of Human Rights*, Vol. 1, ed. David P. Forsythe, New York: Oxford University Press, 2009, pp. 260–272; see especially p. 270.

2. Ibid., p. 271.

3. Jack Donnelly, "Hinduism," in *Encyclopedia of Human Rights*, Vol. 2, ed. David P. Forsythe, New York: Oxford University Press, 2009, pp. 384–393; see especially p. 389.

4. Ibid., p. 392.

5. Ibid.

6. Abdullahi Ahmed An-Na'im, *Muslims and Global Justice*, Philadelphia, PA: University of Pennsylvania Press, 2011).

7. Sumner B. Twiss, "Confucianism," in *Encyclopedia of Human Rights*, Vol. 1, ed. David P. Forsythe, New York: Oxford University Press, 2009, pp. 394–403; see especially p. 395.

8. Ibid., p. 395.

9. Ibid., p. 401.

10. United Nations Development Program, *Human Development Report 2001*, New York: UNDP, 2001, pp. 226–229.

11. Susan Sachs, "Where Muslim Traditions Meet Modernity," the *New York Times*, December 17, 2001, p. B1.

12. Melani Budianta, "The Blessed Tragedy: The Making of Women's Activism during the *Reformasi* Years," in *Challenging Authoritarianism in Southeast Asia: Comparing Indonesia and Malaysia*, ed. Ariel Heryanto and Sumit K. Mandal, New York: Routledge Curzon, 2003, pp. 145–177; see p. 153.

13. For more on the case of Indonesia, see Mahmood Monshipouri, *Muslims in Global Politics: Identities, Interests, and Human Rights*, Philadelphia, PA: University of Pennsylvania Press, 2009, Chapter 9.

14. Clinton Bennett, "Religious Minorities: Challenge or Threat," available at http://www.religiousfreedom.com/Conference/Germany/bennett2.htm. Last accessed on November 28, 2003.

15. Khalid Baig, "On Religious Tolerance," posted on March 21, 2001, available at http://www.albalagh.net/food_for_thought/tolerance.schtml. Last accessed on November 28, 2003.

16. David L. Neal, Esq., and Ashraful Hasan, "The Distinctions between Muslims and Dhimmis: The Human Rights of Non-Muslims under Islamic Law," in *Human Rights Dilemmas in Contemporary Times*, ed. Ashraful Hasan, New York: Austin & Winfield Publishers, 1998, pp. 9–49; see especially p. 25.

17. Ibid., p. 33.

18. Ibid., p. 35.

19. Ibid., pp. 40–41.

20. Ibid., p. 46.

21. Ibid., p. 47.

22. Paul Marshall, *Religious Freedom in the World: A Global Survey of Freedom and Persecution*, New York: Broadman & Holman Publishers, 2002, p. 285.

23. Kristen Chick, "Egypt's Troubled Christians," *The Christian Science Monitor*, January 17, 2011, pp. 8–9.

24. Mahmood Monshipouri, "Islam and Human Rights: From Authenticity to Modernity," *American Muslim Quarterly*, Vol. 1, No. 1, Fall 1997, pp. 19–32; see pp. 23–25.

25. The UAE is a federation of seven states, termed emirates: Abu Dhabi, Ajman, Al Fujayrah, Dubai, Ra's al Khaymad, Sharjah, and Umm al Qaywayn.

26. According to the UAE's National Bureau of Statistics, the first population census in the UAE was conducted in 1968 by the Council of Developing Trucial States. http://www.uaestatistics.gov.ae. Even then a large percentage was expatriate Persian. See Frauke Heard-Bey, "The Gulf in the 20th Century," *Asian Affairs*, Vol. 33, No. 1, 3–17 (2002). See also Fred Halliday, "Labor Migration in the Middle East," MERIP Reports, No. 59, pp. 3–17 (Aug., 1977); Frauke Heard-Bey, "The United Arab Emirates: Statehood and Nation-Building in a Traditional Society," *Middle East Journal*, Vol. 59, No. 3, Democratization and Civil Society, pp. 357–375 (Summer 2005); Onn Winckler, "The Immigration Policy of the Gulf Cooperation Council (GCC) States," *Middle Eastern Studies*, Vol. 33, No. 3 (1997), pp. 480–493.

27. "Preliminary Results of the General Census for Population, Housing and Establishments 2005," available on the official website of the 2005 UAE census, www.tedad.ae. Last accessed on June 28, 2010.

28. United Nations Treaty Collection, available at http://treaties.un.org/Pages/ViewDetails.aspx?src=TREATY&mtdsg_no=IV-13&chapter=4&lang=en. For a discussion of the Middle Eastern countries' poor record of CMW ratification, see Mariette Grange, "The International Convention on Migrant Workers and its Relevance for the Middle East," paper presented to the Irish Center for Human Rights 2009 Summer School, December 18 (2009), available at http://www.december18.net/sites/default/files/MWCinME.pdf.

29. Federal Law No. 8 for 1980, Article 112 provides in part: "If the employee has been charged with premeditated crime, such as his involvement in a physical assault or robbery of property or other offenses such as the abuse of honesty, breach of trust or strikes, the said employee may be temporarily suspended from work."

30. In fact, a recent ministerial resolution directed only at migrant workers banned them from employment in the country for at least one year in case of "an illegal strike or its instigation." Ministerial Resolution 707 of 2006 Regarding Rules and Regulations of Employment in the Country (UAE) for Non-Citizens, September 6, 2006, Article 13.

31. See, generally, Anthony Cordesman, *Bahrain, Oman, Qatar, and the UAE: Challenges of Security*, Boulder, Colorado: Westview Press, 1997; "United Nations Expert Group Meeting on International Migration and

Development in the Arab Region," Population Division, Department of Economic and Social Affairs, United Nations Secretariat (May 2006), available at http://www.pfcmc.com/esa/population/meetings/EGM_Ittmig_Arab/P02_Kapiszewski.pdf; and Sean Foley, "The UAE: Political Issues and Security Dilemmas," *Middle East Review of International Affairs*, Vol. 3, No. 1 (March 1999).

32. John Willoughby, "Ambivalent Anxieties of the South Asian-Gulf Arab Labor Exchange," in *Globalization and the Gulf*, ed. John W. Fox, Nada Mourtada-Sabbah, and Mohammed al-Mutawa, London: Routledge, 2006, pp. 223–243; see p. 232.

33. Richard A. Falk, *Human Rights Horizons: The Pursuit of Justice in a Globalizing World*, New York: Routledge, 2000, p. 155.

34. Hatem Bazian, "Palestine," in *Encyclopedia of Human Rights*, Vol. 4, ed. David P. Forsythe, New York: Oxford University Press, 2009, pp. 175–186; see especially p. 179.

35. Stephen Zunes, "Tunisia's Democratic Revolution," *Truthout*, January 19, 2011, available at http://www.truth-out.org/tunisias-democratic-revolution66977. Last accessed on January 20, 2011.

36. Jonathan Githens-Mazer, "The Blowback of Repression and the Dynamics of North Africa Radicalization," *International Affairs*, Vol. 85, No. 5, September 2009, pp. 1015–1029; see especially p. 1016.

37. Lise Storm, "The Persistence of Authoritarianism as a Source of Radicalization in North Africa," *International Affairs*, Vol. 85, No. 5, September 2009, pp. 997–1013.

38. Nicolas Pelham, "The Battle for Libya," *The New York Review of Books*, April 7, 2011, pp. 77–79.

39. "Veering from Peaceful Models, Libya's Youth Revolt Turns Toward Chaos," *The New York Times*, available at http://www.nytimes.com/2011/03/13/world/africa/13opposition.html?_r=1&scp=5&sq=Libya%20funerals&st=cse. Last accessed on April 10, 2011.

40. For a compelling argument along this line, see Abdulaziz Sachedina, *Islam and the Challenge of Human Rights*, New York: Oxford University Press, 2009.

PART I

INTRODUCTION I: PROBLEMS WITH THE CURRENT FRAMEWORKS

Many have questioned whether or not the modern liberal position on human rights, which underscores individual rights established by a contract between rulers and ruled, is capable of accounting for the most basic challenges that human rights struggles present in the Middle East. Although most liberal democracies accept socioeconomic rights and manifest large welfare states, some Western countries adopt a liberal thinking in their foreign policy that privileges a particular account of human rights—placing civil and political rights above social and economic rights. This approach may or may not be widely shared in the non-Western world. The debate has further raised the issue of how domestic and international contexts hinder or advance respect for human rights standards across the globe. One core set of contemporary problems concerns the navigation between domestic cultural legitimacy and international standards. Legitimacy has many potential sources, and the legitimacy that supposedly stems from following internationally recognized human rights may, to some, be trumped by the legitimacy that comes from faithfulness to a conservative interpretation of Islam. Another one relates to the difficult task of preserving cultural diversity while at the same time moving toward forging a genuine normative consensus on the definition and implementation of human rights.

And yet another one revolves around enforcement of rights. Even if there is a consensus on upholding certain rights, such as women's rights, the implementation of some rights—for example, rights contained in the Convention on the Elimination of All Forms of Discriminations against Women (CEDAW)—has faced a number of obstacles, the most obvious one is the charge of cultural imperialism. Many Muslim states have thus ratified the Convention with reservations that protect their religiously based laws and cultural traditions.

Although there is no consensus on how each problem should be resolved, it is imperative to explore the possibilities for compatibility—or their absence—between universal human rights norms and the tremendous diversity of cultural traditions, local and national identities, as well as socioeconomic and political conditions. Without taking into account the entire array of factors contributing to human rights violations or improvements, it is not possible to identify variables and policies that often affect human rights practices in the region in major ways. Despite a significant transformation of economic systems and the trend toward political democracy in much of the world, the modern states in the Middle East still operate on the basis of conventional premise of state sovereignty. It is in this context that we argue that while human rights are essentially moral claims, they must ineluctably be staked out in the political arena. It is the legislative process that creates law, and this process is always political—featuring a clash of power and policy options. In reality, rights have never been above politics, and the latter has always been influenced largely by local factors.

Lawrence Davidson argues that there is no such thing as a priori human rights. Historically all rights have local origins and have been shaped by the customs and traditions of particular groups. The notion that rights are customized by natural localism, however, is challenged by those who argue that internationally recognized human rights were negotiated by a variety of state representatives from all regions of the world, in 1948 and thereafter, and that the application of these norms was affected by particular and varying contexts, including local customs—everywhere, including in the West. In addition, the provincial nature of human life has opened the notion of rights to manipulation by power elites who control local, regional, and/or state information environments and thereby can construct thought collectives that lead to deep and persistent discrimination. Human rights, Davidson points out, are regularly violated by both nondemocratic and democratic states. In part, this is because natural localism is a constant of the human condition. For all the talk of globalism, people still live primarily within localized areas that are their hometowns and neighborhoods. There are no "natural rights." Human rights do not descend down to us from the heavens. They are products of our own making and we distribute them as we see fit. The goal of distributing them to all is indeed the business of all of humanity. Critics argue that grassroots experience in "neighborhoods" is indeed important—all politics is local—but the fact that there are international factors, such as a universal conception of human rights plus pressures to take them seriously, must be taken into account in any systematic study of the interplay of international and local factors.

Manochehr Dorraj argues that Islam provides the cultural prism of perception and the language of legitimation in the Muslim world. It is not the necessary cause or the explanation for the social realities, including the abysmal record of human rights in much of that region. It can be interpreted to improve the state of human rights, as it was done under President Khatami's interlude in Iran, or it can be interpreted to suppress it, as it was the case under Mulla Umar and the Taliban rule in Afghanistan. Islam is neither responsible for rights violations nor the core basis for advancing rights. It is worth noting that as a faith, Islam is not frozen in time and space. What Muslims have made and continue to make of Islam is historically and socially conditioned. Given this reality, our analytical gaze instead should be focused on social and political developments and on the state and its exercise and abuse of power.

Halim Rane underscores the importance of *Shari'a* (Islamic law) within local contexts, proposing that Islamic law continues to be of particular importance to Muslims. In some cases, classical interpretations of the Qur'an have resulted in a perceived incompatibility between Islam and certain human rights norms. While Muslim states have adopted various human rights and other conventions that have been developed as part of modern international norms, they have not necessarily been accepted on an Islamic basis or as part of contemporary Islamic legal thought.

Unlike Dorraj, who sees a neutral role for Islamic faith insofar as advancing human rights conditions are concerned, Rane allows for the possibility of accommodation of a wide-ranging set of rights between Islamic and Western world traditions. Rane presents an Islamically legitimate methodology that synthesizes the contextualization of faith and a dignified life on the one hand and *maqasid* (objective-oriented approach to reading and interpreting the Qur'an) on the other. He posits that when examined through the lens of context and higher objectives based on a comprehensive, thematic, and inductive reading of the Qur'an, extensive compatibility between modern standards of human rights and Islam's sacred text is evident.

Reconfiguring the debate on minority rights, Turan Kayaoglu offers a framework that can satisfy both the demands of Muslim identity activists who are concerned about the effects of Islamophobia and liberals who are worried about the potential implications of hate speech regulation on freedom of speech. Kayaoglu goes on to make a compelling case that an international norm protecting minority religions from defamation has significant potential to contribute not only to freedom of expression and religion but also to the political participation of religious minorities. Kayaoglu attempts to strike a middle ground: while some normative differences between the supporters and the critics of the United Nations Resolution "Combating Defamation of Religions" remain, shifting the debate from free speech versus defamation of religions to a focus on the protection of minority religions can bring Muslims and those in liberal democracies closer. Moreover, a liberal political theory that emphasizes multiculturalism and the needs of minorities may potentially accommodate government's role in combating the defamation of minority religions.

CHAPTER 1

FRAMING THE HUMAN RIGHTS DISCOURSE: THE ROLE OF NATURAL LOCALISM AND THE POWER OF PARADIGM

Lawrence Davidson

THE PROVINCIAL NATURE OF RIGHTS

The major thesis of this chapter is that rights are local in origin and application and therefore not normally seen or accepted by states as natural or universal. Thus, there has always been a real-life difference between the application of rights (which in practice is almost always a local affair) and assertion of human rights (which can be a universal claim). One can see this when analyzing the precedents usually cited for our contemporary notion of human rights. For example, the Magna Carta (1215), the English Bill of Rights (1689), the French Declaration of the Rights of Man and the Citizen (1789), and the U.S. Constitution and Bill of Rights (1791) were all, despite occasional language to the contrary, local and specific in their intent and application. That is they were promulgated for the benefit of some humans, and not all humans.

This conceptualization of rights in terms of groups is therefore normative, and despite occasional efforts to the contrary, remains so to this day. That is why it has been so difficult to create international treaties that even partially impose the notion of universal human rights,[1] and why we witness the frequent violation of those treaties that do exist.[2] Indeed, the very existence of these treaties, such as the Geneva Conventions, was characterized as "obsolete" and "quaint" by President George W. Bush's White House Counsel, Alberto Gonzales, in 2004.[3] Such people, now referred to as neoconservatives, insist on the proposition that only the nation-state can "best guarantee peace and respect for human rights" because there is an explicit connection of rights and organized groups within states.[4]

The Phenomenon of Natural Localism

Why would rights be persistently thought of as locally acquired and applicable? One contributing factor is a phenomenon I call natural localism. Under normal conditions, most people will naturally focus on their local environment. On a day-to-day basis, it is our immediate environment that is most important to all of us. The local environment supplies the vast majority with their arena of work and sustenance, and is where one finds friends, peer groups, and one's immediate family circle. To use a Darwinian formula, it is the local environment that supplies the majority with knowledge necessary to make useful predictions, and thus a concentration on this arena has survival value. One consequence of this natural orientation is that interpersonal bonding is also a local affair. In terms of human evolution it is the family, followed by the local community that is a source of culture and identity. Rights flow from these cultural roots and are bounded by community identity. So strong can that identity become that it operates like an ideology defining the nature of reality.

While there are rational reasons for people to concentrate their interest and knowledge on their immediate environment, there are also dangers inherent in this provincialism. "Tuning out the rest of the globe,"[5] as Alkman Granitsas puts it, and concentrating on one's locality means that most of us live either in ignorance or often with stereotyped and generalized, untested perceptions about what is going on beyond the proverbial next hill. This can result in a sense of insecurity that, under the right circumstances, can be transformed into anger and aggression. The ignorance about things beyond the community also, by necessity, causes a large number of citizens to rely on others who, it is popularly assumed, know what is going on beyond the local realm. These others: government officials, news reporters and "pundits," religious leaders, and other "reliable experts" may or may not have vested interests that lead them to present a biased picture of events from afar. In either case, it is this limited category of "opinion makers" who are almost automatically sought out by the mainstream media to produce the interpretations upon which locally bound citizens rely in order to make sense of nonlocal events. Thus a general ignorance of outside events leads to the citizens' dependence on media-edited news and "establishment" experts.

The result of this situation is often the creation of a "Closed Information Environment." After all, media that automatically relies on government officials and nonobjective "experts" is also often a skewed media. In the case of the United States, which prides itself on having the "most free media in the world," information flows to the public from for-profit businesses owned by individuals and corporations supportive of (or at least responsive to) the very same interest groups that shape often rights-violating or otherwise violent and aggressive policies. And, almost all of news outlets have financial reasons not to frighten off advertisers by becoming associated with positions that challenge the status quo. Thus, America's mainstream media outlets are not ones that will usually give the public all sides of a story. In many other countries media outlets are simply the direct mouthpieces of the government and their job is specifically to assure public loyalty to the perceptions supported by the ruling clique. Natural localism makes the job easier.

Therefore, unless a citizen takes the trouble to look for alternative points of view, one is likely condemned to a "closed information environment." However, it is yet another aspect of the provincial nature of the citizenry that most, even when confronted with important events, will feel no need to go searching for alternative sources of information. Most will feel comfortable with their traditional sources—local newspapers and news magazines, radio talk shows, and especially television. This is simply because, unless the information supplied by the media and/or the government is capable of being contradicted *within the local environment*, most people will have no context from which to call it into question.

If this process of indoctrination, applied to events beyond one's local setting, is done with consistency across the media spectrum and over a sufficient enough time, it will produce generally similar pictures in the heads of local, regional, or even national populations. What results is a "thought collective."[6] Thought collectives, as the concept is used here, are artificially created, community-wide, points of view that take on added strength from the fact that most people shape their opinions to coincide with those of others around them. People want to fit into their community and sharing outlooks is an important aspect of this. Once the shared perspective is in place, there is a natural tendency to reinforce it by seeking out information that supports it. Ultimately, thought collectives can move populations to action based on firmly implanted assumptions that, in turn, are often based on stereotypes, buzz words, and unanalyzed assertions.

How do the above considerations impact the way people approach the issue of rights? Natural localism reinforces the group orientation of rights and the assumption that rights are tied to local culture and tradition. In other words, rights flow from and are a possession of the community. Natural localism, massaged by often manipulative leaders and an elite-controlled information process, will determine just how people will extend or not extend the notion of rights to those beyond the group.

Of course, the notion of group (and also the notion of localism) can itself broaden over time. The classical description of this has the broadening going from family to clan to tribe to state and so on. Nonetheless, the inherently restricted nature of both our group and our localism creates a precarious setting that functions to produce historically aggressive counterclaims to the notion of universally applicable human rights.

In the modern era, it is the boundaries of the nation-state that serve as the boundaries of rights as well. Despite the efforts of those who promote human rights, it is the nation-state that, for the vast majority of people, represents the broadest notion of community we presently have. Rights, therefore, are citizen-based. Noncitizens within the nation-state usually have restricted rights or no rights at all. And, if one lives under a harsh dictatorship the very concept of rights might be so severely restricted as to become almost meaningless. While certainly not in the same category as dictatorships, democratic countries have their own failings when it comes to awarding and denying rights. Democratic countries of the West are based on a concept of social contract that creates a special, historically evolved, inclusive sense of community identity for everyone within a territorially based state.[7] But this inclusiveness goes only so far. Take, for instance, the United States. Under conditions of manipulated fear the United States has suspended habeas corpus, jailed suspects indefinitely, deported people without a hearing, and thrown privacy rights to the wind. These suspensions of rights did not begin with the so-called war on terror. They began with the Alien and Sedition Acts of 1798 and have been periodically repeated throughout the country's history. If one moves in any direction on the globe and looks at the historical behavior of democracies one will find similar conditions occurring in a cyclical fashion. All of these nations, given enough tension and fear, exhibit episodes of what Robert Hofstadter has called paranoid politics.[8] In all these cases it is resident minorities groups or aliens that are at most risk.

TWO MIDDLE EAST–RELATED EXAMPLES OF PROVINCIAL NATURE OF RIGHTS

There is no lack of group-based struggle for rights in the Middle East. This is because in a majority of countries in the region rights are given or denied, at least in part, on the basis of ethnic, religious, or ideological grounds. Even in those countries with democratic aspirations this is the case. Thus, in newly "democratic" Iraq, rights are contested by Kurds vs. Arabs and Sunnis vs. Shia. In Lebanon, there is a multilevel contest for rights between Christians and Muslims, with the Christians further divided between Maronities and Orthodox Christians, and Muslims further divided among Sunnis and Shia. Then one can add in the

Druzes. In Turkey rights are contested by Turks vs. Kurds. In all cases the key to the possession of rights is control of the nation-state. And then, there is Israel.

I. Israel and the Issue of Rights

More than any other country in the Middle East, the "democracy" of Israel distributes rights according to group membership. At first it might seem odd that those who have taken it upon themselves to defend Israel before the world absolutely refuse to admit this obvious fact. After all, is it not an a priori fact that Israel is a *Jewish* state? As the "law of return" testifies, all *Jews worldwide, and only the Jews*, are virtual citizens of the Israel. This despite the fact that a good number of world Jewry chooses not to live in Israel. The Jewish National Fund holds 92 percent of the nation's land in trust *for the use of the Jewish people*. One can safely assume that all the discriminatory policies that are directed against the Palestinians stem first and foremost from this obsessive drive to make Israel and to maintain it as a Jewish state. Why then should anyone, much less the Zionists themselves, deny that political, economic, and social rights in Israel are accorded first and foremost to Jews?

Nonetheless, if one peruses the website of the major American Zionist organization, the Jewish Virtual Library, under the subheading "Myths and Facts Online—Human Rights in Israel and the Territories," one will find page after page of claims such as "Israel is one of the most open societies in the world" and therefore does not discriminate against its Arab citizens. Although Israel is a Jewish state it has no state religion. It is governed by the rule of law established by an elected parliament. Israel does not act abusively toward Palestinians, even those in prison and suspected of terrorism. Such behavior as torture was forbidden by the Israeli Supreme Court in 1999. Israel does not seek to deny the Palestinians in the Occupied Territories of their political rights, nor has it created a humanitarian crisis for them. And on it goes.[9]

Why should most Zionists in Israel and the Diaspora be so determined to deny what is increasingly obvious to others? The answer is twofold. First, historically it is the Jews, or more accurately the Jews of the West, who have suffered the most from the assigning of rights based on group membership. Prior to the Napoleonic conquests, Europe's Jews, as a people, were mostly restricted to ghettos and, further east, to the Russian Pale. When Hitler took power in Germany the Jews were persecuted as a collectivity. In other words, anti-Semitism manifested itself by the denial of rights to the Jews as a group. Now the Israeli Jews, with the support of large numbers of the Diaspora Zionists both Jewish and Christian, deny rights to the Palestinians as a group. The Israeli government essentially ghettoizes many of the Palestinians both in Israel and in the Occupied Territories. The cognitive dissonance that this can cause has to be held off somehow. So, many Zionists just deny it is happening, while others will rationalize it as necessary. Thus, the proclamation that the Palestinians want to destroy the Jewish state and so, the denial of rights is an unfortunate self-defense policy forced upon Israel by its adversaries.

The second reason is complementary to the first. It makes no difference if the Zionists claim that Israel is one of the most open societies in the world. Just as it makes no difference if Americans claim that the United States has the freest press in the world. Natural localism means that a majority of citizens have first-hand information about the nature of their world only within the spacial and temporal boundaries of their immediate locales. Beyond that they are likely to exist in a closed information environment that creates story line explanations for what is happening beyond the proverbial next hill. Freedom and openness only means that one is at liberty to search for alternative explanations if one wants to. But the fact is that most people do not bother to do this. In fact, most people are not conscious of any need to do so. Thus, in both Israel and the United States, and elsewhere too, politicians, media executives and other representatives of the "power elite" can maintain a story line that fits into the prevailing stereotypes and biases of the community, particularly when dealing with alleged enemies. In other words, information is self-censored to preserve and strengthen the prevailing thought collective. For the Israelis the all-important story line is (1) the right to and necessity of maintaining a Jewish state, (2) the notion that the Palestinians seek to destroy it, and (3) therefore the unfortunate need of Israel to deny the Palestinian rights. These are the primary elements of the Zionist story line about rights that feed into the prevailing Israeli thought collective.

There is, of course, something deeply illusionary about this aspect of the Israeli thought collective. In practice, the capacity of the Palestinians to actually destroy Israel is just about nonexistent. Therefore, in reality, it cannot be Palestinian actions alone that threaten Israelis. More importantly, it is the Palestinian mind-set that denies the legitimacy of Israel, labels Israeli actions as persecution, and reflects the determination to resist oppression. Because the Palestinian condition is representative of the human condition for many people, I choose the following quote from the Irish nationalist Roger Casement (executed by the British for treason in 1918) to best characterize it:

> Where all your rights become only an accumulated wrong; Where men must beg with bated breath for leave to subsist in their own land, to think their own thoughts, to sing their own songs, to garner the fruits of their own labors, . . . then surely it is a braver, and saner and truer thing, to be

a rebel in act and deed against such circumstances as these than tamely to accept it as the natural lot of men.[10]

It is the persistent resistance of the Palestinians that threatens the myths of the Israeli thought collective. That is, it threatens the self-image of Israel and its Zionist supporters worldwide. The Palestinian mind-set accuses Israel of being a product of a racist, militarist society. In clinical terms, Israel is accused of being the product of a "battered child syndrome." Having been historically conditioned by being battered by anti-Semitism, the Israeli Jews turn around and now batter the Palestinians.

"Not so," say the Zionists. It is the Palestinians who are in fact the epitome of latter day Nazis. "We allowed the original Nazis to drag us off to the concentration camps in the 1930 and 40s. We will not allow these modern Nazis to attempt to destroy us again." Thus, the motto, "never again" becomes operative in destroying Palestinian resistance to Israeli colonization and ethnic cleansing. This being the case, the Israelis and their supporters will do what they must to protect themselves against Palestinian violence (resistance) and, if necessary, expel the Palestinians (ethically cleanse them) from the land of Israel (Palestine). For the Israelis this has been metamorphosed into a matter of self-defense. The Palestinians have forced them to behave as they do.

In the meantime it is easy for the Palestinians to see, and document, the consequences of Israel's group-based denial of rights. Much of this evidence has been documented by the Palestinian Center for Human Rights (http:www.pchrgaza.org/index.htm). The Israelis dismiss any evidence provided by their enemies, but that evidence is substantiated by multiple independent sources. For instance, evidence of the systematic, group-based denial of rights to Palestinians is given by Human Rights Watch (http:www.hrw.org/en/middle-east/n-africa) and by the United Nation Relief and Works Agency (http://www.un.org/unrwa). The Zionists charge these organizations with bias. Yet, in Israel too there is a minority of Jewish citizens who have escaped the society's thought collective and are no longer subject to its closed information environment. Thus, those who represent B'TSelem, The Israel Information Center for Human Rights in the Occupied Territories (www.btselem.org/english/ statistics/Index.asp), The Association for Civil Rights in Israel (*www.acri. org.il/eng*), and others as well have been able to document the fact that "Arab citizens of Israel face entrenched discrimination in all fields of life. In recent years the prevalent attitude of hostility and mistrust toward Arab citizens has become pronounced with large sections of the Israeli public viewing the Arab minority as both a fifth column and a demographic threat."[11] The Association for Civil Rights in Israel also has the answer to the apparent contradiction between the reality of group-based denial of rights and the Zionist assertion that Israel is guided, in the Western style, by the rule of law. ACRI has documented the fact that, more often than not, the Israeli police and security forces simply do not enforce the few laws that might protect the Palestinians.[12] This makes today's Israel a democracy in the same way that the American South was a democracy for African-Americans prior to the Civil Rights Acts of the 1960s.

Israel is the most notable denier of equal rights in the Middle East and the situation is made all the worst by the fact that practices approaching ethnic cleansing and cultural genocide are being carried out by a people who, in their recent history have suffered both. Nonetheless, there are other Middle East cases of the assignment and denial of rights based on group identity. They aren't as drastic or tragic as the Israeli case, but they exist. One such case is found in Saudi Arabia.

II. Saudi Arabia and the Issue of Rights

The Kingdom of Saudi Arabia has a population of roughly 27.5 million people (figures are as of 2007) one-third of which are noncitizens. These are foreign nationals who have small chance of ever gaining citizenship.[13] This exclusion includes foreigners who are Muslims as well as those, Muslim or not, who have resided in the country for generations. Thus, noncitizens who happen to be born in the country do not automatically become citizens. The differential in terms of rights is great and foreign residents are sometimes segregated from the indigenous population. However, they are not persecuted as is the case of Palestinian Arabs under Israeli control. Indeed, foreigners are resident in Saudi Arabia mostly in hope of enjoying an improved level of economic well-being. Nonetheless, the aim of restrictions on citizenship and the restriction on full rights are the same in both cases. That is, to shape and control the demographic and cultural landscape for the benefit of one well defined group. This means encouraging the provincial outlook that flows from natural localism, setting your group off from other groups and seeing them as, at the very least, cultural threats. Some other Arab Gulf states operate similarly.

THE POWER OF THE HUMAN RIGHTS PARADIGM

The cultivation of natural localness, closed information environments and thought collectives, all profoundly associated with the modern nation-state, renders true Hannah Arendt's observations that up until recently, our world "found nothing sacred in the abstract nakedness of being human."[14] If that is true, then what hope can we place in the victory of human rights? Arendt concludes the following, "The right to have rights, or the right of every individual to belong to humanity, should be guaranteed by humanity itself. It is by no means certain this is possible."[15]

The uncertain effort to overcome the natural localness of rights and establish truly international humanitarian law has been going on for about a century and a half (if we are to date the process from the first Geneva Conventions set forth in 1864). However, it is only since the end of World War II that human rights have begun to be an influential paradigm—a conceptual framework for overcoming the worst aspects of nation-state behavior. Why is this so? An answer can be suggested at least in terms of the contemporary West. And that has to do with the Holocaust. It is the Holocaust that created a truly epoch-altering, existential shock to the Western state system. Why did it take so long for Western civilization to see the practice of genocide as a manifest danger to itself? It might very well be that World War II and its death camps, where the technology of modernity that so characterized European civilization was turned to the mass killing of subsets of the Europeans themselves, was just too shocking to rationalize away. In other words, Europeans would not take the issue of genocide (and concomitantly transnational rights) seriously as long as it did not impact their own local lives. As long as the victims of genocide were non-Europeans no serious official attention was paid to such organized slaughter. This was so even when, as in the colonies, the perpetrators were agents of the West. Distant geography and myriad rationalizations that ranged from the racial inferiority of the victims to the manifest destiny of the imperialists and even the sanctification of a supposed superior religion, sufficed to bury the issue. However, by the 1930s the Nazis had, in effect, brought the racial stereotyping and prejudice that had made possible colonial slaughter back home to Europe. By inventing the Aryan race and designating its primary area of activity to be Europe itself, the Nazis came to see not just the non-Western world but Europe too as a land full of inferior peoples to be bullied, enslaved, and murdered for the benefit of a superior people with its own overweening locally produced ideological view of things. If, under this new order, the Jews were to be slaughtered, then the Poles and the Russians were to be enslaved. And what of Western Europeans such as the French? Well, ultimately, they were to be treated by the Nazis in the same manner as the French themselves had treated the native Algerians. Upon the defeat of the "master race" in 1945, the populations of the West were sufficiently shocked by all of this that they recognized there were important lessons to be learned from Nazi behavior and the Holocaust.

Still, drawing the proper lessons was not automatic: it took a conscious and concerted effort to present the lessons in ways that would lead to treaty-based, legal prohibitions on genocide. If you will, a law asserting the transnational human right of ethnic group existence. Much of this effort was put forth by the idealistic and cosmopolitan Polish Jewish jurist Raphael Lemkin. It is he who helped the Western nations take a big step toward institutionalizing human rights as a way of reining in their genocidal impulses.

Lemkin was born in 1900 in what was then Russian-controlled Polish territory. He studied law at the University of Lvov and eventually became a city prosecutor in Warsaw. In 1939 he left Poland as a consequence of the Nazi invasion and made his way to the United States. Eventually he was employed by the War Department as an expert on International Law. During this time he wrote the book *Axis Rule in Occupied Europe*, published by the Carnegie Endowment for International Peace in 1944. In this 721-page book Lemkin sought to undermine what he considered to be a dangerous silence in the face of the brutalization of occupied Europe. In it he gave an exhaustive accounting of the decrees and laws used by the Nazis to legitimize mass murder.

It was in this work that he coined the word genocide (genos = the Greek for race or tribe and cide = the Latin for killing). In Lemkin's description, genocide did not necessarily require a direct use of force to immediately destroy the victim group. It could start out, at least, much more insidiously, as "a coordinated plan of different actions aiming at . . . the disintegration of the political and social institutions, of culture, language, national feelings, religion, and economic existence of national groups, and the destruction of the personal security, liberty, health, dignity . . . of the individuals belonging to such groups."[16] In this description Lemkin pointed out that genocidal actions directed against individuals had nothing to do with their personal behavior. They were targeted solely due to their group membership. In other words, there was no change in behavior that could possibly ward off the attack.

Lemkin's efforts to generate laws against genocide took a big step forward in the years immediately following the war. Nazi behavior had forced Western official opinion to move toward Lemkin's position. For instance, Justice Robert H. Jackson, the lead American prosecutor at the Nuremberg trials, stated that the actions of the Nazi defendants were "so calculated, so malignant, and so devastating, that civilization cannot tolerate their being ignored, because it cannot survive their being repeated."[17] Yet Jackson went on to qualify his words by stating, "We think that it is justifiable that we . . . attempt to bring retribution to individuals or to states only because the concentration camps . . . were in pursuance of a common plan or enterprise of making an unjust or illegal war. . . . "[18] And, in fact, no conviction of a Nazi criminal was achieved for any action taken prior to the outbreak of World War II (September 1, 1939). Still, it was during the immediate postwar period that Lemkin would be able to separate the crime of genocide from the notion of an unjust war and therefore achieve a partial limitation to national sovereignty's ability to act as a cover for genocidal atrocities.

The United Nations met at Lake Success, New York, in October 1946 and Lemkin was there. He sensed that the time was finally right for him to begin an intensive lobbying campaign for a genocide treaty. As a consequence, on December 11, 1946, the General Assembly resolved that genocide was "an international crime and that a treaty should be drawn up" making the designation legally binding. Genocide was defined as "a denial of the right of existence of entire human groups, as homicide is the denial of the right to live of individual human beings."[19] Then, on December 9, 1948, the vote was taken that transformed intention into reality. On that day the Convention on the Prevention and Punishment of the Crime of Genocide was passed. It should be noted that the next day, December 10, the General Assembly proclaimed the Universal Declaration of Human Rights.

Lemkin was happy to get the treaty. It separated the act of genocide from the act of war and specifically recognized that it could occur in peace time. It made those charged with genocide subject to extradition thus making it harder to run from justice. And, it broadened culpability to include actions taken with the "intent to destroy, in whole or in part, a national, ethnic, racial or religious group."[20] Yet when all was said and done, Lemkin understood that this was only a beginning. Many other crimes and violations of human rights, deserved to be outlawed at the international level. In addition, as we will see, Lemkin's achievement would prove to be a precarious one.

AN UNEXPECTED THREAT TO THE HUMAN RIGHTS PARADIGM

As it is described above, the factor that pushed the West into a path of marginally restricting national sovereignty and thereby opening legal space for transnational human rights law was the experience of the Holocaust. Thus, support for human rights is connected to the memory of and attitude toward this seminal historical event. To the extent that the memory of that event fades with time, or is otherwise compromised, support for human rights is potentially jeopardized.

Unfortunately this may in fact be happening. And, ironically, the source of this problem lies once more with Israel and its Zionist supporters. For most of the world's Jews the ultimate justification of Israel's existence lay with the history of anti-Semitism culminating in the Holocaust. There is some justification for this, for the Holocaust was the ultimate fate of stateless people (primarily Ashkenazim or European Jews)— people, as Arendt put it, denied the right to have rights. It was the logical conclusion of the Zionists that if the Jews were to have any future at all, they had to have a secure guarantor of group rights and for that they would need a state of their own.[21] Therefore, it was probably inevitable that that state would then be seen by most Jews, for an indefinite future, as a bulwark against anti-Semitism in general and, in particular, any new Holocaust.[22] Inevitable perhaps, but unfortunate. For, in adopting this point of view, the Zionists transformed a catastrophe of universal importance, in that it symbolized the extreme inhumanity that natural localism (manifested as the Nazi ideology) can result in, into an axiom of another natural localism (that manifested by Zionist ideology). Add to this their tireless justification of all Israeli behavior in terms of preventing another Holocaust and you get the conditions that have led many, mostly non-Western peoples, to become skeptical of the historical validity of the Holocaust itself—that is, skeptical of the greatest historical manifestation of the need for institutionalized transnational human rights.

Thus, it is the Zionist use of the Holocaust as a justification of their own behavior that has led their adversaries, such as the Iranian leader Mahmoud Ahmadinejad to call the Holocaust into question, and millions of anti-Zionists, particularly Muslims, to take this seriously. As such, the Zionists have done the cause of human rights a great disservice. Obviously, the establishment of a universal "right to rights" is not their program. Such an assertion of a universal claim to rights would certainly have to be shared with the Palestinians. The Zionist program, however, is every bit a local, nationalist one.

CONCLUSION

From the point of historical practice, there is no such thing as a priori human rights. That is why Jean Jacques Rousseau could look around him in 1762 and marvel at the fact that, while people are allegedly born with natural rights, they appeared to be "everywhere in irons."[23] Historically all rights have local origins and have been shaped by the customs and traditions of particular groups. That is, rights are customized by natural localism. In addition, the provincial nature of human life has opened the notion of rights to manipulation by power elites who control local, regional and/or state information environments and thereby can construct thought collectives that lead to deep and persistent discrimination.

As long as the consequences of this reality led to the persecution of marginalized subgroups, such as the Jews, or semigenocides and massacres against distant peoples of relatively limited numbers such as the Armenians, the situation pertaining to rights saw little change. Even the mass murders and enslavements of colonial times did not move the majority of Western leaders (the power elites of the modern age) or the Western peoples they ruled (whose perceptions were the product of closed information environments) to reexamine the notion of rights. Only the disaster of Nazi rule tripped a balance. Only when the Nazis brought genocide and mass murder into the heartland of Europe and spread these practices beyond the German borders did the leaders of the West and their respective populations come to a reluctant conclusion that some restriction on the concept of national sovereignty had to be instituted. The result was the successful campaign of Raphael Lemkin for the Convention on the Prevention and Punishment of the Crime of Genocide, which was soon followed by the Universal Declaration of Human Rights.

While these measures are certainly great steps forward, and have been complemented with the creation of the International Criminal Court, they have not resulted in worldwide respect for human rights. As the cases addressed above, particularly that of Israel, demonstrate, human rights are regularly violated by both democratic states and non-democratic states. In part, this is because natural localism is a constant of the human condition. For all the talk of globalism, people still live primarily within localized areas that are their hometowns and neighborhoods. Within those areas, they can usually make valid judgments based on experience. Beyond them, things become more shadowy and people must rely on others who claim valid knowledge of those nonlocal realms. This opens the majority of any given population to the manipulation of information environments and the creation of thought collectives.

The conclusion drawn from this sociohistorical situation is that humankind is involved in a very long-term struggle to spread out the definition of who has the "right to have rights." The goal is to bestow rights on all people by virtue of their humanity rather than by virtue of membership in this or that family, clan, tribe, religion, or nation-state. However, because of the still exceedingly stubborn and powerful counterforces of natural localism, mostly in the forms of nationality and national sovereignty, the struggle is far from won. And, it is very worrisome that steps advancing the cause of human rights usually come only as the result of instances of catastrophic denial of rights leading to slaughter and mayhem.

Yet this is the reality of our age. There are no "natural rights." Human rights do not descend down to us from the heavens. They are products of our own making and we distribute them as we see fit. The goal of distributing them to all is, as Hannah Arendt told us, the business of all of humanity. Unfortunately, thanks to natural localism, closed information environments and thought collectives that are exclusive rather than inclusive, a lot of humanity does not want to extend rights in a universal manner. Thus, those that do must struggle constantly, without let up. To cease to struggle means that there will always be those who do not have the right to have rights, those who do not have the right to be human beings.

NOTES

1. See, for example, the short description of the struggle of Raphael Lemkin to achieve an international genocide treaty in Dan Eshet, *Totally Unofficial: Raphael Lemkin and the Genocide Convention* (Facing History and Ourselves Foundation, 2007).

2. See the information provided by Human Rights Watch at www.hrw.org. Accessed on August 9, 2011.

3. "Memorandum on the Geneva Conventions," on the web at www. americanprogress.org/issues/kfiles/b79532.html. Accessed on August 9, 2011.

4. See Roger Scruton, *The Need for Nations* (Civitas, Folsom California, 2004), p. 1.

5. Alkman Granitsas, "Americans Are Tuning Out the World," Yale On Line (11/24/05) http://yaleglobal.yale.edu/article.print?id=6553. Accessed August 9, 2011.

6. This term was first used by Ludwik Fleck to describe a socially determined collective approach to scientific research. See his book *The Genesis and Development of a Scientific Fact* (Chicago, IL: University of Chicago Press, 1979). My usage of the term is considerably broader.

7. See an analysis of the work of Roger Scruton entitled, "Is the Nation Obsolete," at www.brusselsjournal.com/node/1101. Accessed on August 9, 2011.

8. Richard Hofstadter, "The Paranoid Style in American Politics," *Harper's Magazine* (November 1964), pp. 77–86.

9. Http://www.jewishvirtuallibrary.org/jsource/myths/mf18.html. Accessed on August 9, 2011.

10. Statement made at the conclusion of his trial, London, June 29, 1916.

11. http://www.acri.org.il/eng/story.aspx?id=499. Accessed on August 9, 2011.

12. See (1) http://www.acri.org.il/eng/aspx?id=577 and (2) http://www.acri.org.il/eng/aspx?id=547. Accessed on August 9, 2011.

13. The restriction is even greater in Kuwait where among a population of some 3.5 million only 1.5 million are citizens.

14. Peter Baehr, ed., *The Portable Hannah Arendt* (Harmondsworth, UK: Penguin Books, 2000), p. 31.

15. Ibid., p. 39.

16. Ibid., p. 20.

17. Ibid., p. 29.

18. Ibid., p. 30.

19. Ibid., p. 35.

20. Ibid., p. 36.

21. The idea that Israel is a product of the Holocaust is incomplete at best. Zionism predates the Holocaust, as does anti-Semitism. It can be reasonably argued that Israel would have eventually been established even if there had been no Holocaust. Nonetheless, it is accurate to assert that the Holocaust has taken center stage in the minds of Zionists as a justification for Israel and its questionable behaviors.

22. At the Yad Vashem memorial in Israel a "Pillar of Heroism" was erected following the 1967 Six Day War. The pillar represents the belief that that war was "the antithesis of the Holocaust." See http://www.jewishvirtual library.org/jsource/Holocaust/israelmons.html. Accessed 9 August 2011.

23. Jean Jacques Rousseau, *Social Contract*, Book 1, Chapter 1. Pacific Publishing Studio, Seattle, Washington, 2010.

CHAPTER 2

ISLAM AND HUMAN RIGHTS:
IDEALS AND PRACTICES

Manochehr Dorraj

The debate over compatibility of Islam and human rights has raged among theologians, scholars, intellectuals, and the public at large for generations in the Muslim World as well as in the West. This discourse, however, has become more intense since the proclamation of 1948 United Nations Universal Declaration of Human Rights (UDHR). That declaration pronounced that all human beings are born free and are equal in dignity and rights.[1] Article 2 of the UDHR stipulates: "Everyone is entitled to all the rights and freedoms set forth in this Declaration, without distinction of any kind, such as race, color, sex, language, religion, political or other opinion, national or social origin, property, birth or other status." The rights entailed in the UDHR are indivisible and inalienable and include wide-ranging civil-political, as well as economic, social, and cultural rights. These universal rights include such rights as to life, liberty, and security of person; freedom from slavery and servitude; freedom from arbitrary arrest, detention, or exile; freedom of thought, conscience, and religion; freedom of opinion and expression; right to education; right to work; right to a nationality; and right to own property. According to the UDHR, all people are entitled to these rights by virtue of their humanity.

In other words, these rights are "independent of obligations, undefined by role and unconditional on status or circumstances. Rights are legitimate claims or entitlements and as such they imply corresponding duties. . . . Since human rights are inalienable they constitute the starting point for political morality in any human society that purports to respect them. Collective or group rights are meaningless if they imply the disregard of individual rights."[2]

The fact that much of the Muslim World has proven to be inhospitable to democracy and human rights in twentieth and twenty-first centuries has fueled the presumption that violation of human rights is rooted in Islamic culture in general and in Islam n particular. In this chapter, we would address the complexities and the nuances surrounding the vexing question of compatibility and would discuss the contending perspectives on the issue, concluding with some observations on theoretical implications of the debate. However, since many Islamists who oppose human rights do so under the pretext of cultural authenticity, arguing that human rights are embedded in Western cultural experience and as such their implementation would compromise the creation of an ideal Islamic society, we must first address the issue of Cultural relativism.

THE DILEMMAS OF CULTURAL RELATIVISM

Human rights by definition are universal—applied to all human beings at all times in all places. As stated at the 1993 World Conference on Human Rights in Vienna, "their protection and promotion is the first responsibility of governments."[3] Yet, since states can choose to not sign an international human rights treaty, and to impose restrictions on the implementation of these treaties within their borders, it seems much more likely that human rights are relative in acceptance rather than universal.

A core of humanness links every human being, whether it is through common experience, common ideas of evil, or common ideas of good. Human rights, according to this standpoint, are not relative but universal. Such rights as right to life, to justice and fair treatment, to aid, to freedom from arbitrary repression of a lawless state are universal. Without protection of such rights, the social contract between the ruler and the ruled, the government and citizens become meaningless. People may not agree about what makes something good but they agree that it is good.[4] While good and evil may be defined differently in variant cultures, a predisposition toward good and aversion toward evil is something that cuts across cultures. As Michael Perry has observed, "There is nothing culture-bound in the great evils of human experience, reaffirmed in every age and in every written history and in every great tragedy and fiction: murder and destruction of life, property, imprisonment, enslavement, starvation, physical pain and torture, homelessness, friendlessness."[5] Without human rights, citizens have no stand in the political system and become dispensable subjects.

Despite the universality of human rights discussed above, there are different categories and concepts of human rights. First is the so-called first generation of rights. These are civil and democratic rights often associated with individualism and individual rights, pervasive in many Western societies. The second generation of rights refers to socioeconomic rights, rights to a decent living and freedom from hunger and abject poverty and access to basic necessities of life. These rights are considered to be more relevant in the Third World. The third generation of rights refers to such rights as protection of environment, species, and animals, as well as the right to peace and humanitarian intervention. Because of pervasiveness of poverty and malnutrition in many parts of the developing world, these rights are not perceived as salient by many who live in those countries. In general, the West has traditionally emphasized political rights whereas the non-Western world has been preoccupied with social and economic rights. Thus, the right to survival and well-being has taken precedence over basic freedoms associated with civil-political rights.[6] Increasingly, however, this dichotomy has proven false given that living in a globalizing age has made that distinction virtually useless.

In addition to desperate notions of human rights, there is also the assertion that the predominant ideas of human rights have their origins in intellectual and cultural experience of the West. More specifically, it is a by-product of Western Renaissance, rationalism, humanism, individualism, and enlightenment. Hence, since historically international human rights law is derived from Western legal heritage, it is not deemed relevant to the historical experience of the non-Western world where individualism and individual rights are not paramount on the list of social priorities. The case is also made that since human rights seem to thrive in democratic societies, we should not expect their implementation in nondemocratic ones. The advocates of such nativist perspectives in the developing world often wrap their arguments against universal application of human rights in flags of nationalism or claims of Western cultural imperialism. While human rights are universal, their implementation takes place at national and local levels. Thus the opponents of universality of human rights use the pretext of cultural exceptionalism or religious sanctity and specificity and even cultural rights and cultural autonomy to refute it.[7] The detractors of human rights in the Muslim World argue that its observance would lead to decline of morality, ushering in decadence and the decline of cultural authenticity. Through a reactive rhetoric, they shift the attention from human rights as an entitlement against possible abuse of power by the state to a right of state to safeguard cultural and religious identity against the West.[8] Such cultural relativist arguments often discard the fact that while the origin of human rights is Western, its ethical and legal claims are universal.

Western ideas of individualism, individual freedoms, and the separation of religion and politics often lack resonance in some non-Western societies such as Islamic, Hindu, Buddhist, and Confucian cultures. For the purposes of this chapter, we shall focus on the tension between Western ideas of human rights and Islamic societies.

ISLAM AND HUMAN RIGHTS: MUSLIM TRADITIONALISTS VS. MUSLIM MODERNISTS

Due to the fact that all the independent human rights monitors list the Arab World among the globe's worst violators of human rights in the past century,[9] questions have emerged if pervasiveness of political authoritarianism, police states, and violation of democratic rights in the region are due to predominance of Islamic culture and religion. When the question of compatibility of Islam and human rights is raised, however, one should ask which Islam, who is interpreting it, in what historical and social context, and for what purpose. In other words, the understanding of Islamic texts must be accompanied with an understanding of the context as the understanding of deeds done under the name of Islam must be put in a broader social context that animates such modes of behavior. Hence, the immense diversity that defines the Muslim World must also be taken into account. Without it our knowledge and assessment of Islam is incomplete and superficial.

Scholars, the lay intellectuals, the clergy, and the public at large in both the Muslim World and the West differ substantially on the question of compatibility of Islam and human rights. On one side of the divide are those who interpret Islam in essentialist terms, as if it was a religion frozen in time and space and devoid of social context and evolution, thus dogmatically clinging to their own preconceptions about Islam. On the other side of the divide are those who see Islam and its survival and viability since its inception in the seventh century inseparably linked to its ability to transform through *Ijtihad* and reinterpretation and remain relevant to the lives of many Muslims in the modern times.

The advocates of incompatibility of Islam and human rights, in whose ranks Muslim traditionalists figure prominently, argue that in orthodox Islam God is the ultimate sovereign and the granter of rights, any human-conceived notion of right by nature is inferior and would lead to Muslims deviating from the righteous path. Since the word Islam means "submission," and one must submit to the will of God, the only legitimate law is the one based on Islamic law and derived from the *Shari'a*. Because of *Shari'a*'s divine inspiration, it is superior to any fallible human reason and notion of law and because the pious clerical leaders represent God's will, by definition, they are just.[10]

In the totalizing and totalitarian interpretation of Islam, the *Shari'a* should govern all aspects of a Muslim's life. Since some of its principles and edicts are deemed as permanently valid, there are limitations on its reinterpretation. Thus, any alternative interpretation of law, including secular law, is shunned. At times such hostilities to democratic principles, human rights, and democracy assumes a blatant character. Ali Belhadj, one of the contemporary leaders of Islamist movement in Algeria, makes this very explicit: "Beware of those who pretend that the concept of democracy exists in Islam . . . democracy is *Kofr* (blasphemy). . . . There is no democracy because the sole source of power is Allah, through the Qur'an and not the people. If people vote against the law of God, this is nothing but blasphemy. In this case, one must kill these non-believers for the good reason that they want to substitute their authority to the authority of God."[11]

In addition, traditionalists divide the society into *Dar al Islam and Dar al Harb* (the realm of Islam and the realm of nonbelievers, the realm of war). Believers are worthy of protection and nonbelievers are not. As such, Islam discriminates between believers and nonbelievers and is unable to accommodate one of the basic principles of human rights, freedom of religion. Muslim traditionalists regard disseminations of other religions within Muslim territories and the conversion of Muslims to other religions as "crimes" (apostasy), which are punishable by death. Saudi Arabia's abstention, for example, from voting on ratification of the Universal Declaration of Human Rights was done on the grounds that it found the Articles 16 and 18 that establish freedom of thought and religion, including the right to change one's religion objectionable.[12] Hence, Muslim traditionalists regard men and women as unequal and discriminate against women, thus violating another cardinal principle of human rights, equality before the law and equality of gender.[13] These types of backward-looking interpretations of Islam abound in particular among Wahhabis and the Salafis, (the two sects) in the contemporary Muslim World, but by no means are they confined to them.

The preoccupation with Western imperial penetration and the ensuing defensive posture of the Muslim World in the colonial and postcolonial era, and the anxiety about Islamic identity became a major preoccupation for Muslim intellectuals. Many of them returned to "Islamic self" to resolve their identity crisis and to anchor themselves in what they perceived to be their authentic culture. One of the most influential Muslim traditionalists of the post–World War II era was Sayyid Qutb.

Sayyid Qutb who was influenced by Mawdudi of Pakistan was one of the most significant Muslim traditionalists of the 1950s and the 1960s. He was a major theoretician of the Muslim Brotherhood in Egypt. After his death in Nasser's prison in 1966, his stature was elevated as a martyr saint and is regarded by many as the intellectual precursor of modern day Islamic militancy and extremism. Qutb regarded Islam as a self-contained, self-sufficient, and a total religion, encompassing the public as well as the private realms of life that should regulate the life of the faithful from cradle to grave.[14]

Unlike Mawdudi who was sympathetic to the idea of a synthesis between Islam and democracy, Qutb regarded all forms of popular sovereignty that derives its inspiration from secular ideologies and fallible human reason as illegitimate. But Qutb also opposed theocracies that would be ruled by clergy who may abuse their religious authority. Since he regarded human beings as sinful, he argued in any government that is based on "a group of people legislating for others, equality and absolute dignity cannot be realized."[15] Qutb was also highly critical of the Western notion of human rights that was associated with individualism and primarily focused on political and civil rights. He gave primacy to economic rights and believed real emancipation and liberty is only possible when one is free from hunger and disease. He makes this very explicit when he asserts, "who will dare to claim that those millions of hungry, naked, barefoot peasants whose intestines are devoured by worms, whose eyes are bitten by flies and whose bloods are sucked by insects are humans who enjoy human dignity and human rights (as the capitalist slogan claim?). . . . Who will dare to claim that the hundreds of thousands of disabled beggars, who search for crumbs in garbage boxes, who are naked, barefoot, with faces crusted with dirt . . . who will dare to say that they are the source of authority in the nation, based on democratic election?"[16]

Qutb regarded an Islamic order superior to both Communism and Capitalism. Whereas a Communist system is preoccupied with satisfaction of material needs of its citizens and its atheism condemns the people under its rule to moral depravity, Capitalism is exploitative and lacks lofty morals. In contrast, an Islamic government would provide for the material as well as the spiritual needs of the *Umma* and ensure their salvation. Qutb also believed protecting the sanctity of Muslim community takes precedence over individual rights.

On the other end of the divide is the Muslim modernists' perspective that adheres to compatibility of Islam and democracy. The advocates of this view attempt to find precedence for human rights in Islamic precepts and principles or examples of the prophet and Imams. For example, they argue that Islam's insistence that every individual determines his/her destiny, is personally responsible for his/her actions, and can communicate with God directly without the need for the priestly mediation indicates that each individual should be treated as equal and autonomous, thus affirming many individual rights.[17] Hence, it is asserted that the emphasis on Muslims living their lives according to *Shari'a* law is an indication that Islam is opposed to arbitrary rule. They contend that authority in early Islam was based on a delicate dialectic between the ruler and the ruled in which the ruler governs through *Shura* (consultation) and derives his power from the community of the faithful, *Umma*, through their consensus (*Ijma*). Other interpreters use the precept of *Ikhtilaf* (difference and opposition) present in early and medieval Islam and conclude since honoring different opinions was rooted in Islamic history, Islam embraces pluralism. Thus, the precept of *al-Huquq al-Shar'iyya* (rights stipulated in *Shari'a*) is used as a precedent for modern concept of human rights.[18] The foundation of *Shari'a* is based on certain necessities known as *darruriyat al-khams* that obligate Muslims to strive to preserve their religion (*al- Din*), themselves (*al- Nafs*), reason (*al- Aql*), their families (*al- Nasl*), and their properties (*al- Mal*). In so far as the individual fulfills these obligations and other stipulated duties, they are entitled to certain rights including fair treatment and to live their lives in dignity and peace.[19]

Furthermore, Islamic history provides example of Muslim philosophers such as Al-Farabi (d. 950) and Ibn Rushid (d. 1198) who shunned blind embracement of revelations and orthodoxy, saw reason and rationalism as a window to truth, and advocated a reasoned faith. In addition, it is argued that pristine Islam was also concerned with economic equality; as such, its notion of rights is broader as compared to its Western counterpart. To prevent a rift between rich and poor, Muhammad introduced Islamic alms (*Khoms* and *Zakat*) and charitable giving (*Saddaqah*). Thus, many Muslim modernists argue that the notion of rights and equality existed in early Islam and Muslims can fall on their own tradition to find precedence for human rights.[20]

Some scholars argue that in the same way that the Western notions of civil and human rights law evolved from the divine law and the divine rights, it is likely that human rights in the Muslim World may emerge out of evolution in Islamic law.[21] However, the dilemma many Muslim modernists face is that they are torn between the allure of ideals of Western civil and human rights that grant individuals protection against the abuse of power by the state and their abiding loyalty to their Islamic identity and cultural traditions. For many modernists of the early twentieth century, the reconciliation of these two aspirations proved to be an arduous task at best and problematic at worst. Many Muslim modernists have criticized secular democracy on the ground that while it values individuals and individualism, it pays no attention to spiritual enrichment of individual.[22] They assert individual rights, including human rights, should be subordinated to the collective rights, such as economic and social well-being and the welfare of the society at large. Hence, for them the interests of Islam were more significant than preserving the interests of the individual.[23]

Some of the contemporary Muslim modernists' views on human rights are more accommodating and far-reaching than of those who lived in early twentieth century. Among them is Abdul Karim Soroush of Iran, a philosopher and an early ideologue of the Islamic revolution of 1979 who initially defended the absolute rule of the Jurist (*Valayat-i Faqih*), and subsequently broke with that institution and theocracy, labeling it as a stepping stone to religious despotism. Soroush is an advocate of primacy of reason and freedom as the two major universal pillars of human development. Disillusioned with the outcome of Islamic revolution in Iran, where according to him the spiritual essence of Islam was sacrificed at the altar of power politics and certain layers of clergy used religion for self-enrichment and power grab, he advocated separation of religion and state as the only path to maintain the dignity of Islam as a sacred faith. Soroush has called for a full-fledged Islamic reformation as the solution to a sense of malaise that pervades the Muslim World.

To remain viable and relevant in a postmodern world, Soroush asserts, Islamic tradition has to be reinterpreted. Likewise, religion should not be used to suppress democratic and human rights. Neither the pretext of maintaining doctrinal purity nor political expediency is justifiable end to suppress rights and liberties. To maintain their legitimacy and relevance in the modern world, Muslim societies must democratize and protect civil and human rights. Since God is compassionate, merciful, and just, as vice-regents of God on earth, pursuit of social justice is a part of the divine duty of all Muslims. Therefore, Islam must serve human welfare and well-being and the ideal Islamic state must submit to the will of majority.[24]

A new generation of Muslim scholars, such as Abdullahi Ahmed An-Na'im, who best represent and capture modernist interpretation of Islamic law and propose new ethical foundations tend to argue that rights are not proclamations but social construction facilitated through dialogue and discourse. Such discursive engagements are likely to lead to an overlapping cultural consensus.[25] On balance, however, Muslim modernists have yet to meet the challenge of bridging Islamic law and modern human rights standards by defining what is properly "universal" and what is precisely "cultural."[26] Thus addressing ways to reconcile Muslim countries' domestic law and international human rights law is the right place to start. Without sincere commitment at the top of power structure in most Muslim majority countries, this task is immensely difficult. Ultimately, the move toward reforming Islamic laws might be more political than religious in nature. Herein lies the greatest challenge facing modernists in the Muslim World.

A SHADE OF GRAY: DEBATING THE DEBATE

One point of tension between Islamic law and international human rights law is that whereas the former is based on a sacred faith, the latter is secular in its inspiration and orientation. Some orthodox Muslims refuse to accept principles of international human rights law because it fails to recognize religion as a legitimate source of authority. Hence, some of the freedoms and liberties spawned by human rights law are perceived to be against proper moral values that Islam promotes. Thus, they deem imposition of limitations on individual rights in order to protect public morality as justified. While they concede that Islam values human life, they also assert that Islam stipulates that Muslims should live a good and pious life that can only be guaranteed if they live their lives according to *Shari'a*. For example, some Islamic governments curtail free expression, conferred by *fitan* (sedition) in Islamic law. This gives the Muslim governments wide latitude to suppress their political opponents and deny them their democratic and human rights.

A problem that Muslim traditionalists who regard themselves as the guardians of Islamic orthodoxy face is the reality that *Shari'a* emerged in seventh to ninth century after the death of Muhammad and it represents an interpretation of Muslim jurists of the time regarding the legal and social application of the prophet's teachings and conduct. It reflects the premodern customs and values. Essentially, it has not been fundamentally reinterpreted since then. Therefore, many of its legal injunctions are outdated and inapplicable in modern times.[27] For example, such *Hadd* punishments as the amputation of the hands of a thief or stoning to death someone suspected of adultery is regarded by modern standards of human rights as inhuman and cruel.[28]

Moreover, the traditionalists leave a number of questions unresolved. Who would interpret the *Shari'a* and implement "God's sovereignty"? How would one safeguard against abuse of power by self-proclaimed intermediaries between humans and God? How can God's sovereignty be reconciled with people's sovereignty? How can a sacred faith that proclaims monopoly over the truth consent to the idea of ideological pluralism and the free competition in the marketplace of ideas? Can a faith be self-sufficient and self-contained, as the traditionalists contend, in a postmodern world? These philosophical questions notwithstanding, in recent years we have witnessed important political gain for Muslim traditionalists as demonstrated by the examples of Front for Islamic Salvation's parliamentary electoral victory in Algeria in 1989–1990 and Muslim Brotherhood's electoral victory in the occupied territories in Palestine (HAMAS) and their impressive political showing in Egypt. Equally impressive is the rise to power of the Islamic Justice and Development Party in Turkey, which used a modernist discourse and political agenda to outmaneuver and outflank Turkey's secular parties in a state with a relatively strong secular tradition. Institutionalization of the modernist interpretation of Islam, which is perhaps in no small part due to looming Ataturk's secular legacy, may partially explain the turn of events in that country. But in the final analysis the answer to the question why these political parties performed so well may not lie in Islam per se, but on the failure of secular parties to deliver on their promises.

Going beyond the preoccupation of Muslim traditionalists with religious orthodoxy, more sober and balanced assessments of Islam indicate that while Islam did not go through the experience of Protestant Reformation that made religion a private matter, thus providing a religious justification for the idea of individual rights, there is nothing in Islamic history that matches the persecution of non-Christians that we have witnessed during the Crusades, the Spanish Inquisition, the Holocaust and the other religiously spawned carnage. While Jews were being confined to the life of Ghetto and during the Second World War many of them were murdered in Hitler's gas chambers, prior to the rise of state of Israel in 1948, Jews for the most part lived peacefully in Islamic societies.[29] Putting this history in proper perspective may provide some ground for optimism in regard to compatibility of Islam and human rights.

Modernists are more likely to rely on reason rather than revelation, rationalism rather than blind embracement of faith. They believe that the gates of *ijtihad* are open and it should be utilized to renew Islam in each epoch in order to maintain its relevance. Clearly, Islam gives precedence to the community over the individual and regards the preservation of *Umma's* sanctity more important than individual. However, this is not a valid argument to refute application of human rights in Islamic societies. Although human rights enlarge the scope of individual freedom, they are by no means individualistic. They are not meant to lead to an "atomistic society" devoid of communitarian solidarity.[30] A purely individualistic concept of religious liberty, for instance, would almost amount to a contradiction in terms, because religious life in Islam is hardly conceivable outside of religious communities.

What is at stake in human rights is not an abstract individualism but rather the principle of equal freedom that always affects individuals and communities simultaneously. In fact, according to Islamic tradition, once the duties of the individual, as stipulated by the *Shari'a*, are fulfilled, then as a rightful member of the *Umma* the individual is entitled to certain rights. These rights come with certain obligations to the community and its well-being, including commanding the good and forbidding evil. Although the Qur'an is primarily preoccupied with the duties and the obligations of the faithful and the language of rights is lacking in it, this has not prevented some of the modern Muslim thinkers from the ranks of both traditionalists and modernists to adopt its language. Hence, since Islamic tradition contains both an egalitarian and a hierarchical element, it can be interpreted to accommodate equal rights as well as political authoritarianism.[31]

Muslim modernists take the Qur'anic phrase that "there shall be no compulsion in religion" to mean that Islam respects religious tolerance. Islam regards Christians and Jews as "the people of the book." As such, they have enjoyed certain rights as "protected minorities." However, this has not prevented most governments in Muslim lands (secular or religious) to declare Islam as the state religion and deny religious minorities equal rights.

For example, interreligious marriages continue to be restricted in accordance with traditional *Shari'a* law,[32] even though this clearly violates Article 16 of the Universal Declaration of Human Rights that explicitly recognizes the right to marry without any limitation due to race, nationality, and religion. Hence, traditional Islam has no doctrine of human rights and the very notion of a bill of rights would be regarded contrary to the spirit of *Shari'a* in which only God has rights and Muslims have duties and obligations. In this scheme, the moral obligation of a rightful Muslim leader is to uphold God's law, not be at the whim of the electorate and concede to the popular will.

While some scholars regard human rights to be rooted in Judeo-Christian ethics and Greco-Roman statecraft and law, and regard liberal democracy as the only protector of it,[33] many people in the Muslim World regard the Western notions of human rights, its preoccupation with individual rights and the negligence of social and economic rights as misplaced. It is argued, West privileges the individual over the community whereas the Muslims prefer communitarian human rights for the benefit of the *Umma* as a whole.[34] They assert that since human rights are more likely to be implemented in democratic societies, their future prospects are linked to the success of democratization and alleviation of chronic poverty and the lack of meaningful political participation in many parts of the Muslim World. Since democratic political systems are more likely to promote and protect human rights, the roots of the problem are social and political; we must focus on the state and its policy rather than on religion.[35]

A MISPLACED QUESTION?

Given the disparity of perspectives on compatibility of Islam and human rights chronicled above, and since there is no monolithic definition of Islam that is shared by all the diverse groups in the Muslim World, the real question remains: Is the categorical question of compatibility of Islam and democracy a legitimate one? If the answer is yes, then why we should not ask the question if Christianity is compatible with human rights? Or for that matter, Judaism or Buddhism is compatible with human rights? After all in many parts of Africa and Latin America where Christianity is the majority religion there are also systematic and widespread abuses of human rights. In case of Israel, should we then attribute the violation of human rights of the Palestinians to Judaism? In case of Burma, should we attribute chronic violation of human rights there to Buddhism?

The question of compatibility of Islam, democracy, and human rights also privileges Islam and assumes its monopoly of public space. Even the modernist Islamists who seem more sympathetic to the idea of human rights do so only insofar as human rights conform to their perception of Islamic morals and piety. As Anthony Chase has aptly observed, to make

Islam as the necessary basis for human rights is problematic. As he puts it, "structurally, such an assertion—no matter how liberal or human rights friendly the intentions—is anti pluralist insofar as it implicitly assumes an Islamic monopoly on public sphere. Thus, as the theoretical foundation of human rights, there is reason for skepticism. To the degree that a liberal Islamic approach monopolizes the framing of the rights discourse in the Muslim World it is likely to be, at best, unproductive. At worst, it is potentially a harmful project in that it risks reifying the same assumptions as political Islam, i.e., that Islam inevitably monopolizes the public sphere and drawing from other sources is somehow irrelevant."[36]

Given the prominent advocacy role, activism, and intellectual contributions that secular forces have made to the human rights discourse and its promotion throughout the Muslim World, Chase's point is on target and poignant. A more pertinent question before the Muslim modernists and traditionalists who are committed to the idea of an Islamic government to ponder is: Can Islam accept ideological pluralism and abandon its position as a sacred faith with a monopoly on truth? Can it surrender to popular sovereignty if it means creation of a secular government? Can Islam regard itself as another ideology in the marketplace of ideas competing on equal footing with secular forces to win hearts and minds as the principle of pluralism connotes? Or by definition Islamism demands a monopoly over the public space as Islamic theocracies in varying degrees have demonstrated in recent years.

In addition, raising the question of compatibility misses the larger issue that Islam is preoccupied with moral duties and obligations of the faithful and their worldly and otherworldly salvation, human rights are concerned with rights and freedoms that should be guaranteed to all citizens under the law. By posing the question as such one is asking a sacred faith to become what it is not. Even a cursory look at the human rights record of secular authoritarian regimes throughout the Muslim World reveals that they fare no better than their Islamic counterpart in respecting the rights of their citizens.[37] This should make it clear that the problem is not Islam per se, but the social conditions that animate its different manifestations. Instead of looking for a monolithic Islam as the culprit or the catalyst, we must look at the socioeconomic diversity, desperate histories and culture, the multiplicity of voices that engulf the Muslim World as the key explanatory factors responsible for the variations in implementation of human rights.

However, given the limitations involved in reinterpretation of Islam to accommodate human rights, and in light of abysmal human rights record of Islamic theocracies and the ensuing disenchantment with them, certain scholars suggest that we have entered the era of post-Islamism, which is not only a condition, but also a project. According to this view, post-Islamism "is a conscious attempt to conceptualize and strategize the rationale and modalities of transcending Islamism in social, political and intellectual domains. Yet, post-Islamism is neither anti-Islamic, un-Islamic, nor is it secular. Rather it represents an endeavor to fuse religiosity and rights, faith and freedom, Islam and liberty. It is an attempt to turn the underlying principles of Islamism on its head by emphasizing rights instead of duties, plurality in place of a singular authoritative voice, historicity rather than fixed strictures, and the future instead of the past. It wants to marry Islam with individual choice and freedom, with democracy and modernity to achieve what some have termed an 'alternative modernity.'"[38] Indeed, the monumental uprisings of millions in the Arab World in 2011, spearheaded by the youth of the region, may have heralded the arrival of post-Islamist era. These uprisings are characterized by the fact that no grand ideology or narrative such as Pan-Islamism or Pan-Arabism or "Arab Socialism" that inspired the movements of the past seems to be the concern or the preoccupation of the current generation. They aspire for jobs, human rights, respect for their dignity, political accountability, an end to corruption and cronyism and they demand good governance. The peaceful nature of these uprisings, the multiplicity of voices, and the centrality of social, economic, and civic rights concerns once again has proven the salience and the universal appeal of human rights and the intellectual bankruptcy of cultural relativism as an excuse to refute them.

CONCLUSION

This chapter has sought to illustrate that Islam provides the cultural prism of perception and the language of legitimation. It is not the necessary cause or the explanation for the social realities, including the abysmal record of human rights in much of the Muslim World. It can be interpreted to improve the state of human rights, as it was done under president Khatami's interlude in Iran, or it can be interpreted to suppress it, as it was the case under Mulla Umar and the Taliban rule in Afghanistan. Islam is neither responsible for rights violations nor the core basis for advancing rights. Ultimately, "Islam is what Muslims make of it."[39]

Perhaps a more pertinent question is: Should there be a shift in the center of authority in Islam whereby the interpretation of the text and tradition, including Islamic law, is no longer the monopoly of the clerical elite whose preoccupation with the past has made them oblivious to the realities and the challenges of a rapidly changing world? There is an urgent need for a new interpretation of Islamic Jurisprudence (*fiqh*) in order to accommodate human rights as a natural derivative of divine rights, not a deviation from it. Furthermore, Islamic applied ethics must be based on a new set of principles that prohibits its reification and instrumentalization in the hands of politicians and clerics alike. Only a transformational change within Islam that includes the restoration of its spiritual essence that embraces human welfare—upholding a new ethical order in which protection of human rights is at the epicenter of its moral structure—can render Islam a positive and relevant force in the discourse of human rights.[40]

As a faith, Islam is not frozen in time and space. What Muslims have made and continue to make of Islam is historically and socially conditioned. Given this reality, our analytical gaze instead should be focused on the social and political developments and the state and its exercise and abuse of power. As the focus of power and the embodiment of the monopoly of force, the state can be potentially a protector of human rights or its violator. The role of power politics from above, however, is one side of the equation. Perhaps the more significant factor determining the faith of human rights in the region is the struggle of marginalized and the powerless people for political empowerment. As the political uprisings against dictatorships in Tunisia in December of 2010 and in Egypt in January-February of 2011 that have now spread to other countries in the region have demonstrated, the real impetus for human rights has to come from below and from within Muslim societies themselves. Rights are not granted from above by some benevolent dictator, they are won through sweat, blood, and tear—that is, through the concrete social struggle of people from below, as they attempt to re-create their societies in a world in which the appeal of human rights is increasingly borderless and universal.

NOTES

1. General Declaration of the United Nations, "The Universal Declaration of Human Rights of the United Nations." Resolution 217 A (111) of December 10, 1948. http://www.un.org/Overview/rights.html. Accessed on April 17, 2011.
2. Katerina Dalacoura, *Islam, Liberalism and Human Rights: Implications for International Relations* (New York: Macmillan, 2007), 6.
3. Michael J, Perry, *The Idea of Human Rights: Four Inquiries* (New York: Oxford University Press, 2000), 70.
4. Ibid., 64.
5. Ibid., 71.
6. Jack Donnelly, *International Human Rights* (Second Edition) (Boulder, CO: Westview Press, 1998), 32.
7. Reza Afshari, "An Essay on Islamic Cultural Relativism in the Discourse of Human Rights," *Human Rights Quarterly*, Vol. 16, No. 2 (May 1994): 246.
8. Ibid., 247. See also Bassam Tibi, "Islamic Law/Shari'a, Human Rights, Universal Morality and International Relations," *Human Rights Quarterly*, Vol. 16, No. 2 (May 1994): 286–287.

9. Anthony Chase, "Human Rights and Agency in the Arab world," in *Human Rights in the Arab World*, ed. Anthony Chase and Amr Hamzawy (Philadelphia: University of Pennsylvania Press, 2008), 7.

10. Ann Elizabeth Mayer, "Islam and Human Rights: Tradition and Politics," in *Human Rights and Religion: A Reader*, ed. Liam Gearon (Portland: Sussex Academic Press, 2002), 124.

11. Lucas Helie and Aimee Marie, "What Is Your Tribe?: Women's Struggles and the Construction of Muslimness." In *Religious Fundamentalism and Human Rights of Women*, ed. Courtney Holland (New York: St. Martin's Press, 1999), 22.

12. Susan Waltz, "Universal Human Rights: The Contribution of Muslim States," *Human Rights Quarterly*, Vol. 26, No. 4 (November 2004): 814–815.

13. Ann Elizabeth Mayer, *Islam and Human Rights: Tradition and Politics* (Boulder, CO: Westview Press, 1991), 157. See also Fatema Mernissi, *Islam and Democracy: Fear of the Modern World* (Cambridge, MA: Perseus Books, 2002), 51.

14. Sayyid Qutb, *This Religion of Islam* (Palo Alto, CA: Almanar Publishers, 1967), 97. See also William E. Shepard, *Sayyid Qutb and Islamic Activism: A Translation and Critical Analysis of Social Justice in Islam* (Leiden: E. J. Brill, 1996), 19–24.

15. John L. Esposito and James P. Piscatori "Democratization and Islam," *Middle East Journal*, Vol. 45, No. 3 (Summer 1991): 435.

16. Mehran Tamadonfar, *The Islamic Polity and Political Leadership: Fundamentalism, Sectarianism, and Pragmatism* (Boulder, CO: Westview Press, 1989), 42.

17. Richard W. Bulliet, "The Individual in Islamic Society," in *Religious Diversity and Human Rights*, ed. Irene Bloom, Paul J. Martin, and Wayne L. Proudfoot (New York: Colombia University Press, 1996), 176.

18. Ahmad S. Moussalli, *The Islamic Quest for Democracy, Pluralism, and Human Rights* (Gainesville: University of Florida Press, 2001), 7–167. See also Esposito and Piscatori, "Democratization and Islam," 434.

19. Ibid., 126.

20. Louise Marlow, *Hierarchy and Egalitarianism in Islamic Thought* (New York: Cambridge University Press, 1997).

21. John L. Esposito and John O. Voll, *Islam and Democracy* (Oxford, UK: Oxford University Press, 1996), 28.

22. Abbott Freeland, "View of Democracy and the West." In *Iqbal: Poet Philosopher of Pakistan*, ed. Hafeez Malik (New York: Columbia University Press, 1971), 155–175.

23. Ibid.

24. Abdolkarim Soroush, *Farbeh Tar az Ideology* (Sturdier than Ideology), (Tehran: Sara Cultural Institute, 1994), 235–283. See also by Abdolkarim Soroush, *Reason, Freedom, and Democracy,* translated and edited by Mahmoud Sadri and Ahmad Sadri (New York: Oxford University Press, 2000).

25. Abdullahi A. An-Naim, *Toward an Islamic Reformation: Civil Liberties, Human Rights, and International Law* (Syracuse, NY: Syracuse University Press, 1990).

26. Mahmood Monshipouri, *Muslims in Global Politics: Identities, Interests, and Human Rights* (Philadelphia, PA: Pennsylvania University Press, 2009).

27. Timur Kuran, *The Long Divergence: How Islamic Law Held Back the Middle East.* (Princeton, NJ: Princeton University Press, 2011).

28. Abdullahi A. An-Na'im, "Qur'an, Shari'a, and Human Rights: Foundations, Deficiencies and Prospects." In *Human Rights and Religious Values: An Uneasy Relationship?* Ed. Abdullahi A. An-Nai'm, Jerald D. Gort, Henry Jansen, and Hendrik M. Vroom (Grand Rapids, MI: William B. Erdemans Publishing, 1995), 229–242.

29. Ahmad Moussali, "The Classical and Modern Roots of al-Huquq al-Shari'yya and Its Modern Islamic Conceptions as Human Rights," in *The Islamic Quest for Democracy, Pluralism and Human Rights* (Gainesville, FL: University of Florida, 2001), 147.

30. Heiner Bielfeldt, "Muslim Voices in the Human Rights Debate," *Human Rights Quarterly*, Vol. 17, No. 4, November 1995, 591.

31. Mayer, *Islam and Human Rights*, 83.

32. Bielefeldt, "Muslim Voices in the Human Rights Debate," 599.

33. Paul A. Winters, *Islam: Opposing View Points* (San Diego, CA: Greenhaven Press, 1995), 103.

34. Mahmood Monshipouri, *Muslims in Global Politics*, 45.

35. Julie Chernov Hwang, *Peaceful Islamist Mobilization in the Muslim World: What Went Right* (New York: Palgrave Macmillan, 2009), 161–174.

36. Anthony Chase, "Liberal Islam and 'Islam and Human Rights': A Skeptic's View." In *Religion and Human Rights* (Leiden: Koninklijke Brill NV, 2006), 3.

37. For a comparison, see Reza Afshari, *Human Rights in Iran: The Abuse of Cultural Relativism* (Philadelphia: University of Pennsylvania Press, 2001). See also, "From Exporting Terrorism to Exporting Repression: Human Rights in the Arab Region," Annual Report, 2008. Cairo Institute for Human Rights Studies, 17–223.

38. Asef Bayat, *Making Islam Democratic: Social Movements and the Post-Islamist Turn* (Stanford, CA: Stanford University Press, 2007), 94.

39. Anthony Chase, "Human Rights and Agency in the Arab World," 24–25.

40. Tariq Ramadan, *What I Believe* (New York: Oxford University Press, 2010), 3–48.

CHAPTER 3

HUMAN RIGHTS THROUGH THE LENS OF ISLAMIC LEGAL THOUGHT

Halim Rane[1]

INTRODUCTION

The successful implementation of modern standards of human rights in the Muslim world depends on the extent to which they are regarded as not a product of the West but genuinely possessing Islamic legitimacy and authenticity. This chapter contends that the challenge is not simply to demonstrate Islam's ability to adopt what are widely regarded as "Western" norms, but for them to be identifiable as legitimate and normative within the Islamic texts and traditions. It is a positive first step for Muslim states to agree to certain human rights conventions but it is far more meaningful if such standards were met on an "Islamic" basis through their integration into "Islamic" legal thought. This chapter presents a methodology for Quranic interpretation that concentrates on higher, universal objectives or *maqasid* in Arabic. This methodology is both grounded in the Islamic tradition and responsive to the need for Islamic legitimacy and authenticity in instituting human rights in the contemporary Muslim context.

The methodological approach to the interpretation of Islamic law is a critical factor in the resultant legal position. An examination of the human rights norms associated with the Islamic tradition shows that they are frequently based on premodern customs and norms rather than any textual authority from the Quran or the Prophetic traditions. This chapter explores the implications of addressing the question of human rights in the Muslim world through the contextual-*maqasid* methodology interpreting the Quran. It details the origins, Islamic legitimacy, and process of the contextual and *maqasid* approaches. This chapter then demonstrates the extensive compatibility of modern standards of human rights with Islam's sacred texts that emerges when examined through the lens of context and higher objectives.

1 HUMAN RIGHTS IN ISLAM AND THE MUSLIM WORLD

Since the 1990s, much has been written about Islam and human rights (Monshipouri 1998; Ali 2000; Mayer 2006; Baderin, Monshipouri, Mokhtari and Welcham 2006; Baderin 2003; Oh 2007; Akbarzadeh and MacQueen 2008). A large part of this effort has been toward the reconciliation of Islamic and Western norms. The work of Mahmood Monshipouri (1998), for instance, makes an important contribution to synthesizing Islamic and secular values in the promotion of such central aspects of human rights as equality and dignity. More recently, a sharper focus has been made on the issue of interpretation of Islamic law in relation to human rights, including Mashood Baderin's (2003) *International Human Rights and Islamic Law* and Adbullahi An-Na'im's (2008) *Islam and the Secular State.*

The main problem for the application of human rights in the Islamic context is the absence of a legitimate "Islamic" basis for ratification in terms of law. Baderin (2003) writes that "while Muslim states participate in the international human rights objective of the UN, they do not enter declarations and reservations on grounds of the *shariah* or Islamic law when they ratify international human rights treaties" (p. 2–3). However, the representatives of Muslim states do make their arguments against various articles of human rights charters on the basis of Islamic law (Baderin 2003). It must be noted that the principles of the *shariah* and even Islamic law as manifested in premodern times are essentially compatible with contemporary standards of human rights (An-Na'im 2008). The general consensus of scholarship on the subject identifies three main exceptions: gender equality, rights of religious minorities, and freedom of religion.

The work of An-Na'im (2008) looks to the core of the problem concerning Islam and human rights. In his words, he is "trying to promote an understanding of *shariah* that Muslims can actually live by, instead of maintaining an unrealistic ideal that is honoured only in theory but not in practice" (p. 107). As noted by Baderin (2003), An-Na'im (2008), and others such as Hashmi (2002), Muslim states have signed various international human rights covenants and have even included human rights provisions in their states' legislation and constitutions. The issue, however, remains that this needs to be done as a matter of Islamic law if human rights are to attain the requisite normative authority in the

Muslim world. As An-Na'im (2008) contends, for most Muslims "their motivation to uphold human rights is likely to diminish if they perceive those norms to be inconsistent with Islamic precepts. Conversely, their commitment and motivation to protect those rights will increase if they believe them to be at least consistent with, if not required by, their belief in Islam" (p. 111).

An-Na'im (2008) offers a thorough analysis of the compatibilities and incompatibilities of classical interpretations of Islam and contemporary standards of human rights. He advocates an approach to interpretation that allows for Islamic law to be more aligned with contemporary human rights norms. Indeed, he quotes extensively from the Quran to demonstrate that the potential for accommodation on the basis of Islam's sacred text and that alternative formulations of *shariah* principles are merely possible but valid "if accepted by Muslims" (p. 135). As per his earlier work (1990), *Towards an Islamic Reformation*, An-Na'im (2008) continues to advocate a methodology of interpretation based on reverse abrogation: "a shift in the basis of social and political aspects of *shariah* from verses included in the Medina phase of the revelation of the Quran (622–632) to those revealed during the Mecca period (610–622)" (p. 135). The rationale of this approach is that it would facilitate the development of alternative *shariah* principles based on the universal teachings of Islam found in the Meccan period rather than those of the Medinan period, which are more concerned with the specific historical, social, and political contexts of the Prophet Muhammad and his companions. This approach has been advocated by An-Na'im for the past two decades but is yet to gain legitimacy in Islamic legal thought.

As a consequence of classical interpretations of Islamic sources, certain "traditional barriers" for human rights in the Islamic context have been identified (Baderin 2003, p. 10). Religious interpretations that have been used by Muslim states to argue against certain human rights provisions as in the case of the Saudi Arabian representative who opposed certain articles on the Universal Declaration of Human Rights concerning freedom of human conscience in religion as well as those concerned with the rights of women on the basis of Islamic law (Little, Kelsay, and Sachedina 1988). Baderin (2003) is part of a growing list of contemporary scholars who endorse a *maqasid* or objective-oriented approach to interpreting Islamic texts in response to the challenges and complexities of the modern world. He writes that "taking cognizance of the object and purpose of the *shariah (maqasid al-shariah)* . . . is an important holistic approach for realising the proper and benevolent scope of Islamic law" (p. 40). In terms of human rights, he advocates the *maqasid* approach as a means of ensuring the protection of human rights by way of appeals to the higher objectives and general welfare (*maslaha*) that overcome classical interpretations that either violate or disregard contemporary standards of human rights. However, his analysis of the International Covenant on Civil and Political Rights and the International Covenant on Economic, Social, and Cultural Rights fails to effectively or systematically apply the *maqasid*. To his credit, Baderin's analysis identifies specific areas of incompatibility between Islamic law and international law that a *maqasid*-oriented approach would effectively resolve but his work lacks a clear methodology for interpretation and application of this approach.

2   THE CONTEXTUAL-MAQASID METHODOLOGY

Issues concerning the Muslim world need to be addressed within the Islamic tradition if they are to be viewed by Muslims as legitimate and accepted. This cannot be achieved by a simple return to the *shariah* rulings of the past, at least not until what is referred to as *shariah* is realigned with contemporary realities and conditions. Mohammad Hashim Kamali (2006) explains that "this would necessitate imaginative reconstruction and *ijtihad* (intellectual reasoning) entailing revision and modification of the rules of *fiqh* so as to translate the broad objectives of the *shariah* into the laws and institutions of contemporary society" (p. 33). Central to this point, the late Fazlur Rahman (1984) emphasizes that for an approach to interpretation to be successful, it must "flow from the teaching of the Quran and Sunnah as a whole"; otherwise it "will not solve a given problem or apply to a given situation Islamically" (p. 23).

As I have documented elsewhere, the classical *usul* methodology along with classical approaches to *ijtihad* have been deemed inadequate to meeting the challenges posed by modernity (Rane 2009). Increasingly, scholars of Islamic studies are endorsing two approaches, *maqasid* and contextualization. In his renowned work *Islam and Modernity*, Fazlur Rahman (d.1988) explains that the failure to appreciate the unity of the Quranic verses resulted in the emergence of an alternative worldview from that intended by the Quran. Historically, Islamic law has suffered from "the lack of an adequate method for understanding the Quran" (p. 2). Central to this shortcoming is a failure to appreciate the "underlying unity of the Quran . . . coupled with a practical insistence upon fixing on words of various verses in isolation," referred to as the "atomistic" approach. The overriding problem with this approach is that "laws were often derived from verses that were not at all legal in intent" (p. 2–3). This view is reinforced by others, such as Kamali (2006) who observes an "overtly legalistic tendency" among latter day Muslim jurists, which he contends has developed at the expense of the spirit of Islam (p. 1).

Istiqra

I will elaborate on the *maqasid* approach in a moment and discuss the contributions of one of its most influential proponents, the fourteenth-century-Islamic scholar Abu Ishaq al-Shatibi (d.1388). At this point however, it is important to explain the concept of *istiqra* and how it is used in the methodology I propose. Like many after him, Shatibi emphasized the danger of conducting *ijtihad* on the basis of particulars in isolation rather than universals in context. He argues that both universals and particulars must be considered together (Raysuni 2006). He left a robust methodology for analyzing and identifying the *maqasid* of the Quranic text on the basis of induction. Induction is for Shatibi "one of the most crucial, powerful tools with which to identify the objectives of the Law" (Raysuni 2006, p. 280). In fact, Shatibi regards induction as yielding "complete certainty" as an inductive reading is not based on a single piece of evidence but upon numerous such pieces, which together "convey a single message which is thereby invested with complete certitude" (p. 281). It is through this method that Shatibi bases his conviction that Islamic law is best explained in terms of the preservation of human interests or *maslaha*.

The method of induction developed by Shatibi has been refined by the late Muhammad al-Tahir Ibn Ashur (2006). His method, "thematic inference" or *istiqra*, identifies the objectives of the law through inductive analysis of the text as a whole by focusing on provisions and commands with stated effective causes (*ilal*) or explicit indication or allusion to a specific objective (*maqsad*), and comparing rules and commands with a common *ratio legis*. As Shatibi, Ibn Ashur, and others contend, *istiqra* is the most reliable method for understanding the Quran and identifying the intent, objectives, and purpose of its content. The value of a thematic reading of the Quran, in order to acquire a more holistic and comprehensive understanding of the book, is also endorsed by Fazlur Rahman (1989) and best represented in his famous work, *Major Themes of the Quran*. While a *maqsad* may not be identifiable from a single verse of the Quran, the reading of multiple verses on a certain issue will reveal an associated purpose, intent, or objective. Kamali (2006) explains:

> There may be various textual references to a subject, none of which may be in the nature of a decisive injunction. Yet their collective weight is such that it leaves little doubt as to the meaning that is obtained from them. A decisive conclusion may, in other words, be arrived at from a plurality of speculative expressions (p. 124).

Maqasid

I will now proceed to elaborate on the *maqasid* and contextualization approaches. The *maqasid* approach offers a framework to guide the contextualist approach and to ensure consistency with the spirit of the Quran. It emphasizes the goals, purpose, intent, and objectives of the text rather than the specific words and verses. Kamali (2006) writes that the *maqasid* are "rooted in the textual injunctions of the Quran and the Sunnah . . . their main focus is the general philosophy and objectives of these injunctions often beyond the particularities of the text" (p. 130). This approach makes the *shariah* more accessible by avoiding the literalism, atomism, and conditions associated with the *usul* methodology. In this context, it should be recalled that the laws deduced from the *shariah* are not imposed for their own sake but for the purpose of realizing certain objectives and benefits and avoiding certain harms. Kamali (2006) writes that "when there is change of a kind whereby a particular law no longer secures its underlying purpose and rationale, it must be substituted with a suitable alternative. To do otherwise would mean neglecting the objective of the Lawgiver [God]" (p. 51–52). Herein is the importance of the *maqasid* approach today.

To appreciate the relevance of the *maqasid* in light of the challenges and complexities of the contemporary world, it is useful to consider its origins and development. Reference to the *maqasid* peaked at times of social, political, and economic challenge. While the concept of higher objectives can be seen in the approach and ruling of rulers as far back in Muslim history as the second caliph, Umar (d.644), the actual term *maqasid* was not used in the writings of jurists until 300 years after the death of the Prophet Muhammad, when Abu Abd Allah al-Tirmidhi al-Hakim (d.932) became the first scholar to use the term *maqasid* and to write specifically on the topic.

It was not until more than a century later that Abd Allah al-Juwayni (d.1085), who extensively used the term *maqasid* along with its derivatives in his book, *al-Burhan*, classified the three categories of *maqasid: daruriyyat, hajiyyat*, and *tahsiniyyat* (essentials, needs, and enhancements). He is also credited as having been the first to define the major essentials as the protection of religion, human life, faculty of reason, progeny, and wealth. His student Abu Hamid al-Ghazali (d.1111) expanded and developed these ideas in his famous works *Shifa al-Ghalil* and *al-Mustasfa*. Al-Ghazali defined the five objectives of *shariah* as the preservation of religion, life, faculty of reason, chastity/progeny, and material wealth in relation to their corresponding prescribed punishments or *hudud*. A sixth objective, preservation of honor, was subsequently added by Shihab al-Din al-Qarafi (d.1285).

Al-Ghazali outlined the central objectives of Islamic law in terms of intents and interests, both "spiritual" and "worldly." His work is attributed with having set the parameters for the understanding and application of the *maqasid*. Although these parameters were somewhat reshaped by Abu Ishaq al-Shatibi, they have continued to influence and constrain the thinking of *maqasid* even until today. In the two centuries between al-Ghazali and Shatibi, the influence of al-Ghazali can clearly be seen in terms of the direction in which the theory of *maqasid* developed. As Ahmad Raysuni (2006) documents, the contributions of the scholars during this period basically served to elaborate the model developed by al-Ghazali. Some scholars, however, did depart from the framework constructed by al-Ghazali, including Izz al-Din Abd al-Salam (d.1261), al-Qarafi, Ibn Taymiyyah (d.1328), Ibn al-Qayyim (d.1350), and al-Shatibi. Abd al-Salam's work on the *qawa'id al-ahkam* or "legal maxims" broadened the discussion of *maqasid* in terms of all that promotes benefit and prevents harm.

The concept of *maqasid* was expanded in the fourteenth century by Ibn Taymiyyah, who identified a more open-ended list of values that included fulfilment of contracts, preservation of kinship ties, honoring the rights of one's neighbors, sincerity, trustworthiness, and moral purity. He raised objection to the *usuli* position that limited the essential objectives of Islamic law to the five expounded by al-Ghazali, going so far as to state that these five or six do not represent the highest or most significant of objectives. The work of Shatibi, however, made a profound contribution to developing the theory of *maqasid* by focusing on the concept of *maslaha* or public interest as an approach to overcoming the rigidity imposed by literalism and *qiyas* (analogical reasoning).

In the modern era, the most significant contribution to the *maqasid* was made by Ibn Ashur. First published in 1946 in Tunis, Ibn Ashur's *Maqasid al-Shariah al-Islamiyyah* is arguably the most important attempt of the twentieth century to further develop the theory of *maqasid*. Expressing the need for an objective-based approach to Islamic law in light of modern realities, he introduces to the theory of *maqasid* the preservation of the family system, freedom of belief, orderliness, natural disposition, civility, human rights, freedom, and equality as objectives of Islamic law. In contemporary times, Yusuf Qaradawi has further extended the *maqasid* list to include social welfare support, freedom, human dignity, and human fraternity, while Kamali has added to this list the protection of fundamental rights and liberties, economic development, along with research and development in science and technology. Like their predecessors, both scholars based their additions on relevant supporting texts of the Quran and Prophetic Traditions. Kamali (2006) contends that the *maqasid* remains dynamic and open to expansion according to the priorities of every age.

In isolation, however, the theory of *maqasid* remains deficient to the extent that it does not systematically address the issue of context. Abdullah Saeed (2006), for instance, regards the *maqasid* as an important theoretical basis for context-based interpretation but contends that its historical formulation has rendered it "too restrictive to be considered as a basis for liberal interpretations of the Quran" (p. 127). The major obstacle for the *maqasid* approach in Saeed's opinion is the authoritative method of *usul al-fiqh*, which does not allow for interpretation on the basis of context, intent, purpose, or circumstances, in the case of clear instructions or statements in the Quran or Prophetic traditions. Commenting that the demand of the *usul* method for following the text negates a *maqasid*-oriented approach, Saeed laments that "*maqasid* is thus often reduced to a form of empty rhetoric as far as ethico-legal texts are concerned" (p. 127).

Contextualization

It is my contention, such reservations as those expressed by Saeed can be overcome by a methodology that incorporates contextualization, both in the historical and contemporary context. Contextualization is an approach to interpreting the Quran that requires consideration of the text as a whole, the position of verses within the text, the circumstances or conditions of the Prophet Muhammad and the early Muslim community at the time of the revelation, and the contemporary situation or issue for which the Quranic guidance is sought. Diversity in interpretation is to be expected with differing experiences, beliefs, prejudices, and values of different interpreters.

There has been a realization among some contemporary Muslim scholars that if the Quran is to remain relevant to Muslim societies and conditions, given the dramatic changes that have occurred since the seventeenth century, a contextualist approach is necessary. A large number of contemporary scholars including Abdullahi An-Na'im, Khaled Abou El Fadl, Louay Safi, and Sohail Hashmi have discussed the need to read and understand the Quran in light of historical and contemporary contexts. Among those who have developed methods of contextualization are Fazlur Rahman, Abdul Hamid Abu Sulayman, and Abdullah Saeed.

Rahman (1984) advocates a contextualist process of interpreting and applying the Quran that he refers to as a "double-movement." The process involves a movement from a contemporary issue to Quranic times (first movement) and then back to the present (second movement). The first movement requires one to first "understand the import or meaning of a given statement by studying the historical situation or problem to which it was the answer" (p. 6) This step, along with the general, preliminary, historical study, is necessary for an understanding of the "meaning of the Quran as a whole in terms of the specific tenets that constitute responses to specific situations" (p. 6). The second step is the generalization of the specific answers and to enunciate them as "statements of general moral-social objectives that can be distilled from specific texts in light of the sociohistorical background and the often stated *rationes legis*" (p. 6).

Following this perspective and referring to what he calls the "time-space dimension," Abu Sulayman (1993) explains that the pervasive usage and acceptance of *qiyas* (analogical reasoning) particularly during the Abbasid period was due to the fact that the empire was globally dominant and, therefore, content with the status quo. It, therefore, sought a methodology that would maintain the model that developed in the last years of the Prophet's life when conflict with the tribes of Arabia was particularly intense (p. 106). In this respect he also argues against reading historical events in legal terms. Rather, he advocates an analysis of the political and strategic significance of the events. Abu Sulayman writes that it was the Prophet's realism, "with its wide margin of political manoeuvrability, rather than legalism and formalism, that explains the Prophet's successful conduct of external affairs" (p. 75–79). The Prophet's actions, peaceful and forceful, were guided by what was necessary in any given circumstance and the ultimate goal of ensuring the survival of the Muslims and the prosperity of Islam, all within Islam's moral and ethical framework, which later became legal.

A more recent contribution to the contextualist approach is that of Abdullah Saeed (2006). In his book *Interpreting the Quran*, Saeed presents a comprehensive argument for the replacement of the traditional "legalistic-literalistic" approach to interpreting the Quran, particularly the ethico-legal verses, with an approach-based contextualization. Saeed has developed a three-fold framework for a contemporary approach to interpreting the Quran involving a new classification of Quranic verses, a new hierarchy of Quranic values, and a new model for interpretation. Saeed's four-stage model for interpretation begins with the text of the Quran in its context, followed by a linguistic and literary examination of the words of the text, then an examination of the original meaning of the text for its first recipients in their sociohistorical context, and finally the meaning of the text in reference to contemporary circumstances.

The methodology of interpreting the Quran proposed by this chapter integrates the *maqasid* and contextualization approaches derived from a reading of the Quran on the basis of *istiqra*. As I have demonstrated in *Reconstructing Jihad amid Competing International Norms*, these approaches are most effective when applied as part of a single methodology. This methodology involves reading all of the relevant Quranic verses on a particular issue on the basis of *istiqra* or thematic induction, considering the historical, social, and political context in which they were revealed, and ascertaining the overriding objectives that emerge from this reading. Once the higher objectives (*maqasid*) of a collection of verses concerning a particular issue are identified, interpretation of particular verses should then be made on the basis of these objectives and should not be made in contradiction to the identified *maqasid*. This methodology has the potential for broad application to a range of issues concerning

Islam and modernity, including human rights. The next section of this chapter will apply this methodology to the issues of gender equality, rights of religious minorities, and freedom of religion.

3   APPLICATION AND RECONCILIATION

For the purpose of demonstrating the application of the contextual-*maqasid* methodology proposed by this chapter, I have limited the key search terms and will provide only a brief analysis of gender equality, rights of religious minorities, and freedom of religion in the Quran. The following analysis is based on Muhammad Asad's English translation of the Quran via the online Quran search engine at www.islamicity.com/Quransearch/.

Gender Equality

For the purposes of this discussion, I have used "women," "woman," "mate," "wife," "wives," "daughter," "mother," "queen" as well as the names of women mentioned in the Quran, such as "Mary," as search terms. This yielded almost 200 verses that we can consider to be most relevant to understanding the Quran's view of gender issues.

Many of the Quranic verses concerning women arise in the context of family matters, namely, marriage, divorce, and inheritance. In such verses the Quran establishes certain rules of marriage (Quran 4:22–24, 33:50, 2:221, 2:235, and 60:10), guidelines for divorce (Quran 2:229–241, 4:20, 4:130, 4:128, 65:1, and 66:5), and details of inheritance (Quran 4:7, and 4:11–12). The underlying principle of these verses is that a woman is an independent entity with rights (Quran 2:233 and 4:32) whose will is acknowledged (Quran 2:231–232) and who is in charge of her own affairs (Quran 33:50). Men are regarded by the Quran as carers of women (Quran 4:34) but that women should have a say in decision making is expressed as normative (Quran 28:26). Moreover, the relationship between spouses is intended by the Quran to be a partnership (Quran 42:11) and the expectation is that women should be treated with kindness and fairness (Quran 4:25 and 33:49).

The most apparent theme of the Quran's perspective on gender relations is equality. The Quran repeatedly stresses the equality of believing men and women and the equal rewards they should expect to receive for their good deeds (Quran 3:195, 33:35–36, 40:40, 16:97, 48:5, 48:25, 49:11, 57:12, 57:18, 85:10, 71:28, 47:19, and 9:72). However, the Quran acknowledges that both men and women are capable of both good and bad (Quran 48:6, 57:13, 24:26, 33:73 and 9:67–71). Certain women are criticized in the Quran for their faithlessness, namely, with wives of Noah and Lot (Quran 29:32–33, 66:10, 7:83, and 11:81), while others are highly praised, such as the wife of the Pharaoh (Quran 28:9 and 66:11) and Mary the mother of Jesus (Quran 5:75, 5:110, 23:50, 66:12, and 3:42). The Quran does not accept the idea of original sin or ascribe specific blame to women. Rather, the book elaborates on the creation of man and woman in terms of equality (Quran 2:35, 7:19, 20:117, 39:6, 4:1, and 7:189). It also ridicules customs underlined by notions of gender inequality (Quran 6:139) as well as the idea that sons are superior to daughters (Quran 6:100, 37:149, 37:153, 43:16, 43:18 and 52:39).

In the context of marriage and divorce, the equality of men and women is continually emphasized. The very basis of marriage according to the Quran is "love and compassion" (Quran 30:21). The Quran advocates that marriage should take place based on equitable terms (Quran 4:3–4, 4:25, and 4:127). Similarly, divorce should be conducted on the basis of equality and fairness (Quran 4:130, 4:128, 65:1, 65:6, 2:231–232, and 2:241).

In addition to equality, the other major theme of the Quran's perspective of women is dignity. The upholding of the dignity of women is repeatedly emphasized by the Quran (Quran 24:3–4, 24:23, 24:31, 24:60, 33:55, 33:58–59, 4:25, 5:5, and 2:241). The Quran imposes a harsh penalty for those who make slanderous accusations against a woman (Quran 24:4). It encourages modesty in dress for women in public as a means of protecting their dignity and protection from harassment (Quran 24:31 and 33:59). However, the Quran considers the participation of women in society as normative (Quran 28:23, 12:30–33, 12:51, and 3:61). It accepts a role for women in economic affairs (Quran 2:282) as well as their political participation (Quran 60:12). The book even gives legitimacy to female leadership through its discussion of the Queens of Sheba (Quran 27:36–38) and particularly the description of her throne as "mighty" (Quran 27:23).

Taking these verses collectively, the spirit of the Quran is one of gender equality, the upholding of women's dignity, and her social, economic, and political participation as normative. All verses of the Quran concerning women should be read in this light. Thus, such verses as 2:282, which on the surface may suggest that the testimony of a woman is worth half as much as that of a man should be read in the social and historical context of seventh-century Arabia. Economic participation and witnessing business contracts was a male privilege. The Quran legitimized the involvement of women in such activities. The provision of one male to two female witnesses should not be seen as a matter of female inferiority but a tactical response to prevailing social norms. The full and equal participation of women is consistent with the overall message of the Quran.

Similarly, for verse 4:34 to be read as an endorsement of women's subservience to man is to read this verse in contradiction to the spirit of the Quran. The prevailing norms of seventh-century Arabia meant that the well-being of women was dependent on men, their fathers, brothers, and husbands. The Quran, however, makes provision for the full and equal social, economic, and political participation of women and is therefore open to change in social norms that would allow women to be more independent of men. The ability of women to inherit, own property, and remain in charge of their own affairs suggests that the Quran supports this level of equality.

Minority Rights

Using "Jew," "Christian," "people of the book," and "unbeliever" as search terms, yields almost 100 verses that we can consider to be most relevant to understanding the Quran's view of non-Muslims. It is important to note from the outset that the Quran is not a text that details matters of social organization. What can be drawn from the Quran on matters of minority rights or the place of non-Muslims in Islam is derived from stories of ancient relations between God and certain religious communities and relations between Muhammad and non-Muslims in the context of seventh-century Arabia.

The dignity of all human beings is a principle established by the Quran irrespective of religion. It states that God has conferred dignity on the children of Adam and preferred them above other creations (Quran 17:70). From this perspective, all human beings are entitled to be treated justly and equitably (Quran 60:8). Moreover, the Quran advocates good relations between all human beings; the religious convictions of people are not meant to be a determinant of relations or conduct toward one another (Quran 4:94).

This is not to suggest that the Quran is uncritical of certain non-Muslims. The Quran discusses the rivalry between Muslims, Christians, and Jews over such matters as ancestry and relations with God (Quran 2:120, 2:135, 2:139, 2:140, 3:140, 3:67, and 5:18). Jews are especially criticized in the Quran for hostility toward the Muslims (Quran 5:82) and distorting the meaning of God's word (Quran 4:46 and 5:41). The Quran even advises Muslims against taking non-Muslims as protectors or allies (Quran 5:51). However, the Quran clarifies that this instruction on allies refers to those who were fighting against the Muslims because of their faith and drove them from their homes (Quran 60:9).

The verses that suggest adversarial relations between Muslims and non-Muslims were revealed in the context of war between Muslims and non-Muslims (Quran 66:9 and 9:73). The Quran is unambiguous concerning the rationale of fighting. Muslims were given permission to fight against non-Muslims not because of faith but in response to aggression and oppression (Quran 22:39–40, 9:17, 8:39, and 8:34). Even the so-called sword-verse (Quran 9:5) is followed by two verses that instruct

Muslims to give protection to non-Muslims who seek their protection (Quran 9:6–7). Moreover, the Quran advocates that upholding a treaty with non-Muslims takes priority over the obligation to protect people from their oppression (Quran 8:72).

Such verses that address hostility between Muslims and non-Muslims do not detract, however, from the Quran's declaration that all human beings are accountable to God (Quran 2:139, 4:42, and 22:17) and that all those who believe and do good deeds, including Christians and Jews, shall be rewarded by God (Quran 2:62, 5:69, and 22:17). In sum, Quranic verses critical of non-Muslims, including those concerning matters of faith, occur in reference to particular historical contexts. Others that appear to encourage hostility between Muslims and non-Muslims occur in the context of war and relate to treaty obligations, aggression, oppression, and freedom of religion. The *maqasid* established by the Quran regarding all human beings, non-Muslims included, are treatment of others with dignity, fairness, and equality.

Freedom of Religion

A search of the Quran for such words as "religion" and "faith" results in a total of almost 380 verses. Only in a couple of dozen verses does the Quran use the term religion or *din* in Arabic. In over 360 verses, however, the Quran uses the term faith or *iman* in Arabic. Although in not a single verse of the Quran is there a provision for any sanction or punishment for those who choose not to profess Islam, exclusivist and intolerant claims by Muslims vis-a-vis other religions stem from a repeated statement of the Quran that the only religion accepted by God is Islam (Quran 3:19, 3:85, 5:3, 9:33, and 48:28). These verses seem to stand in contrast, however, with others that express that there is no coercion on religion (Quran 2:256, 10:99, and 109:6), declare great rewards for all those who have faith in God and do righteous deeds (Quran 2:25, 3:57, 4:122, 5:9, 6:82, 7:42, 8, 74, 9:88, 10:4, 20:82, 24:55, 30:15, 41:8, 48:29, 57:7, 65:11, and 95:6), and even advocate jihad for the defense of other religions that worship God (Quran 22:39–40).

How to reconcile these apparent contradictions? Perhaps consideration should be given to the words used in their literal sense. If read in this way then what the Quran is saying is that the only "way of life" (*din*) accepted by God is "submission to God" (*islam*). The Quran uses this very approach in settling the dispute between Muslims, Christians, and Jews, as to the religion of previous Prophets. The Quran states that they were *"Muslims"* as they submitted themselves to the will of God (Quran 3:67 and 2:140). Moreover, the Quran repeatedly states that religion or the way of life involving submission to God was the same throughout history (Quran 26:137, 2:132, 2:183, and 42:13).

As far as the concept of faith is concerned, the Quran provides extensive descriptions of faith (none of which preclude non-Muslims), including being conscious of God (Quran 2:212, 3:102, 3:35, 9:119, 33:70, 57:28, and 59:18), loving God above all else (Quran 2:165), enjoining what is just and forbidding what is unjust (Quran 3:110), doing righteous deeds (Quran 98:7 and 103:3), being constant in prayer and giving charity regularly (Quran 2:43, 2:254, 4:162, 5:55, 8:3, and 14:31), being fair and kind to one's spouse (Quran 4:19), being patient in adversity (Quran 103:3 and 3:200), and honoring pledges and being true to one's word (Quran 5:1and 61:2).

The Quranic verses that may be read in support of a hostile response to non-Muslims and the supremacy of Islam (such as Quran 9:5 and 9:29) should be read in their historical context. Specifically, the wars that raged between the Muslims and non-Muslim Arab tribes during the last decade of the Prophet Muhammad's life that involved acts of overt aggression, expulsion from homes, and a denial of the right to freedom of religious conviction. Even within the context of such hostilities, the Quran maintained that hatred of others should not prevent them being treated justly (Quran 5:8), that non-Muslims may be invited to accept Islam (Quran 9:6–7) but not compelled to accept (Quran 10:99), treated with forgiveness (Quran 45:14), kindness, and equality (Quran 60:8), and that peaceful relations should be pursued (Quran 4:90 and 8:61).

Outside of the context of war and hostility, the Quran does not endorse a posture of adversity toward non-Muslims. Submission to the will of God is regarded as a preferable way of life for human beings but is regarded as a matter of conviction that some human beings will embrace, while others remain free to reject. In sum, the *maqasid* of these verses are the preservation of conditions under which human beings are free to choose their religious convictions.

CONCLUSION

Islamic law continues to be of particular importance to Muslims. In some cases, classical interpretations of the Quran have resulted in a perceived incompatibility between Islam and certain human rights norms. While Muslim states have adopted various human rights and other conventions that have been developed as part of modern international norms, they have not necessarily been accepted on an Islamic basis or as part of contemporary Islamic legal thought. This chapter has presented an Islamically legitimate methodology that synthesizes the contextualization and *maqasid* or objective-oriented approach to reading and interpreting the Quran. When examined through the lens of context and higher objectives based on a comprehensive, thematic, inductive reading, extensive compatibility between modern standards of human rights and Islam's sacred text is evident.

NOTES

1. Dr. Halim Rane is the Deputy Director of the Griffith Islamic Research Unit and Senior Lecturer in the National Centre of Excellence for Islamic Studies at Griffith University. Dr. Rane is the author of a number of books including *Reconstructing Jihad amid Competing International Norms* (Palgrave Macmillan, 2009) and *Islam and Contemporary Civilisation: Evolving Ideas, Transforming Relations* (Melbourne University Press, 2010).

REFERENCES

Abu Sulayman, A. A. 1993. *Towards an Islamic Theory of International Relations: New Directions for Methodology and Thought* (Herndon: International Institute of Islamic Thought).

Akbarzadeh, S., and B. MacQueen. (eds.). 2008. *Islam and Human Rights in Practice: Perspectives across the Ummah* (London: Routledge).

An-Na'im, A. A. 2008. *Islam and the Secular State: Negotiating the Future of Sharia* (Cambridge, MA: Harvard University Press).

———. 1990. *Toward an Islamic Reformation: Civil liberties, Human Rights, and International Law* (New York: Syracuse University Press).

Baderin, M. 2003. *International Human Rights and Islamic Law* (Oxford: Oxford University Press).

Baderin, M., M. Monshipouri, S. Mokhtari, and L. Welcham, (eds.). 2006. *Islam and Human Rights: Advocacy for Social Change in Local Contexts* (New Delhi: Global Media Publications).

Esposito, J. 2005. *Islam: The Straight Path* (Oxford: Oxford University Press).

Feldman, N. 2008. "Why Shariah?" *New York Times*. http://www.nytimes.com/2008/03/16/magazine/16Shariah-t.html?ref=world. Accessed September 1, 2009.

Hashmi, S. (ed.). 2002. *Islamic Political Ethics: Civil Society, Pluralism, and Conflict*. (Princeton, NJ: Princeton University Press).

Ibn Ashur, M. T. 2006. *Treatise on Maqasid al-Shariah*. (London: International Institute of Islamic Thought).

Kamali, M. H. 2006. *An Introduction to Shariah* (Kuala Lumpur: Ilmiah Publishers).

Little, D., J. Kelsay, and A. A. Sachedina. 1988. *Human Rights and the Conflict of Cultures: Western and Islamic Perspectives on Religious Liberty* (Columbia: University of South Carolina Press).

Maududi, A. A. 1981. *Human Rights in Islam* (London: Islamic Foundation).

Mayer, A. 2006. *Islam and Human Rights* (Boulder, CO: Westview).

Monshipouri, M. 1998. *Islamism, Secularism, and Human Rights in the Middle East* (Boulder, CO: Lynne Rienner).

Oh, I. 2007. *The Rights of God: Islam, Human Rights and Comparative Ethics* (Washington, D.C.: Georgetown University Press).

Rahman, F. 1984. *Islam and Modernity: Transformation of an Intellectual Tradition* (Chicago: University of Chicago Press).

———. 1989. *Major Themes of the Quran* (Kuala Lumpur: Islamic Book Trust).

Rane, H. 2009. *Reconstructing Jihad amid Competing International Norms* (New York: Palgrave).

Raysuni, A. 2006. *Imam al-Shatibi's Theory of the Higher Objectives and Intents of Islamic Law* (Kuala Lumpur: Islamic Book Trust).

Saeed, A. 2006. *Interpreting the Quran: Towards a Contemporary Approach* (London: Routledge).

Shaheen, A. 2000. *Gender and Human Rights in Islam and International Law* (Leiden: Brill).

CHAPTER 4

ISLAMOPHOBIA, DEFAMATION OF RELIGIONS, AND INTERNATIONAL HUMAN RIGHTS

Turan Kayaoğlu

Since 1999, under pressure from Muslim majority states, the United Nations passed a series of resolutions asking states to combat the defamation of religions. This initiative raises the question: Should there be an international norm against hate speech targeting a religion? In particular, is the United Nations Resolution "Combating the Defamation of Religions" a step forward in developing such a norm? So far these questions have polarized international society by setting Muslims against Western liberal democracies. After 12 years of campaign, the supporters of the Resolution decided not to pursue defamation resolution and joined major Western states to pass a joint resolution on religious tolerance and freedom.

While now defunct, this campaign has been important as an example of both Muslim majority states' engagement with international human rights discourse and the substantial issues about hate speech it raised. In an attempt to circumvent the political and normative polarization the Resolution has created, I argue that an international norm protecting minority religions from defamation has significant potential to contribute not only to the freedom of expression and religion but also to the political participation of religious minorities. I reconfigure the debate by putting the rights of the religious minorities at the center and offer a framework that can satisfy the demands of both Muslim identity activists who are concerned about the effects of Islamophobia and liberals who are worried about the potential implications of hate speech regulation on freedom of speech.

I proceed in three sections. I first describe the politics of the Defamation Resolution and the way it has polarized international society. Second, I highlight the differences between the Western states and NGOs and the Organization of Islamic Conference (henceforth "OIC") on this issue. Third, I argue how refocusing of the debate can narrow, if not totally eliminate, the differences, making the defamation of religions an acceptable human rights concern in liberal political theory.

I THE POLITICS OF THE DEFAMATION RESOLUTION

The idea that religious minorities need specific protections is not new in international society. From the treaties of Westphalia (1648) to the various "minority" treaties of the nineteenth century, international law has advanced the rights of religious minorities. Modern international human rights law also aims to protect the freedom of religion and to eliminate religious discrimination; this is most notably embodied in the UN Declaration on the Elimination of All Forms of Intolerance and of Discrimination Based on Religion or Belief (1981).[1] Yet religious hatred and public defamation of religions abound, as exemplified by the persistence of anti-Semitism, the association of Judaism with financial domination and power, by the growth of Islamophobia, the association of Islam with violence and terrorism, and the presence of Christianophia, the association of Christianity with Western political and military domination. The United Nations Special Rapporteur maintains that in all the above cases, the defamation of religion demonizes the followers of these religions, creates fear and hatred of them, and thus establishes the political and ideological context for the violation of the human rights of their believers.[2]

The rise of Islamophobia in Europe illustrates the relationship between religious hatred and violation of human rights. Various human rights reports show how Muslims in Europe continue to suffer widespread discrimination resulting both from Europe's historical anti-Islam prejudices and the post-9/11 political environment. According to the report of European Monitoring Centre on Racism and Xenophobia (EUMC), "Muslims in the European Union: Discrimination and Islamophobia" (2006), Islamophobia is a form of racism. For that claim, EUMC uses the definition of racism developed by the European Commission against Racism and Intolerance: "the belief that a ground such as race, colour, language, religion, national or ethnic origin justifies contempt for a person or a group of persons, or the notion of superiority or a person or a group of persons."[3] Viewing Islamophobia as a form of racism, the EUMC reports increasing Islamophobia in the post-9/11 political and social environment; Muslim communities in Europe are subject to widespread prejudices ranging from manifesting of negative stereotyping to varying degrees of violence and harassment. Since 9/11 and the increased efforts to fight international terrorism, certain visible minorities, like Muslims, "have become particularly vulnerable to racism and/or racial discrimination across many fields of public life including education, employment, housing, access to goods and services, access to public places and freedom of movement."[4] According to the report, negative stereotypes marginalize and discriminate Muslims.[5] Muslims often face prejudice and hatred in the form of verbal threats that can escalate to physical attacks on people and property.[6] More than half of Western Europeans view Muslims with suspicion.[7]

A second EUMC report, "Perceptions of Discrimination and Islamophobia" (2006) tells that European Muslims complain about the media's negative portrayal of Muslims through distortions or selective reporting. While respondents concede that the majority of attacks suffered are mostly verbal rather than physical violence, they note that they are "worn down" by such daily experiences that are far more likely to happen when a person is visibly Muslim, such as when wearing a headscarf.[8]

The Defamation Resolution

The prior neglect of religious hate speech in international human rights is puzzling given the origins of the modern human rights movement, which grew out of a response to the Holocaust.[9] The current Muslim-promoted debate revolves around a series of UN resolutions created first at the Commission on Human Rights (CHR) and then passed to the current UN Human Rights Council (HRC) after the dissolution of the former body. The CHR first accepted an earlier version of the Resolution in 1999, and the UN General Assembly (UNGA) passed the Resolution for the first time in 2005.[10] Marking its Islamic pedigree, the 1999 version was "Combating initially proposed as of Islam." Over time the name and content of the resolution changed. The changes were also the result of new issues in international relations, like 9/11 and post-9/11 politics in the West. Also, criticisms voiced by major international actors, such as the European Union, seem to have influenced the text.[11] Although UNGA resolutions are nonbinding, they do have significant moral authority as they both reflect and shape the collective expectations of the international community. These shared expectations of acceptable standards of behavior in international relations are what legal scholars call "soft" law and what political scientists call international norms. For example, the Secretary General of the OIC, Ekmeleddin İhsanoğlu, argues that the resolution is now "the opinion of international community" and thus has "international legitimacy."[12] This view, as I argue later, is heavily contested by Western states and NGOs.

According to the supporters of the Resolution, various UN human rights documents justify a norm for combating the defamation of religions. Invoking the UN Charter, the Universal Declaration of Human Rights, the International Covenant on Civil and Political Rights, and the Convention on the Elimination of Racial Discrimination, supporters link their demand for a norm against religious defamation to existing human rights norms such as combating racial discrimination and the incitement to religious hatred. Furthermore, supporters refer to various UN initiatives such as the Global Agenda for Dialogue among Civilizations, the Millennium Declaration, and the Durban Declaration, which all urge the international community to combat racism, xenophobia, and religious discrimination.

Compatible with these initiatives, the Resolution claims to combat defamation of religions, particularly Islamophobia. Yet the Resolution lacks definitions of its key terms such as "combating," "religion," and "defamation." Ambiguity regarding "defamation" is particularly troublesome due to its implication for the free speech. Without knowing what constitutes defamation, how would states combat it and how would the international community assess if states are genuinely combating religious defamation or suppressing free speech? Short of a definition, the text of the resolution enumerates examples of the defamation of religions. These examples hint at the intention of the Resolution's sponsors. Some of the examples of the defamation of religions are general: negative stereotyping of religions, their adherents and sacred persons; attacks on businesses, cultural centers, and places of worship; dissemination of racist and xenophobic ideas and material aimed at any religion or its followers; incitement of religious hatred, hostility, and violence; acts of hatred, discrimination, intimidation, and coercion; and targeting people on the basis of their religions. Additionally, the text provides two examples that are specifically about Islam: the identification of Islam with terrorism and the profiling of Muslims after 9/11 through laws controlling and stigmatizing Muslims. These examples include a wide range of behaviors and expressions as defamation. While some of them, like "negative stereotyping of religions" suggest that the resolution may stifle religious criticism in violation of the freedom of expression, others, like incitement to religious hatred, are under the purview of internationally established norms of human rights.[13]

The Resolution makes sweeping assertions about the broader problems of international society, namely, the polarization along cultural and religious lines similar to what is expressed in Huntington's clash of civilization thesis. In response, the resolution stresses the importance of religious dialogue, tolerance, and diversity and argues that the defamation of religions stands as a major impediment in realizing the coexistence of civilizations. Bringing religions in the international agenda with a religiously positive framework, the resolution pleads for the recognition of positive contributions of *all* religions to modern civilization and international society. It stresses the importance of tolerance of and respect for religion and belief and calls on states, NGOs, religious bodies, and the media to acknowledge the realities and the importance of cultural diversity and pluralism.

The Resolution's Discontents

Despite its declared intentions, the resolution further divided international society and became the part of the clash of civilizations it aimed to prevent. The HRC and UNGA voting patterns show how Muslim majority and Western states disagreed. The only votes against the Resolution came from Western states. Muslim states had some allies—China, Russia, and Cuba—all supported the Resolution. Other states in Africa, Asia, and Latin America either supported the resolution or abstained (see Table 4.1).

The Resolution's most vocal opponents, like the International Humanist and Ethical Union,[14] argued that the polarized voting record proves that the Resolution is an Islamist *jihad* against Western norms of free speech. While plausible, this argument ignores that the Resolution received support from non-Muslim majority states in Africa, Latin America, and Asia. Furthermore, Muslim majority states like Turkey, Tunisia, Indonesia, Algeria, Senegal, and Mali that are not Islamist are also supporting the Resolution. Finally, the European and North American states' rejection of the Resolution does not stem from a belief that free speech should never be restricted. Many anti-Resolution states have their own laws that prohibit hate speech targeting groups on the basis of race, and also increasingly, religion. Although the United States is the major exception in this category, the Holocaust denial laws in France and Germany are examples of how these Western states accept restrictions on the freedom of speech in some instances to protect a religious minority.

II THE NORMATIVE DIVERGENCE
IN INTERNATIONAL SOCIETY

In addition to political polarization, the Resolution caused a normative polarization with both Muslims and those in Western liberal democracies claiming to have human rights on their side. Even if Western states and NGOs agree with the principle that religious hatred must be prevented,

Table 4.1 Voting Patterns at the HRC and UNGA

	In favor	Against	Abstaining	Non-voting
Human Rights Council Votes				
2010	20	17	8	
2009	23	9	13	
2008	21	10	14	
2007	24	14	9	
Human Rights Commission Votes				
2005	31	16	5	
2004	29	16	7	
2003	32	14	7	
2002[i]	30	15	8	
2001	28	15	9	

2009 Votes at the HRC for the Resolution[ii]

In favor	Against	Abstaining
Azerbaijan	Canada	Argentina
Bahrain	Chile	Brazil
Bangladesh	France	Bosnia and Herzegovina*
Cameroon	Germany	Burkina Faso
Djibouti	Italy	Ghana
Egypt	Netherlands	India
Gabon	Slovakia	Japan
Indonesia	Slovenia	Madagascar
Jordan	Switzerland	Mauritius
Malaysia	Ukraine	Mexico
Nigeria	United Kingdom	Republic of Korea
Pakistan		Uruguay
Qatar		Zambia
Saudi Arabia		
Senegal		
Angola		
Bolivia		
China		
Cuba		
Nicaragua		
Russia*		
Philippines		
South Africa		

United Nations General Assembly Votes for the Resolution

	In favor	Against	Abstaining	Non-voting
2010	79	67	40	10
2009	80	61	42	13
2008	86	53	42	11
2007	108	51	25	8
2006	111	54	18	9
2005	101	53	20	17

[i] Commission on Human Rights, Combating Defamation of Religion. UN Doc. E/2002/23-E/CN.4/2002/200

[ii] http://www2.ohchr.org/english/bodies/hrcouncil/docs/10session/edited_versionL.11Revised.pdf. Shaded states are members of the Organization of Islamic Conference; States with * have observer status at the OIC.

they do not believe that the Defamation Resolution is an appropriate means to achieve that. These actors object to the Resolution because they claim it aims to protect religious doctrine not individuals, it legitimizes the suppression of free speech, and it can lead to more religious hatred. Although the disagreements reflect real political and moral conflicts and make an easy compromise difficult, the shared discourse grounded in human rights that the anti- and pro-Resolution groups invoke to frame their positions indicates a desire to deliberate, negotiate, and contest each others' positions within the existing human rights discourse.

Western States and NGOs: Protection of Free Speech

The American government has led the Western opposition to the Resolution. This American leadership makes a compromise unlikely because of the absolutist view Americans take with regard to free speech, a view that is exceptional among the Western states. This absolutism draws its strength from the First Amendment not from international human rights. American government offers several criticisms to the Resolution.[15] To begin with, the American government points to the futility of hate speech restrictions in preventing religious hatred; apart from some shallow and illusionary changes speech restrictions may bring, religious hatred would likely remain because of deeper and more structural causes. State Department officials seem to believe that the best way to combat hate speech is less through government restriction, regulation, and intervention but rather to let hateful ideas fail on account of their intrinsic lack of merit. The American government believes that the resolution is incompatible with human rights law since according to the American government the Resolution aims to protect religions and not individuals. The U.S. government argues that this misplaced protection can undermine human rights because it permits censorship, which limits freedom of expression, a fundamental and more important human right than protection from religious hatred. Finally, and more ominously the U.S. government claims that antidefamation attempts would backfire, producing more religious strife, not less, because "it would lead to numerous legal claims and counterclaims between majority and minority religious communities or dissenting members of a faith. Instead of fostering tolerance, such a standard would almost certainly lead to a greater conflict and intolerance."[16]

Many NGOs also condemned the Resolution. Among the NGOs that submitted opinions to the HRC, all but one strongly opposed the Resolution. In their submissions, The Becket Fund for Religious Liberty,[17] the American Center for Law & Justice, the European Center for Law & Justice,[18] the International Humanist and Ethical Union (IHEU), the International Center against Censorship, and the Cairo Institute for

Human Rights Studies[19] all called the Resolution an attack on free speech. They also noted that the Resolution could jeopardize already vulnerable religious minorities within Muslim majority states; in particular, the Ahmadi Muslims in Pakistan and the Bahais in Iran may suffer because the Resolution would offer a cover for the blasphemy laws in these countries. Blasphemy laws justify government discrimination and persecution of these religious minorities whose views differ from the orthodox Islam. In response to concerns about the freedom of speech and to fear about blasphemy laws,[20] several NGOs formed an advocacy network, Coalition of Defending Free Speech, to oppose the Resolution. For the same purpose, another NGO, UN Watch, initiated the "Joint NGO Statement on Danger of U.N. 'Defamation of Religions' Campaign." The Campaign website shows that the statement has been signed by 239 NGOs.[21]

Some of these broadly liberal concerns relate to the content of the Resolution itself. To begin, the NGOs argue that the concept of "defamation of religions" is flawed since it is individual believers and nonbelievers alike who have rights, not religions. Because of the ambiguity resulting from giving rights to religions, not individuals, the NGOs fear that the Resolution empowers states to suppress the much-needed criticism of religions. Also, these NGOs dispute the necessity of a new international norm for "combating defamation of religions" because they claim that the existing human rights system already urges states to combat the incitement to religious hatred. Furthermore, they believe that any speech short of the incitement to religious hatred, however defamatory, should be protected not punished.

The NGOs have also concerns external to the substance of the Resolution. Namely, they point to some disturbing practices among the supporters of the Resolution. The NGOs note divergent voting patterns: states with good human rights records tend to oppose the resolution, while states with bad human rights records tend to support it. According to the NGOs, what is more worrisome is that some pro-Resolution states use blasphemy and heresy laws to suppress the free speech and to discriminate against minority religions. These critics fear that the Resolution will legitimize these blasphemy laws, and, at worse, result in their spread.

The Organization of Islamic Conference: Muslim Minority Rights

Representatives of the OIC reject allegations that the Resolution is designed to stifle criticism against Islam. The supporters of the Resolution note that the definition "defamation" of religions has been narrowed to a more acceptable category: the incitement to religious hatred. They also point to the protections the Resolution accords to religious minorities.

For example, the OIC representative to the U.N. in Geneva, Ambassador Babacar Bo, asserts that the OIC supports freedom of expression within the context of other human rights, stating that he supports the "rights of all religious minorities, enabling them to lead a life of respect and enjoy their economic and social rights in an environment free of coercion, fear and threat."[22] Another OIC diplomat, Mojtaba Amiri Vahid, justifies the OIC's efforts for a norm against defamation of religions by invoking the rights of Muslims threatened with Islamophobia. He argues that the freedom of expression must be regulated so that it cannot be used to undermine the freedom of others. To that end, Vahid suggests the compromise of adding a protocol or declaration (to the freedom of speech articles of the International Covenant on Civil and Political Rights specifically to Articles 19 and 20); his proposed statement would affirm that the freedom of expression comes with human responsibilities.[23]

The strongest rejection of the charge that the Resolution is an OIC attempt to ban the criticism of Islam comes from Secretary General Ekmeleddin İhsanoğlu. In an interview appearing in *Jyllands Posten*, the Danish newspaper with Mohammad Cartoons, İhsanoğlu stated, "We are neither against criticism of any religion nor calling for banning criticism of religions." However, he distinguishes criticism from "campaigns of insults with apparent or declared intent to incite hatred against the followers of" a religion. According to İhsanoğlu, such behavior is not an exercise in criticizing a religion, but an abuse of the freedom of expression. Once the purpose of such behavior is "to ridicule and demonize with the intention to sow seeds of hatred against a group of peoples or citizens," this incitement to hatred is an abuse of the freedom of expression that violates the rights of others. İhsanoğlu thinks thatIslam and Muslims are, in particular, being targeted with hostility:

> What we are saying is that incitement for hatred should not be allowed, as long as this specific act constitutes a crime within the parameters of international human rights documents, particularly article 20 of the 1966 International Covenant on Civil and Political Rights, which requests the governments to take measures at the national level against incitement of religious hatred. What we are against is not the criticism of religion per se but rather the intended objective of this criticism which is, in this case, jeopardize Muslim rights, by creating an atmosphere of hostility and rancor which make their life unsafe and strewn with prejudices of all kinds, and this what international law prohibits.[24]

Essentially, the OIC objects to the comparison of the Resolution with blasphemy laws. The OIC defines "defamation" of religions narrowly as the vilification of a religion in a way that constitutes the incitement to hatred toward the followers of that religion, as in the case of Islamophobia. The OIC has started to document Islamophobia with monthly reports, and has found that such Islamophobia is widespread in Western countries.[25] In this context, "Islamophobia" is defined as a form of religious hatred that creates a political and ideological environment that normalizes anti-Muslim policies and trivializes Muslim suffering. Like EUMC reports I have discussed earlier, the reports of several other human rights NGOs and IGOs and a series of United Nations Reports on racial and religious hatred show that this hatred has grown since 9/11 and the terrorist attacks in London and Madrid.[26]

In sum, both the supporters and critics of the Resolution seem to agree on the need to protect members of minority religions from the incitement to hatred. In practice, this would mean like combating Islamophobia in the West, anti-Semitism in Muslim states, anti-Bahaism in Iran, and anti-Ahmediaism and Christianophia in Pakistan. Shared concern about minority religions can form the basis for a compromise about limiting the freedom of speech in order to protect the rights of religious minorities. If refocused in this way, the Resolution may move beyond the polarization it has created. However, any compromise will also need to reconcile the freedom of speech with the freedom of religion in the context of political liberalism. Political liberalism is the foundation for the dominant human rights philosophy and dominant political attitude in Western states.

III   RELIGIOUS DEFAMATION AND POLITICAL LIBERALISM

Can there be an argument grounded in liberal political theory that justifies the state suppression of free speech in order to protect minority religions from being defamed? There are at least two liberal answers to this question: traditional and multicultural. The traditional approach emphasizes individual autonomy and abhors state intervention to regulate free speech. Multicultural approach emphasizes group rights and accommodates, and may even require, state intervention to establish equality between groups and to secure the cultural rights of groups. While some multicultural policies raise questions about the illiberal implications of such policies for the even more vulnerable members, like women, in the minorities, state intervention to prevent powerful groups' hate speech defaming minority religions is not associated with similar problems, thereby establishing a strong multicultural argument for the state intervention to limit free speech in order to protect minority religions.

Freedom of expression is essential in the traditional liberal theory of human rights, due to both its substantive importance in political and social liberties and its instrumental value in achieving other rights. The most well-known defense of free speech is offered by John Stuart Mill who contends that the suppression of speech, particularly political speech, is wrong because the silenced opinion might be true and that, moreover, all opinions contain some element of the truth. Even a speech false in its totality should not be suppressed because such speech is instrumental in reminding people of the truth and its justification.

The binary categories of truth and falsehood are not the only possible categories of speech; traditional liberal theory does not deny the existence of hate speech. It, however, does deny the government's role and efficiency in addressing hate speech. Similar to liberal skepticism about the government's intervention into free markets, this traditional view maintains that the remedy for hate speech is not regulation but more speech. In the "marketplace" of speech, every idea will be judged based on its own merit and good ideas will drive bad ones out of the public sphere. In this theory, the biggest threat to the freedom of speech comes from the government, silencing speech and thus limiting the exchange of ideas.

In extreme cases, the liberal theory concedes that the government can restrict speech only for cases in which speech creates immediate danger and violence. This is similar to First Amendment jurisprudence in the United States: While the First Amendment of the U.S. Constitution guarantees freedom of speech without qualifications, the U.S. Supreme Court's interpretations acknowledge some limitations, such as the government's obligation to regulate so-called fighting words if a speaker uses them with the intention of causing immediate danger and violence. These exacting requirements create a very high threshold for government restriction of speech in the United States.

Building on traditional liberal theory and First Amendment protections, the U.S. government and NGOs stress the importance of freedom of speech for the members of minority groups. An environment of free speech empowers vulnerable groups because it allows them to voice their demands without fear of persecution and to achieve other rights as a consequence of speaking about the inequalities and discrimination they experience. Thus, not surprisingly, in their taxonomy of human rights, Jack Donnelly and Rhoda E. Howard label freedom of expression as an "empowerment" right through which individuals can realize their human rights.[27]

I agree that minority groups would be more disadvantaged in the absence of free speech. But the free speech also creates some unfavorable consequences for the minorities. An absolute free speech environment without attention to unequal power relations in the society or to the differential ability of groups to access the media can further disempower and harm vulnerable groups. For example, in an environment characterized by patriarchy, homophobia, and racism, free speech empowers male, heterosexual, white perspectives and marginalizes female, gay, and black perspectives. This is because power in society is relational; that is, it exists as a matter of relationships—not as an individual quality—between speakers and the groups with which the speakers are identified. Although group identities and positions in society are socially constructed, disproportionate access to media and politics allows already dominant groups to construct the subordinate groups' identities and positions.[28]

While supporters of free speech paint the free market of ideas in idealistic terms, in the real world the market does not allow all participants to have their voices heard. Paradoxically, the practice of free speech reinforces the status quo by ensuring the validity of dominant views and silencing and dismissing the views that challenge the power structure.[29] By sustaining existing social, cultural, and linguistic inequalities, free speech has the potential to become a tool for powerful groups to target and silence vulnerable groups.[30] Without any checks, powerful groups would continue to marginalize and demonize lesser groups. Various forms of subordination would be perpetuated through hate speech and its power to define—and defame—identity and place in society. In other words, in addition to *what* is said, one should think about *who* says what to *whom* with an awareness of the history and power relations between them to assess whether particular expressions constitute incitement to hatred.[31] With these contextual elements, some forms of speech can constitute an incitement to religious hatred and can thus cease to be protected speech.

The arguments of the critical race theorists with respect to blacks and the arguments for the feminist theorists with respect to women also describe the situation of Muslims in the West. In the Western public sphere, the Muslim identity has been constructed not by Muslims but by Islamophobic groups.[32] Debates concerning Islam often become one-sided generalizations about Islam and Muslims with ideologically and politically committed Islamophobic groups dominating the media, politics, and religious organizations. Some of these generalizations attribute criminalizing qualities to Muslims through Muslim identity markers: *jihad* as a holy war, Muhammad as a pedophile, the Quran as a fascist book, Islam as fascism, and Muslims as terrorists. This rhetoric and its implications lead to a perception within "the Muslim community that they cannot 'defend their side' without being accused of being terrorists" or being seen as disloyal to their states in the West. Thus, Islamophobia creates an environment that denies Muslims the right to freedom of expression, including defining who they are and what they believe. Muslims, a group whose political and civil rights are more at stake than those of any other group in the West in the post-9/11 environment, often lack access to media and politics to participate effectively in deliberations about the issues that influence them the most. Conversely, combating Islamophobia can contribute to a healthy public debate, particularly in situations where the entrenched disparities of media, organizational frameworks, and financial capabilities prevent religious minorities from accessing the means of deliberation and thus experiencing the genuine implementation of freedom of expression and speech.

Combating Islamophobia is also important to create conditions for debates within Muslim communities in the West. Islamophobia inflames emotions and religious zeal; rather than the growth of reasoned discussion it results in the empowerment of radicals and the weakening of moderate Muslims. It empowers radicals by justifying their positions regarding the irreconcilable animosity of non-Muslims toward Muslims. In an environment of defamation, moderate Muslims resist raising critiques of their coreligionists both for the fear of their position being identified with Islamophobic groups and for the fear of giving Islamophobic groups arguments that they can use against Islam and Muslims. Islamophobia undermines moderate Muslim voices and prevents debates among Muslims, serving to unite all Muslims around the common interest created by defending themselves from Islamophobia.

The traditional approach to freedom of speech often neglects the harm hate speech can inflict on members of already marginalized groups. Even if the vulnerable minority groups have ability to response hate speech with speech, speech cannot prevent both the possibility of hate speech leading to hate crimes and the possibility of hate speech inflicting pain and humiliation. For example, according to U.N. Special Rapporteur on the Promotion and Protection of the Right to Freedom of Opinion and Expression, many Muslims in Denmark believe that the Muhammed drawings were part of a systematic campaign to denigrate Muslims and affirm the supremacy of Danish values. Due to this Islamophobic environment, "Muslims in Denmark reportedly decided to adopt a very low profile in public life, an attitude that was defined as self-censorship, as they thought that they could easily have become target of harsh criticism even without any specific reason."[33] This paradox of the effects of free speech in silencing marginalized and vulnerable groups, such as religious minorities, requires an analysis that considers the unequal power relations when evaluating utterances about one's identity and religion.

Political theorist Geoffrey B. Levey and sociologist Tariq Modood assert concisely that "context is everything" and illustrates this point within the experience of European Muslims: "One can image cases where the mere depiction of Muhammad might constitute hate speech; for example, if streets in a Muslim neighborhood were adorned with posters of Muhammad's image under cover of darkness."[34] The history of Islamophobia in the West and power relations between largely immigrant minority Muslim communities facing a hostile social and political environment characterized by powerful Islamophobic groups creates a context that requires lowering threshold for hate speech targeting Islam in these countries.

This protection is important in environments where dominant groups demonstrated a tendency to use religious hate speech to provoke racism and xenophobia. The remarks of Geert Wilders and Susanne Winter are examples of these types of speech in which antireligious rhetoric become a cover for racial and xenophobic speech. Similar rhetoric can be seen in the propaganda of the British right-wing party, the British National Party. The Party replaces racist speech with anti-Islamic messages to avoid legal action under the British Racial Act law. This excerpt from the Party's website, featured in an article called 'The Islamic Menace" shows how an attack on the Prophet Muhammad becomes a means to demonize and attack Muslims as a group: "The hidden epidemic of molestation, abductions and rape of scores of white girls in northern English cities, all show the inherent tendency that the teachings of the pedophile Muhammed have had on some of his followers."[35] Considering the context—the racist orientation of the Party and Muslims' position in England as a marginalized minority—the statement about "the pedophile Muhammad" is a rhetorical device conjuring for Muslims-as-sex-criminals. The entire statement thus becomes anti-Muslim hate speech targeting a religious minority in England, rather than a speculation about historical Muhammad to be considered under protected speech.

There seems to be growing acceptance regarding the idea of preventing hate speech targeting religious minorities in liberal democracies that emphasize multiculturalism. Rhoda E. Howard-Hassmann's study of Canadian civic leaders shows that these civic leaders often distinguish between blasphemy targeting minority religions in Canada, like Islam and Judaism, from speech aimed at majority religions. These civic leaders readily agree that blasphemy against a minority religion constitutes hate speech.[36] Their conviction seems to be based on the belief that identity is essential to one's self-respect and that these individuals in minority should be protected from speech that violates that identity, particularly if such violations perpetuate prejudice and discrimination.[37] According to Howard-Hassmann, these civic leaders take a moral position of equal concern and respect, and they want to protect religious minorities from hate speech even if that requires limiting the free speech of majority.[38]

A 2006 British law balances freedom of speech with protections against hate speech. The United Kingdom's Racial and Religious Hatred Law outlaws the incitement of hatred against persons on religious grounds. The law stipulates that "[a] person who uses threatening words or behavior, or displays any written material which is threatening, is guilty of an offence if he intends thereby to stir up religious hatred." The law distinguishes the legitimate criticism and insults of religion from the criminal act of inciting hate through a double requirement: a test of content, not merely the criticism of any religion but the actual threatening words or behavior; and a test of intention, the objective of stirring of religious hatred. Some Muslim groups criticized the legislation because the requirement of intention to cause hatred created a very high standard of proof.[39] There are also questions if the legislation can withstand challenge from free speech groups at the European Court of Human Rights.[40]

CONCLUSION

While the OIC-led campaign for "Combating Defamation of Religions" was defeated by liberal state and pro-free speech groups, the political and normative debates around the Resolution highlight the need for strong protection of religious minorities than the current international human rights system provides. In this chapter I raised two arguments: First, while some normative differences between the supporters and the critics of the United Nations Resolution "Combating Defamation of Religions" remain, shifting the debate from free speech versus defamation of religions to a focus on the protection of minority religions would have brought Muslims and those in liberal democracies closer. Second, a liberal political theory that emphasizes multiculturalism and the need of minorities may potentially accommodate government's role in combating the defamation of minority religions.

NOTES

1. UN Doc. A/36/684 (36/55) Adopted by the General Assembly on November 25, 1981. Also see *The Challenge of Religious Discrimination at the Dawn of the New Millennium*, ed. Nazila Ghanea, 2003. Leiden: Martinus Nijhoff Publishers.

2. The report of the UN Special Rapporteur of contemporary forms of racism, racial discrimination, xenophobia, and related intolerance. UN Doc. A/HRC/9/12.

3. European Monitoring Centre on Racism and Xenophobia. Muslims in the European Union (2006). http://fra.europa.eu/fraWebsite/attachments/Manifestations_EN.pdf (accessed on August 20, 2011), pp. 13–15. The report invokes the ECRI's General Policy Recommendation (No. 7). The report also invokes Council of Europe's two General Policy Recommendations of European Commission against Racism and Intolerance (ECRI): General Policy Recommendation No. 5 combating intolerance and discrimination against Muslims (CRI (2000) 21) and General Policy Recommendation No. 7 on national legislation to combat racism and racial discrimination (CRI (2003) 8). The European Monitoring Centre on Racism and Xenophobia was replaced by the European Union Agency for Fundamental Rights (FRA) in 2007. FRA's annual report (2008) contains a section on anti-Semitism but not on Islamophobia.

4. Ibid., p. 14.

5. European Monitoring Centre on Racism and Xenophobia. Perceptions of Discriminiation and Islamophobia. (2006). http://fra.europa.eu/fraWebsite/attachments/Perceptions_EN.pdf (accessed on August 20 2011), pp. 3–4.

6. Ibid., p. 8.

7. Ibid., p. 10.

8. Ibid., pp. 8–9
9. Micheline R. Ishay. 2004. *The History of Human Rights*. Berkeley: California University Press. Pp. 241–243.
10. UN Doc. A/RES/60/150.
11. See the latest version of the resolution, UN Doc. A/RES/62/154. For EU criticism of Combating Defamation of Religions (November 20, 2007), see http://www.europa-eu-un.org/articles/fr/article_7543_fr. htm (accessed on March 1, 2009).
12. See the interview of the Secretary General with *Jyllands Posten* (October 28, 2008). http://www.oicun.org/uploads/files/articles/Jyllands%20Posten%20 Interview.pdf (accessed on August 20, 2011).
13. Patrick Thornberry, "Form of Hate Speech and the Convention on the Elimination of All Forms of Racial Discrimination (ICERD)," 19. UN Doc. A/RES/62/154.
14. See appendix B of report by International Humanist and Ethical Union and UK National Secular Society "Concerns about Undue Religious Influence and Religious Activities Compromising Human Rights" (July 31, 2007), http://www.secularism.org.uk/uploads/3546cec0d096448823933094. pdf (accessed on March 17, 2009).
15. "United States Government Response to the United Nations Office of the High Commissioner for Human Rights Concerning Combating Defamation of Religions" (July 11, 2008), http://geneva.usmission.gov/Press2008/July/0715DefamationReligions.html (accessed January 15, 2009). European Union's position is also similar to that of the American position. See EU Presidency's explanation of vote on Combating Defamation of Religions (November 20, 2007), http://www.europa-eu-un.org/articles/fr/article_7543_fr.htm (accessed March 1, 2009).
16. United States Government Response to the United Nations Office of the High Commissioner for Human Rights concerning Combating Defamation of Religions.
17. Becket Fund for Religious Liberty. Issue Brief on "Combating Defamation of Religions," http://www.becketfund.org/files/a9e5b.pdf (accessed on March 19, 2009).
18. For its report, see http://www.eclj.org/PDF/080626_ECLJ_submission_to_OHCHR_on_Combating_Defamation_of_Religions_June2008.pdf (accessed on August 20, 2011).
19. UN Doc. A/HRC/9/NGO/15.
20. Also see, Steve Edwards. 2008. "The Trouble with Religious Hatred Laws," *Policy* 24(3): 38–46.
21. http://www.unwatch.org/site/apps/nlnet/content2.aspx?c=bdKKISN qEmG&b=1330815&ct=6859557 (accessed on August 20, 2011).
22. Cited in Marc Perelman, "U.S. Mounting Effort to Counter Limits on Speech Critical of Islam," (October 2, 2008), http://www.forward.com/articles/14318 (accessed on March 1, 2009).
23. Remarks by Mojtaba Amiri Vahid at the Concluding Session of the Seminar on Articles 19 and 20 (Geneva, October 2, 2008), at http://www.oic-un.org/document_report/Amiri_15_oct_2008.pdf (accessed on March 5, 2009).

24. Interview of the Secretary General with *Jyllands Posten* (October 28, 2008). http://www.oicun.org/uploads/files/articles/Jyllands%20Poste n%20Interview.pdf (accessed on August 20, 2011).

25. For First OIC Observatory Report on Islamophobia, see http://www. oic-un.org/document_report/observatory_report_final.doc (accessed on August 20, 2011).

26. UN Doc. A/HRC/9/12 and UN Doc. A/HRC/2/3.

27. Jack Donnelly and Rhoda E. Howard. 1988. "Assessing National Human Rights Performance," *Human Rights Quarterly* 10(2): 214–248.

28. Chris Demaske. 2009. *Modern Power and Free Speech*. Lanham, MD: Lexington Books, p. 74.

29. Ibid., pp. 14–19.

30. Ibid., p. 60.

31. Ibid. p. 7.

32. Maxim Grinberg. 2006. "Defamation of Religions v. Freedom of Expression: Finding the Balance in a Democratic Society," *Sri Lanka Journal of International Law* (18): 1–22.

33. UN Doc. E/CN.4/2005/64, Report of the Special Rapporteur on the Promotion and Protection of the Right to Freedom of Opinion and Expression.

34. Geoffrey B. Levey and Tariq Modood. 2009. "Liberal Democracy, multicultural citizenship and the Danish cartoon affair," in *Secularism, Religion, and Multicultural Citizenship*, ed. Geoffrey B. Levey and Tariq Modood. Cambridge: Cambridge University Press, p. 225.

35. Cited in Kay Goodall, 2007. "Incitement to Religious Hatred: All Talk and No Substance?" *Modern Law Review*, 70(1): 94.

36. Rhoda E. Howard-Hassmann. 2000. "Canadians Discuss Freedom of Speech: Individual Rights Versus Groups," *International Journal of Minority and Group Rights* 7: 109–138.

37. Ibid., p. 133.

38. Ibid. p. 127.

39. Tariq Modood. 2009. "Muslims, Religious Equality and Secularism," in *Secularism, Religion, and Multicultural Citizenship*, ed. Geoffrey B. Levey and Tariq Modood. Cambridge: Cambridge University Press, pp. 171–172.

40. Ben Clarke. 2007. "Freedom of Speech and Criticism of Religion: What are the Limits?" *Murdoch University E Law Journal* 14(2): 94–121.

PART II

INTRODUCTION II: COMMON GOALS AND CASE STUDIES

Throughout history everywhere, minorities and other marginalized groups (e.g., women) have invariably been victimized by elites—especially in war and times of domestic instability. While there is a consensus that it is vitally important that such victims be provided with some basic protection or assistance, the fact remains that the resultant humanitarian reaction has all too often fallen short of meeting this colossal challenge. The question of how to address the inhumane treatment of vulnerable groups in countries that are in conflict, undergoing democratic transition, or under authoritarian rule looms larger today than ever before. In addition to political exclusion, gaping inequalities and social injustice illustrate burgeoning concerns surrounding the protection of rights for minorities and the marginalized. It may be that the rise of a human rights discourse and culture makes these long-standing inequalities and victimizations seem greater.

Contributors to this section argue that the lack of attention to the treatment of nonelites, minorities, and women will have dire consequences. The case studies of the Kurds, Iranian theocracy, women's rights in Turkey, and minorities in Egypt, Iraq, Lebanon, and Turkey will be investigated with an eye toward addressing the most effective way to protect their rights. Perhaps the best approach to dealing with the issue of safeguarding human rights under theocratic systems and protecting the rights of minorities—suffering from ethnicity, sectarianism, and/or gender-based discrimination—is to rely on the acceptability of broad universal principles that avoid pitting one group's rights against those of another. It is important to bear in mind that the key to upholding rights is the principle of universality while allowing for positive distinction or affirmative action as a form of inequality.

Nader Entessar writes that the geostrategic map of the region has changed since the U.S. invasion of Iraq and the overthrow of Saddam Hussein's regime. The Iraqi Kurds have gained a measure of political freedom that had eluded them for much of their recent history, and the Kurdish struggle in the rest of the region continues unabated. The notion of universal human rights has gained increasing currency as a pillar of the obligations that nation-states accept since the end of World War II, and more recently the codification of these rights has begun to challenge the state-centric focus of international law. It should be noted that there are no clear-cut and universally accepted formulae for resolving human rights problems in ethnically heterogeneous societies. The key here is that under the principle of national self-determination, there has never been a set of international rules to specify who precisely is a national people entitled to exercise secession from an existing state. Taking the principle of national self-determination and converting it into a people's collective human right has not changed the fact of absence of specific rules guiding application of the general principle, whether for the Kurds or the Kosovars.

As the Kurdish case demonstrates, intricate political, societal, and historical variables, as well as competing ethnic claims and counterclaims, tend to generate a circular logic that pits one nationality group against another. This logic can contribute to a worst case scenario wherein an ethnic siege mentality can confound the improvement of human rights conditions for many affected people. The application of the principle has to be negotiated, as in the former Czechoslovakia, or fought over, as in the former Yugoslavia. There is, therefore, nothing unique about the Middle Eastern region. Iraqi Kurds face the same options as do south Sudanese: negotiate collective rights or fight over them.

Barbara Rieffer-Flanagan points out that Iran's political system is far from a mature, liberal democracy that guarantees its citizens basic internationally recognized human rights. Although various human rights—including freedom of speech, press, assembly, the right to a fair trial, due process, and bodily integrity—are often violated due to perceived threats to those in power, it is possible to identify some limited progress on many second generation rights such as improved health care and education. Since real and perceived threats account for some of the human rights violations in Iran, removing threats will be essential to improving human rights protection in the future. Given some of the limited progress on second generation rights and the fact that political elites are using the language of international human rights, there is some basis for hope for the future. But critics would argue that the threats to the continued existence and/or dominant position of the authoritarian elite would seem more intractable. Broad political rights are one thing, some relative advances of right to education and health care are entirely different. In this fundamental sense, Iran is not unique compared to China. It appears that human rights discourse and some limited human rights progress can in fact be contained and controlled by elite, allowing more often than not policy-making system to remain authoritarian.

Rieffer-Flanagan concludes that when coupled with the fact that Iran has generally (2009 was an exception) held regular elections in which Iranian citizens are able to vote for a narrow list of candidates, and the fact that the theocracy that Khomeini created is far more inclusive than many of the political systems found in the Middle East, or under the Pahlavi regime, there is some basis for improved human rights protection in the future. While the road is not guaranteed, the less threatened the regime feels, the greater chance there is for improved human rights protections in Iran. The question persists: Will the practice of limited rights spill over into an expanded conception of rights, including rights of full political participation? If the answer is yes, then the issue is not unique to the Middle Eastern region.

Zehra F. Kabasakal Arat turns to the case of Turkey, arguing that subordination of women in Muslim communities and states has been problematized by many, ranging from those Muslim Feminists who focus on sociohistorical factors, to Orientalists who essentialize religion and berate Islam. However, the secularist and republican regime of the predominantly Muslim-populated Turkey has been treated as an exceptional case by many scholars. Some improvement regarding the status of women in Turkey is undeniably observed; however, it bears noting that the country has been far from granting equal rights to women and approaching gender equality. The state agencies and major political actors have subscribed to traditional gender notions, and women face all forms of discrimination and human rights violations. Women in Indonesia, China, or the Islamic parts of India face similar challenges and obstacles. The women's movement, as experts remind us, is weak in relation to the state in Indonesia. Only when the state has been weak, women have had more freedom to organize, but even then they had relied more on their own resources.

The Chinese laws provide equal rights for women in several spheres, including ownership of property, inheritance, and educational opportunities. Women's organizations in China, albeit under the control of the Chinese Community Party (CCP), are able to effectively advocate and promote their agenda. But nevertheless in those situations when women's rights conflict with the interests of the CCP or government policy, the latter prevails. Too often, abuses related to the family planning policy, domestic violence, and sexual trafficking are blocked from being publicly reported in the media—not to mention that the restrictions on the freedom of expression and association have negative impacts on womens' human rights as well. Similarly, women in Muslim communities of India face a myriad of difficulties as citizens of India as well as members of India's largest minority. Their poor socioeconomic conditions and marginal status are emblematic of a lack of social opportunity within the broader context of India's unequal and gender-biased social climate. These examples serve to elucidate the fact that the Middle East is far from unique in its human rights problems.

Examining the case of minorities and marginalized groups in the Middle East, Mahmood Monshipouri and Jonathon Whooley argue that the status of minorities in the Middle East is more heavily influenced by the political, legal, economic, social, and cultural circumstances than religious differences. By conducting a comparative analysis of minorities in Egypt, Turkey, Lebanon, and Iraq, Monshipouri and Whooley demonstrate that to the extent that minorities remain marginal, many policymakers wrongly construct their grievances, activities, and identities as an existential threat to the national security of the countries in which they reside. In virtually all cases examined here, including the Kurdish leaders and groups, parties in Turkey and Iraq, the Druze population of Lebanon, and the Copts in Egypt, participation in the political process may create a sustainable platform for advancing the causes of those minorities. The question arises: Are the Bahais—a religious minority not recognized as the People of the Book by Muslims—a special case precisely because of religion? A narrow or traditional view of Islam sees them as beyond the pale of decent treatment precisely because they are different from Christians and Jews or represent challenges to monotheistic traditions. But has not the state of Israel caused Jews to be more persecuted than prior to when it was formed: 1947–1948? In that case, it is not a narrow view of Islam but a political development that has intensified persecution.

CHAPTER 5

HUMAN RIGHTS AND THE KURDISH QUESTION IN THE MIDDLE EAST

Nader Entessar

HUMAN RIGHTS AND THE ETHNIC QUESTION

The Middle East has undergone significant sociopolitical change since the end of the Cold War. In particular, the geostrategic map of the region has changed since the U.S. invasion of Iraq and the overthrow of Saddam Hussein's regime. The Iraqi Kurds have gained a measure of political freedom that had eluded them for much of their recent history, and the Kurdish struggle in the rest of the region continues unabated. The notion of universal human rights has gained increasing currency as a pillar of the obligations that nation-states have come to accept since the end of World War II when the codification of these rights began to challenge the state-centric focus of international law. This chapter examines the modalities of enhancing the human rights of the Kurds in Iran, Iraq, and Turkey and examines the complexities of issues involved in this process.

Since the end of World War II, the United Nations has made some noteworthy attempts to tackle ethnic and minority abuses, including the adoption of landmark treaties such as the Genocide Convention of 1948, the International Convention on the Elimination of All Forms of Racial Discrimination (adopted by the UN General Assembly in 1965), and the International Convention on the Suppression and the Punishment of the Crimes of Apartheid (passed by the General Assembly in 1973).[1] Of these, the Genocide Convention has the most direct applicability to Kurdish conditions during periods of extreme, overt suppression, for example, in Iraq during the 1991 suppression of the Kurdish uprising.

Genocide, which means "any act committed with the intent to destroy, in whole or in part, a national, ethnical, racial, or religious group,"[2] has been applied to the victims of the Holocaust in Nazi Germany. Article 2 of the Genocide Convention defines this offense as incorporating any of the following acts:

- killing members of the group;
- causing serious bodily or mental harm to members of the group;
- deliberately inflicting on the group conditions of life calculated to bring about its physical destruction in whole or in part;
- imposing measures intended to prevent births within the group; [or]
- forcibly transferring children of the group to another group.[3]

Parties to the Genocide Convention agreed to enact domestic legislation to provide penalties for individuals guilty of committing genocide. In addition, Article 8 of the Convention stipulates that a party to the Convention may call upon the United Nations to take appropriate measures to prevent or suppress acts of genocide.

When analyzing the Kurdish situation, one can argue that the first three acts listed above have, at times, applied to the treatment of the Kurds in Iraq and Turkey, and to some extent in Iran, in the recent past. It would be exceedingly difficult, however, to charge the governments of those countries with genocide against their Kurdish population (with the possible exception of the Anfal campaign conducted by Saddam Hussein's regime) because similar suppression of ethnic minorities occurs regularly in many other member states of the United Nations.

Harff and Gurr have identified 45 instances of genocide and "politicide" committed by states against their populations since World War II.[4] Although there is no universally accepted definition of "politicide," Harff and Gurr have defined the term to mean the promotion and execution of state policies that result in the deaths of a substantial number of members of groups whose political opposition or hierarchical position places them in direct confrontation with the regime in power. Suppression and large-scale killings of members of such groups are labeled as "geno/politicide" committed by the state.[5] In their typology of geno/politicide, Harff and Gurr have identified Iraqi Kurds as victims of "repressive/hegemonic politicide," and Iranian Kurds as victims of "revolutionary politicide."[6] The operational utility of these terms, however, remains questionable and may lead to the vague and problematic extension of genocide to all types of violent suppression of dissent.

Constitutional/Legal Approaches: Federalism as a Panacea?

The foregoing discussion clearly demonstrates the limitations of international legal remedies in enhancing minority rights in an international order dominated by state-centric views and institutions. However, laws can be effectively used to promote constitutional and legal arrangements that can lead to the accommodation of minority rights and the lessening of ethnic tensions in multiethnic societies.[7] For example, constitutional and statutory reforms can be implemented to protect the status of minorities. These reforms can be aimed at specific institutional arrangements to ensure equal treatment for members of ethnic minorities not only by the state apparatus, but also by private institutions and individuals.[8] Nondiscrimination statutes, which have been enacted in the United States since the 1960s, are examples of these reforms. Of course, such statutes should not be duplicated in countries whose legal systems and institutions are vastly different from the Anglo-Saxon model. Nonetheless, legislation already exists to implement indigenously designed "equal rights" in Iran, Iraq, and Turkey. Electoral laws, systems of proportional representation, and the like are useful beginnings in seriously dealing with the integration of the Kurds into the mainstream of sociopolitical life.

A carefully crafted constitutional scheme leading to the establishment of a genuine pluralistic polity is the best means to promote Kurdish rights in Iran, Iraq, and Turkey. Assimilation, which has characterized Turkey's Kurdish policy, may succeed in the short run in stemming the tide of ethnonationalism. In the long run, however, the human and material costs to the state of forced assimilation are likely to be quite high, resulting in, among other things, the rise of armed resistance movements by the affected minority. In addition, assimilation carries a negative connotation because it implies the superiority of the dominant group's culture.

Pluralism, on the other hand, creates a condition of diversity with unity, in which ethnic groups coexist in a territorial state in a relationship of interdependence. In many ways, the multiethnic empires of the Middle East, such as the Persian and Ottoman empires, were characterized by ethnic pluralism. It was only after the creation of the European-style nation-state system that ethnic chauvinism replaced old loyalties and patterns of interaction that had developed over the centuries among various ethnic groups in Iranian and Turkish domains. Furthermore, for pluralism to succeed in multiethnic societies there must be a "large measure of freedom within the state for minorities in the interest of real rather than formal equality."[9] Various autonomy agreements signed between the pre-2003 Iraqi governments and the Kurds failed because of the absence of real equality for the Kurds.

All in all, two desirable techniques, both of which require constitutional restructuring, can be mentioned as desirable ways to reduce conflict between the Kurds and the central authorities in Iran, Iraq, and Turkey. First, the establishment of genuine federal structures and a move away from the strong centralism that characterizes all three countries can help bring about democratic, participatory systems. Nigeria, with its myriad of ethnic and religious groups, has had modest success in reducing ethnic violence through its functioning federalism. In today's Iraq, federalism is still a work in progress and may indeed result in realization of long-sought Kurdish rights in that country.[10] Iraq's 2005 constitution has envisioned a federal system, largely based on the recognition of the country's main ethnic groups. This process must be implemented in stages and not imposed in a short time frame. Imposed federalism would likely fail in the long run, as it did in the former Yugoslavia in 1991. Each country will have to develop its federal structure within its own unique political milieu and with respect to its own unique Kurdish issues.

Second, changes in electoral laws, which can be implemented without a federal system, can help establish a system of proportional representation.[11] Although this system of representation could lead to the proliferation of political parties and unstable coalition governments, it would provide equitable avenues for ethnic groups to develop a stake in the viability of the larger state. In other words, if ethnic minorities were not underrepresented in the decision-making institutions of the national government, as has historically been the case with the Kurds, they would develop greater loyalty to the broader interests of the state. This, in turn, could lead to the development of political alignments that are based on broader interests than the parochial interests of ethnic groups. Ethnic identification, and demands for the recognition of ethnic rights, most likely would persist, even with successful constitutional restructuring. However, such ethnic demands would be less likely to lead to violent conflict if avenues for genuine political participation were open to all groups.

Still, as Reidar Visser has argued, federal schemes in Iraq based on the presumed natural division of the country into Sunni Arabs, Shi'a Arabs, and Kurds may be counterproductive because such a plan reduces Iraqi regionalism as a "residual category forever consigned to a secondary role in Iraqi history and subordinate to 'primordial' ethnic identities, . . ."[12] Visser's thesis is that regional identities in Iraq compete with ethnic identities. As for Iraqi Kurdistan,

> many analysts argue that what was formerly often described as "internal regional tensions" between eastern and western parts of Kurdistan are now a thing of the past. Nevertheless, the process of establishing a Kurdish region within a federated Iraq is in itself an act of regionalism: Kurdish leaders thereby seek a pragmatic role for themselves as Kurds within an

Iraqi federation, separate from the much wider Kurdish world, and at least partially in opposition to pan-Kurdish nationalist sentiment that calls for Kurdish unification on a far larger scale.[13]

Aside from political engineering, some have argued that to promote ethnic peace or ethnic coexistence, governments must reduce their involvement in the country's economy. Steinberg and Saideman have studied the role of economic rents in political competition in multinational societies. Using data from the Index of Economic Freedom and the Minorities at Risk project, they demonstrate that government involvement in the economy of multiethnic countries increases ethnic tension and leads to different forms of ethnic rebellion irrespective of the structure of the government (e.g., federal or unitary).[14]

Federalism, even under the best of circumstances, does not necessarily address the thorny problem of intragroup divisions. In cases of prolonged and violent ethnic conflicts, leaders of contending nationalities seek to mobilize their communities under the banner of "homogeneous interests, or needs, that are argued to be under threat" from without.[15] However, as Caspersen has argued, disunity prevails and factional conflict appears inherent in ethnic politics."[16] Of course, intraethnic rivalry could be based on turf war, distribution of resources, and a host of similar variables. We have already witnessed these types of conflicts among the contending forces in Iraqi, Turkish, and Iranian Kurdistan. In short, federalism, although appealing in theory, may not address fundamental issues that are faced by competing nationalities in the Middle East.

Kurdish Human Rights in the Reform and Post-Reform Eras in Iran

The political changes in Iran since the mid-1990s have coincided with the development of internal fissures in the Kurdish Democratic Party of Iran (KDPI), the largest Iranian Kurdish movement in Iranian Kurdistan. After the September 1992 assassination of Sadeq Sharafkandi, the KDPI's secretary general, in the Mykonos restaurant in Berlin by agents of the Iranian government, the KDPI experienced serious internal friction. Mostafa Hejri (the KDPI's current secretary general) and Abdullah Hassanzadeh challenged each other for the leadership position, with Hejri ultimately prevailing in this power struggle.

The internal Kurdish factionalism in Iran coincided with major political changes in the country. The election of Mohammad Khatami as Iran's president in May 1997 and the defeat of conservative forces in the February 2000 parliamentary elections generated a great deal of expectation for political change in Iran. As Khatami had stated, "We cannot expect any positive transformations anywhere [in Iran] unless the yearning for freedom is fulfilled. That is the freedom to think and the security to express new thinking."[17] Furthermore, Khatami, from the beginning of his presidency, emphasized the notion of inclusiveness, or "Iran for all Iranians" as he called it, and the importance of the rule of law in nurturing and enhancing the foundation of Iran's political system. The Kurds, like many other Iranian citizens, welcomed Khatami's election. The reform movement (the Second of Khordad Movement) that brought Khatami to power and provided him with political backing proved to be weak. In addition to the constitutional limits imposed on the authority of the president, Khatami and his supporters were challenged in all arenas by their conservative opponents. When challenged, Khatami always conceded. The closing down of the reformist newspapers and organizations as well as jailing of supporters of political reform went unchallenged by Khatami, save occasional speeches he delivered denouncing violations of the rule of law.

In Kurdistan, the arrest of officials, some of whom had identified with Khatami's programs, intensified during Khatami's two-term presidency. City council elections were nullified by conservative forces and the credentials of either proreform or independent Kurdish politicians or candidates were routinely rejected when they sought to run for various offices in the province. In a crackdown on Kurdish officials, Abdullah Ramazanzadeh, the governor general of Kurdistan and a Khatami supporter, was summoned before the Special Court for Public Officials in April 2001 and was charged with the "dissemination of lies." Ramazanzadeh's "crimes" were his objections to the nullifications of the votes of two constituencies in the Kurdish cities of Baneh and Saqqez; thus he was accused of libelous statements against the country's powerful Council of Guardians, which had ordered the nullification of the aforementioned constituency votes.[18]

Iran's ninth presidential election in 2005, which ultimately resulted in the election of Mahmoud Ahmadinejad as the country's president, was marked by an open discussion of the "nationality issues" by some of the candidates. This was the first time since the establishment of the Islamic Republic that ethnic and nationality issues were recognized as part of public policy debate, and several candidates openly sought the votes of Iranian nationalities. Dr. Mostafa Moin, the main candidate of the reformist camp, made a special effort to woo voters from non-Persian nationalities and turned Iran's multinational character into an important part of his platform. Moin criticized both those who ignored the country's multinational nature and those who sought to divide the country on ethnic, religious, and linguistic grounds. In this vein, Moin promised complete equality for all Iranian citizens, which is a right guaranteed under the Iranian constitution. Recognizing discrimination as potentially destabilizing, Moin stated that his administration would be composed of all nationalities.[19] Echoing Khatami's campaign slogan, Moin also made "Iran for all Iranians" the centerpiece of his presidential campaign. In addition to Moin, several reformist personalities and writers opined that without recognizing the rights of Iranian nationalities, democracy would not take root in Iran. Furthermore, many reformists welcomed Jalal Talabani's election as president of Iraq and viewed his accession to power in neighboring Iraq as the natural progression of the recognition of nationality rights in the region.[20] The reformist candidates, including Mostafa Moin, were defeated in the first round of the presidential balloting. Unlike the candidates of the reform bloc, Mahmoud Ahmadinejad, the winner of the presidential race, campaigned on the platform of socioeconomic justice. His main target was the country's lower class whose economic conditions had deteriorated under the outgoing reformist Khatami administration. Although Ahmadinejad did not make the issue of nationality rights part of his campaign, he was certainly not an unknown figure among the Kurds. In the early years of the postrevolutionary era, Ahmadinejad was assigned to the Ramazan base of the Revolutionary Guards, with responsibility for military operations in Western Iran, which included the Kurdish regions of the country. Ahmadinejad later served in other capacities in Western Iran, including a stint as a principal adviser to the governor general of the province of Kurdistan.[21]

Given the negative connotation of the activities of the Revolutionary Guards in Kurdistan, it was not surprising that the Iranian Kurds participated minimally in the country's presidential election of 2005. Between the two finalists in the second round of the election, Ahmadinejad received 17,248,782 votes while his opponent Ali Akbar Hashemi Rafsanjani garnered 10,460,701 votes.[22] According to figures released by Iran's Interior Ministry, 62.66 percent of eligible voters participated in the election, with the highest turnout (80.43 percent) in the Ilam Province and the lowest rate of participation (37.37 percent) in the province of Kurdistan. West Azerbaijan, which includes the cities of Mahabad and Uromiyah with their large Kurdish population, recorded the second-lowest participation rate (44.02 percent) in the entire country. Similar results were reported for the 2009 presidential election in which Ahmadinejad only received 20,404 votes as compared to his main opponent, Mir Hossein Moussavi, who garnered 29,902 votes in the Province of Kurdistan alone.[23] In short, the Iranian Kurds expressed their dissatisfaction by boycotting the 2005 and 2009 presidential elections in large numbers. Moreover, the military confrontation between the Kurds and the Iranian government forces has intensified since 2005. For example, Iranian forces and the guerrillas of the newly formed Kurdish Independent Life Party (PJAK), an off-shoot of Turkey's Workers' Party of Kurdistan (PKK), have engaged in a low-level military confrontation inside Iranian Kurdistan with mounting casualties on both sides. The involvement of outside groups in Kurdish affairs in Iran has added an unpredictable twist to the war of attrition in Iranian Kurdistan. For example, the Komala, which has intensified its own low-level warfare inside Iranian Kurdistan, accused PJAK of undermining the legitimate struggle of the Iranian Kurds by its adventurist tactics.[24] The first significant development in Iranian Kurdistan in the post-Khatami era was the grassroots uprising in several Kurdish cities throughout the country. The spark that ignited the Kurdish challenge to the new Ahmadinejad government was generated by the July 11, 2005, shooting of Shavaneh Qaderi, a young Kurdish activist from Mahabad. Subsequently, a number of websites posted photographs purporting to show Qaderi's mutilated body, which contributed to street demonstrations not only in Mahabad but also in several other Kurdish cities, including Baneh, Bukan, Sanandaj, and Saqqez. In addition, Kurdish groups, including university students in Tehran, issued statements supporting the Mahabad demonstrations and condemning the actions of the Iranian security forces, especially the units of the Revolutionary Guards, in suppressing demonstrations of Kurdish grievances. The conditions were further exacerbated by the crackdown on two popular Kurdish-language weeklies, *Ashti* and *Asou*, and the arrest of Roya Tolooi, the editor of the monthly *Rasan* and a well-known activist in Iranian and Kurdish women's rights groups.[25] In mid-2008, a number of Kurdish nationalists, including Farzad Kamangar, Farhad Vakili, Ali Heydarian, Anwar Hossein Panahi, Adnan Hassanpour, and Hiwa Butimar received death sentences that have been challenged by several Iranian and international human rights organizations.

The condition of human rights in several Kurdish cities has deteriorated since the disputed reelection of Ahmadinejad in 2009, and clashes between both Kurdish groups and Iranian forces and infighting among Kurdish forces have resulted in hundreds of casualties throughout the Kurdish province. More ominously, terrorist bombings in Sanandaj, Paveh, and other major Kurdish cities have resulted in the death of scores of both Sunni and Shi'a Kurds in the country. More ominously, discrimination and violence against Kurdish women have contributed to the deterioration of human rights in the Kurdish regions of Iran. According to a recent report by Amnesty International, social problems and deprivation suffered by Kurdish women have led to a high rate of female suicide by self-immolation. The practice of self-immolation "occurs in all the areas of Kurdish settlement, where it is more common than in other parts of Iran. Some alleged suicides may have been staged to cover up 'honour' killings."[26] These abuses have been compounded by the practice of early or forced marriage; targeted killings; discrimination in employment, housing, and education experienced by the Kurds.

The case of Mohammad Sadeq Kaboudvand is symptomatic of the plight of Kurdish human rights activists in Iran today. Kaboudvand is the founder of *Payam Mardom*, the now banned weekly that published articles in Kurdish and Persian on sociopolitical developments in Kurdistan. In 2004 he founded the Human Rights Organization of Kurdistan (KROK), which produced detailed reports on violations of human rights in Iranian Kurdistan. Kaboudvand's campaign and non-violent advocacy of human rights resulted in his June 2007 arrest on ill-defined charges of "disturbing public opinion and societal harmony." A week after his incarceration, Kabouvand was released on bail, but he was rearrested the following week on charges of "acting against national security" of the country and was sentenced to ten years in prison. Notwithstanding the international publicity given to Kabouvand's case and the subsequent granting of the 2009 prestigious Hellman/Hammett award for his courage and commitment to free expression, as of this writing Kabouvand continues to languish in Tehran's Evin Prison.

The execution of Ehsan Fattahian, a 27-year-old Kurdish sympathizer of the Komala, a one-time armed Kurdish guerilla group that now claims to have forsaken armed struggle, highlights a growing concern about the growing climate of fear in the Kurdish province. Fattahian had originally been tried in the first Branch of the Revolutionary Court of Sanandaj and received a ten-year sentence for conspiring against Iran's national security and belonging to an armed opposition group. An appeals court, acting in variance with Iranian law, changed Fattahian's charges to "enmity with God," or *mohareb*, and sentenced him to death. Notwithstanding an international appeal to save Fattahian's life, he was executed on November 11, 2009, at a Sanandaj prison.[27] According to the Campaign to Support Kurdish Political and Civil Prisoners, a "special group" has been set up to supervise the impending execution of imprisoned Kurdish activists. This group, which coordinates its activities with the head of the Kurdish province's judiciary and Sanandaj's prosecutor general, is currently (November 2009) handling cases involving more than 13 Kurdish activists who are awaiting execution.[28] The case of Shirko Moarefi and Habibollah Latifi, two Kurdish activists awaiting execution, has elicited protests from several Kurdish parliamentarians. Even the Iraqi president Jalal Talabani has personally appealed to the head of Iran's judiciary to spare the lives of these two young Kurdish activists.[29]

NEW VISTAS IN KURDISH SELF-DETERMINATION AND HUMAN RIGHTS IN IRAQ AND TURKEY

Notwithstanding major achievements in Iraqi Kurdistan since 2003, there are still several major unknowns or obstacles that may hinder the realization of the Kurdish dream in Iraq. For example, Article 140 of the Iraqi constitution contains several steps that would make it possible for the city of Kirkuk, which many Kurds have always considered as the "heart" of Kurdish Iraq, to be incorporated into the Kurdish region. Article 140 calls for, among other things, the implementation of Article 58 of the Law of Administration for the State of Iraq for the Transition Period, or TAL, which was drafted under the auspices and supervision of the Coalition Provisional Authority (the U.S. government entity that governed Iraq in the immediate aftermath of the overthrow of Saddam Hussein) and signed by the Iraqi Governing Council on March 8, 2004. Article 58 of TAL called for the resolution of the disputed territories, including Kirkuk, between the Kurds and the central government of Iraq based on legal determination of property rights of residents and status of those who had been expelled from these territories during the reign of Saddam Hussein. Iraq's Constitution called for a referendum to be held by the end of December, 2007, to decide the final status of Kirkuk, which the Kurds view as their eternal city. As part of Saddam Hussein's Arabization policy, thousands of Kurds had been forced to leave Kirkuk and were resettled elsewhere in Iraq. In their place, Arabs were given incentives to move to Kirkuk. Article 140 envisions an interim period during which the Kurds will return to Kirkuk and the Arabs would be given incentives to return to their previous towns. At the end of this process, called "normalization," a new census would be taken and a referendum would be held to determine the final status of Kirkuk. Although several thousand Arabs left Kirkuk during the normalization period, few Kurds have returned to Kirkuk, mainly because of the absence of jobs and security in that city. The December 2007 deadline passed without a referendum. Of course, the Kurds hold the majority of Kirkuk's provincial council seats and most senior administrative posts, including security positions, and the Kurdish Regional Government (KRG) pays the salaries of Kurdish civil servants in the city.

In the meantime, the Turkmen and the Arab population of Kirkuk remain wary of their status if and when the city joins the Kurdish region. Thus, they have hardened their opposition to possible changes in Kirkuk's current status. For example, the Iraqi Turkmen Front (ITF), which was established in 1995 and receives funding from the Turkish government and claims to represent the Turkmen people of Iraq, has vigorously contested Kirkuk's status as a Kurdish city. In this vein, the ITF held a rally on April 28, 2007, in Ankara against the proposed Kirkuk referendum. It demanded that Kirkuk be given a "special status" rather than be incorporated into the Kurdish region. At a June 2007 conference in New York, Sadettin Ergec, the ITF's chairman, stated that his party's struggle is aimed at saving Kirkuk as a city for the Iraqi Turkmen.[30] Similarly, Iraq's Assyrian Democratic Movement (ADM) has accused the Kurdish leadership of "executing an orchestrated plan to undermine the national rights of the Assyrian people (as an ethnic group and as indigenous people) in Iraq, in general, and in northern Iraq, in particular."[31] Although there are several Assyrian Christians who are members of the KRG and the Kurdish National Assembly, the ADM has been critical of them because they, like the KRG, advocate "self-rule" in the Nineveh Plains. The critics argue that "self-rule," as proposed by the KRG, requires that Nineveh be linked to the Kurdish region and be under the jurisdiction of the KRG. Instead of "self-rule," the ADM advocates the establishment of a new Nineveh Plains Governorate that would allow its residents freedom to change laws to fit their own unique circumstances and sociocultural structures.[32]

In general, the non-Kurdish minorities in Nineveh province's disputed territories (areas that are contested between the Iraqi central government and the KRG) remain wary of losing their rights under Kurdish rule. In the words of a Chaldean Christian priest in the town of Qaraqosh, the Kurds "have a hidden agenda and are using money to co-opt Christians—it's not because they want to help our people . . . I believe that anyone who disagrees with their agenda puts their life at risk."[33] It is not just the Christian and Turkmen minorities that remain apprehensive about Kurdish rule over their communities. The Shabaks (numbering between 200,000 and 500,000) and the Yezidis (numbering between 500,000 and 800,000), both of which have deep roots in the Nineveh area, have become victims of Kurdish-Arab conflict in today's Iraq. The Shabaks, the overwhelming majority of whom are Shi'a Muslims, have been targeted mostly by extremist Sunni insurgents who view them as heretics and not true Muslims. The Yezidis, who are mistakenly viewed as "devil-worshippers" by outsiders, have also been routinely massacred by Sunni extremists who equate the Peacock Angel, a key symbol of piety among the Yezidis, with the devil in Muslim, Jewish, and Christian theology. Both the Shabaks and the Yezidis have also been victimized by the Kurds because they claim they have resisted attempts to impose a Kurdish identity on them.[34]

On July 22, 2008, the Iraqi parliament, after months of intense debate, finally approved the law on provincial elections. According to this legislation, until elections for the status of Kirkuk are held, there will be a power-sharing arrangement by which key positions will be distributed between the Kurds, Turkmens, Christians, and Arabs. During this interim period, military forces from the center and the south of the country will be in charge of Kirkuk's security, while "a committee of politicians will have until the end of the year to explore solutions to the conflict over the city."[35] This is, at best, a band-aid solution to a festering conflict that will come to a head in the near future.

Endemic corruption, nepotism and violations of human rights have slowed the development of a robust democracy in Iraq's Kurdish region. Human Rights Watch has reported on extensive and systematic torture and mistreatment of detainees at *Asayish* detention facilities. The two major political parties in Iraqi Kurdistan, the Kurdish Democratic Party

(KDP) and the Patriotic Union of Kurdistan (PUK) operate security forces known as *Asayish*, which function with impunity outside the control of the KRG.[36] The *Asayish* operatives routinely violate both Iraqi and international law. These violations include "failure to inform detainees of the grounds for arrest, failure to bring detainees before an investigative judge in a timely fashion, failure to provide a mechanism by which suspects can appeal their detention, . . . holding suspects for prolonged periods of pretrial detention, and extracting confessions through coercion."[37] Human Rights Watch has also documented several cases of torture and ill-treatment of detainees at almost all *Asayish* detention facilities.[38]

In general, the KRG's judicial system is weak and lacks an effective mechanism to allow political prisoners to challenge the legal basis of their imprisonment. In the absence of a strong and independent judiciary, democratic institutions will ultimately wither away. The iron grip of the KDP and the PUK on Kurdish politics has hindered democratic growth in the region. A *Newsweek* article observed, "[A]s the rest of Iraq keeps growing more open and democratic, the enclave [Iraqi Kurdistan] remains stuck in its old ways—and ordinary Kurds are noticing. Businesses grumble at having to form partnership with government cronies; voters are demanding more choice."[39] The Kurdish ruling coalition of the KDP and the PUK has reportedly aligned itself with a group of Nashville-based U.S. evangelical Christian fundamentalists known as Servant Group International (SGI), which has had success in brokering "international business concessions and oil drilling contracts, funneling USAID money into their missions, setting up a chain of 'classical Christian' schools, and producing slick PR videos for the Kurdistan Regional Government that were broadcast in the U.S."[40] In short, festering problems of corruption, cronyism and the general lack of transparency have tempered prospects for meaningful democratic change in Kurdistan. The Kurdish condition in Turkey has presented one of the most daunting challenges to human rights communities both inside and outside the country. For several decades since the establishment of modern Turkey by Mustafa Kemal Ataturk, the Kurds in Turkey had no legal status as Kurds. In fact, they were officially referred to as the "mountain Turks," and any public utterance of the word "Kurd" had been criminalized under the law. Wholesale attacks on Kurdish villages by Turkish security forces were commonplace. However, a combination of factors, including the emergence of a robust Kurdish resistance, led to a gradual change in the country's draconian policy toward its Kurdish citizens.

One of the most significant legal impediments in effectively dealing with Kurdish human rights issues in Turkey has been Article 301 of the Turkish Penal Code. In short, Article 301 made it illegal to "insult" Turkey, Turkish institutions, and Turkish ethnicity. This meant, inter alia, that open manifestation of Kurdish identity would be tantamount to the rejection of "Turkishness," and hence a violation of Article 301. Although a series of changes were made to the law in April 2008 shortly before the opening of a new round of negotiations for possible Turkish membership in the European Union (EU), Article 301 has been used to prosecute a number of Kurdish writers, activists, and other prominent Turkish opponents of the law. For example, the Turkish government brought criminal charges against Orhan Pamuk, Turkey's Nobel Laureate in literature, for publicly stating that some 30,000 Kurds have been killed in his country and nobody dares to acknowledge it. The list of those who have been charged with violating Article 301 because of their nonviolent opposition to Turkey's ethnic policies is extensive, reflecting the continuing challenge to defending "Kurdishness" against the Kemalist notion of "Turkishness."

A possible opening in Turkey's Kurdish policy occured on September 10, 2009, when Yusuf Ziya Ozcan, the president of Turkey's Higher Education Board, announced that the government has approved the establishment of the "Living Languages in Turkey" institute at the southeastern province of Mardin's Artuklu University.[41] In addition to the Kurdish language department, the University is also in the process of establishing a department of Syriac languages and literature with the aim of making Artuklu University into a center of academic scholarship and learning of major Middle Eastern languages, including Arabic and Persian. The Turkish government, which is headed by the Islamic-oriented Justice and Development Party (AKP), has undertaken a number of potentially significant measures in a search for a solution to the country's long-standing "Kurdish problem."[42] As I have discussed in my book *Kurdish Politics in the Middle East*,[43] the Kurdish language had long been banned in Turkey, and in 1967 the government officially outlawed publishing books and other types of printed material in Kurdish. They also made it illegal to record, sing, or otherwise disseminate Kurdish songs and music. As stated above, it was only during the presidency of Turgut Ozal in the early 1990s that the Turkish government acknowledged the Kurdish language as an important component of the country's Kurdish identity. In 2008, the AKP government allowed the establishment of a state television channel to air programs in Kurdish, a measure that the country's Kurdish population had demanded for decades. However, Kurdish critics have argued that the government's restrictions on the Kurdish channel have hampered the free operation of this station. Likewise, many Kurds have taken a wait-and-see attitude toward the recent announcement of the establishment of a Kurdish studies program at Artuklu University. For decades, Kurdish nationalists have demanded that Turkey recognize their legitimate cultural rights by creating a dual educational system where classes are held in both Turkish and Kurdish. The new Kurdish language department at Artuklu University may be a small step in recognition of Kurdish cultural demands as well as a calculated political move to cement Turkey's expanding ties with the Kurdish administration in Northern Iraq.

CONCLUSION

The discussion in this chapter demonstrates the complexities and nuances involved in human rights when it comes to inter- and intra-ethnic relations. Furthermore, it should be noted that there are no clear-cut and universally accepted formulae in resolving human rights problems in ethnically heterogeneous societies. As the Kurdish case demonstrates, intricate political, societal, and historical variables as well as competing ethnic claims, and counterclaims, tend to generate a circular logic that pits one nationality group against another and, in the worst case scenario, creates a siege mentality that compounds improvement of human rights conditions for the affected people. Perhaps the best approach to dealing with the issue of human rights and the ethnic question is to rely on the acceptability of broad universal principles that avoids pitting one group's rights and grievances against another group's claims.

NOTES

1. For a brief review of these treaties, see Gerhard von Glahn, *Law Among Nations: An Introduction to Public International Law*, 5th ed., New York: Macmillan, 1986, pp. 193–194.
2. Ibid., p. 303.
3. Ibid., p. 304.
4. Barbara Harff and Ted Robert Gurr, "Toward Empirical Theoery of Genocides and Politicides: Identification and Measurement of Cases since 1945," *International Studies Quarterly*, vol. 32, no. 3, Summer 1988, pp. 364–365, Table 1.
5. Ibid., p. 360.
6. Ibid., pp. 363–365.
7. Claire Palley, "The Role of Law in Relation to Minority Groups," in *The Future of Cultural Minorities*, ed. Anthony E. Alcock, Brian K. Taylor, and John M. Welton, London: Macmillan, 1979, pp. 120–160.
8. Ibid., pp. 121–126.
9. Patrick Thornberry, *Minorities and Human Rights Law*, London: Minority Rights Group, 1987, p. 4.
10. For a good discussion of the modalities of federal structures and their possible application in Iraq, see Brendan O'Leary, "Power-Sharing, Pluralist Federation, and Federacy," in *The Future of Kurdistan in Iraq*, ed. Brendan O'Leary, John McGarry, and Khalid Salih, Philadelphia: University of Pennsylvania Press, 2005, pp. 47–91. Also, see Liam Anderson, "The Non-Ethnic Regional Model of Federalism: Some Comparative Perspectives," in *An Iraq of Its Regions: Cornerstones of a Federal Democracy?*

ed. Reidar Visser and Gareth Stansfield, New York: Columbia University Press, 2008, pp. 205–255.

11. Donald L. Horowitz, *Ethnic Groups in Conflict*, Berkeley, CA: University of California Press, 1985, pp. 628–633.

12. Reidar Visser, "Introduction," in *An Iraq of Its Regions*, p. 3.

13. Ibid.

14. David A. Steinberg and Stephen M. Saideman, "Laissez Fear: Assessing the Impact of Government Involvement in the Economy of Ethnic Violence," *International Studies Quarterly*, vol. 52, no. 2, June 2008, pp. 235–259.

15. Nina Caspersen, "Intragroup Divisions in Ethnic Conflicts: From Popular Grievances to Power Struggles," *Nationalism and Ethnic Politics*, vol. 14, no. 2, April 2008, p. 239.

16. Ibid.

17. Mohammad Khatami, *Islam, Liberty and Development*, Binghamton, NY: Institute of Global Cultural Studies, 1998, p. 4.

18. Islamic Republic News Agency (IRNA), April 9, 2001.

19. *Emrouz*, www.emrouz.info/ShowItem.aspx?ID=1226&p=1, April 13, 2005. Accessed on May 24, 2008.

20. Ataollah Mohajerani, "Entekhab-e Talabani," *Emrouz*, www.emrouz.info/ShowItem.aspx?ID=1117&p=1, April 7, 2005. Accessed on April 8, 2005.

21. Kasra Naji, *Ahmadinejad: The Secret History of Iran's Radical Leader*, Berkeley, CA: University of California Press, 2008, pp. 29–31.

22. "Final Results of the Ninth Presidential Election," Interior Ministry, the Islamic Republic of Iran, http://www.moi.gov.ir/news.aspx?id=12593, June 25, 2005. Accessed on July 12, 2005.

23. These are official figures released by the Interior Ministry and posted on its website at http://www.moi.ir.

24. Quoted in *Baztab*, http://www.baztab.com/news/27867.php, August 18, 2005. Accessed on September 26, 2005.

25. *Rooz*, August 4, 2005.

26. Amnesty International, *Iran: Human Rights Abuses against the Kurdish Minority*, London: Amnesty International, 2008, p. 22. Also, see Kurdish Human Rights Project, "Human Rights and the Kurds in Iran," *Briefing Paper*, August 26, 2009, and Kurdish National Congress, "Human Rights Violations in Iran," *Briefing Paper*, February 2011, pp. 1–4.

27. For a brief background of Fattahian's case, see Campaign for Human Rights in Iran, http://www.iranhumanrights.org/2009/11/haltfatahianexecution, November 10, 2009. Accessed on November 15, 2009.

28. See *Rooz*, November 19, 2009.

29. See Radio Farda, http://www.radiofarda.com/articleprintview/1880317.html, November 17, 2009, and Radio Farda, http://www.radiofarda.com/articleprintview/1887292.html, November 25, 2009. Accessed on November 26, 2009.

30. For further information about the Iraqi Turkmen Front and its position on Kirkuk, see the organization's website at http://kerkuk.net.

31. Fred Aprim, "Kurds Undermining Assyrian National Interests in Iraq," *Assyrian International News Agency*, http://www.aina.org/guesteds/20080416165822.htm, April 16, 2008. Accessed on May 2, 2008.

32. Ibid.
33. Human Rights Watch, *On Vulnerable Ground: Violence against Minority Communities in Nineveh Province's Disputed Territories*, New York: Human Rights Watch, 2009, p. 25.
34. Ibid., pp. 37–43.
35. Lydia Khalil, "Nobody's Client: The Reawakening of Iraqi Sovereignty," *Analysis*, Lowy Institute for International Policy, Sydney, Australia, March 2009, pp. 11–17.
36. Human Rights Watch, *Caught in the Whirwind: Torture and Denial of Due Process by the Kurdish Security*, New York: Human Rights Watch, 2007, pp. 30–51.
37. Ibid., p. 30.
38. Ibid., p. 41.
39. Lennox Samuels, "The Myth of Kurdistan," *Newsweek*, March 23, 2009, p. 46.
40. Bill Berkowitz, "U.S. Evangelical Christians' Kurdish Crusade," *Z Magazine*, April 2009, p. 11.
41. Sebnem Arsu, "Turkey: Kurdish Studies Approved," the *New York Times*, September 11, 2009.
42. Halil M. Karaveli, "Ankara's New 'Kurdish Opening': Narrow Room for Maneuver," *Turkey Analyst*, vol. 2, no. 14, http://www.silkroadstudies.org/new/inside/turkey/2009/090817B.html, August 17, 2009. Accessed on September 1, 2009.
43. Nader Entessar, *Kurdish Politics in the Middle East*, Lanham, MD: Rowman and Littlefield/Lexington Books, 2010.

CHAPTER 6

THE JANUS NATURE OF HUMAN RIGHTS IN IRAN: UNDERSTANDING PROGRESS AND SETBACKS ON HUMAN RIGHTS PROTECTIONS SINCE THE REVOLUTION

Barbara Ann Rieffer-Flanagan

I INTRODUCTION

There have been serious concerns raised both internally and externally about human rights violations in Iran over the past 30 years. Is there any reason to believe there will be an improvement in the protection of human rights in the future? Risse and Sikkink have suggested that states can be socialized to improve at least part of their human rights record. They argue that Western states, advocacy networks, and international norms can have a positive impact on rights of personal integrity in most if not all non-Western developing countries.[1] Will Iran be socialized to improve its human rights record? This chapter examines both the progress on and the violations of human rights in Iran over the past 30 years. I want to explain why the Islamic regime has restricted the basic rights of its citizens, as well as what accounts for the progress made on some second generation rights. To see further improvements in the protection of human rights this chapter suggests that minimizing threats is a necessary step for further progress. Therefore, this chapter examines Iran's human rights record in the framework of the interplay of international human rights norms and perceived threats.

This chapter begins by examining some of the specific violations of first generation human rights including the right to life and personal integrity.[2] This section explains the motivations and basis of these violations, specifically focusing on threats to the regime and the use of an interpretation of Islam. Then I investigate the condition of some socioeconomic human rights in Iran—specifically the second-generation rights of education and health care.

The second section examines how human rights can be improved in the future. Although some may see the glass as half empty (there are still many basic civil and political rights that are not guaranteed), there are reasons to see a glimmer of hope. Iran's protection of human rights in some areas is better (second generation human rights including health care and education) than some parts of the Middle East. Furthermore, the discourse on human rights has changed over the past 30 years.

II   EXPLAINING HUMAN RIGHTS VIOLATIONS IN IRAN

Various individuals and international NGOs and IGOs have voiced concerns about human rights in Iran. Marking the thirtieth anniversary of the Islamic Revolution, Amnesty International complained: "Despite promises made by Ayatollah Khomeini that all Iranians would be free, the past 30 years has been characterized by persistent human rights violations . . . " Akbar Ganji, an Iranian journalist, also noted the lack of first generation rights:

> We strongly oppose the current laws and policies in Iran, because they do not recognize freedom of thought, freedom of expression, or freedom of religion and assembly. We oppose them because . . . they imprison dissidents and those who live differently . . . They have blocked all democratic methods of reform, and they have deprived our women of many of their civic and political rights.[3]

Freedom House, with its focus on civil and political rights, has consistently rated the theocracy in Iran as Not Free with scores of 5, 6, and 7.[4] The World Bank's Worldwide Governance indicators project also gives Iran low marks.[5] Many in the West including the United States have repeatedly criticized the lack of human rights protections in Iran.[6] Most of these criticisms revolve around first generation rights and are related to perceived threats to the regime.

The Right to Life and Personal Integrity
in the Islamic Republic of Iran

The early years after the revolution saw some of the gravest human rights violations committed against perceived threats to the regime and those considered not sufficiently loyal to Khomeini and the Islamic Republic of Iran. After many of the monarchists were imprisoned, executed, or fled to exile, the revolution turned on its own supporters. The Revolution's diverse mix of secular intellectuals, Islamic clerics, and leftists were united in the initial goal of removing the shah. After this goal was accomplished a power struggle ensued between these three factions over what type of political system would develop and who would control this new government.

Khomeini and his clerical supporters were unwilling to share power with secular elites such as Bazargan, or leftist organizations and this threat to the power of the clerics would result in many violations of the right to life. In response to the repression at the hands of government supporters the Mojahedin (MEK) fought back with a series of assassination attempts some of which were successful. The bomb that went off in June, 1981, at Friday prayers in Tehran seriously injured Ali Khamenei.[7] In August an additional assassination claimed the lives of the new President Raja'i and Prime Minister Bahonar.

In response to these attacks, the government unleashed a reign of terror with numerous executions in the subsequent months. On September 19, 1981, 149 people were executed. The following week saw more bloodshed with 110 people killed in one day.[8] These killings were carried out in part to protect the theocracy from a secular threat to the very existence of the regime. The reign of terror would come to an end in December 1982 at Khomeini's behest.[9]

In addition to executions various individuals have been held in confinement and tortured while in jail. Accounts from opposition figures and dissidents tell of harsh treatment while in custody.[10] Ahmad Batebi, a student protestor, recalled how he was beaten, deprived of sleep, and hung by his arms from the ceiling in an interview after his escape and relocation to the United States.[11]

Political Rights

Freedom of Expression

Freedom of speech (Article 26) or the ability to freely discuss ideas without fear of criminal prosecution is not a right that is protected or guaranteed in Iran despite claims to the contrary by political leaders.[12] Political views that are critical of members of the ruling elite or question the role of religion in the political system have been censored and many individuals voicing political dissent have been arrested and thrown in jail.

In the aftermath of the revolution Ayatollah Khomeini and other religious revolutionaries tolerated very little dissent or criticism.[13] This was also an attempt by Khomeini and the new government to rid the country of Western influence. In *Islamic Government*, he outlined his fears of un-Islamic ideas:

> Although all things contrary to the Shari'a must be forbidden, emphasis has been placed on sinful talk and consumption of what is forbidden, implying that these two evils are more dangerous than all others and must therefore be more diligently combated.[14]

Outspoken critics of the repressive nature of the Iranian regime have repeatedly been harassed. Abdolkarim Soroush, an influential intellectual had been fired from various university positions, physically threatened, and prohibited from teaching and travelling outside of the country.[15] Soroush's ideas are threatening to the clerical regime because he has proposed an alternative interpretation of Islam. He believes that while the texts of holy books such as the Quran do not change, our understanding of them may change:

All of us are fallible human beings. Though religion itself is sacred, its interpretation is not sacred and therefore it can be criticized, modified, refined, and redefined.[16] The notion that religious texts can be reinterpreted does not sit well with many of the clerical elites who insist on the validity of their view of Islam.

University students who have protested against government policies have also encountered many difficulties and have often ended up in Evin Prison in Tehran. The judiciary's closure of the daily newspaper *Salam*—a pro-Khatami, reformist paper—led to student protests in the summer of 1999. The protestors were met by Ansar-e-Hezbollah and many students were beaten. Some were killed in these confrontations.[17] Student protests at Shiraz University in the early months of 2008 also resulted in a harsh crackdown with many arrests.

Presidential Elections in 2009

The large-scale protests that followed the interior ministry's declaration that President Ahmadinejad had been reelected a few hours after the polls closed, was one of the most significant domestic threats to the clerical regime. The millions of protestors who came out in the streets day after day signalled a loss of legitimacy and a political challenge to the regime. The Supreme Leader attempted to end the demonstrations when on June 19, 2009, at Friday Prayers he ordered a halt to the protests.[18] Ironically in this same speech he also used the language of human rights by defending democracy and the rule of law. He said, "The Islamic State would not cheat and betray the vote of the people."[19] In the aftermath of his speech hundreds of Iranians have been detained and many were tortured or killed.

The threats to the regime were material and ideological. If Mousavi and reform-minded politicians were able to gain power they may agree to talk to or compromise with the United States, which would challenge one of the central tenets of the Islamic Revolution of 1979. It could also have a financial impact if certain ministries were no longer controlled by hard-liners. Thus the regime's response to the elections in 2009 demonstrated how the regime when faced with a perceived domestic threat to its political security would respond in a harsh manner.

Women's Civil and Political Rights

The position of women in Iranian society since the revolution has fluctuated with the political winds in Iran. While Iranian women have far greater rights and opportunities than their counterparts in, for example, Saudi Arabia, they do not enjoy complete equality. The mixed and inconsistent messages women have received from the regime are a product of the factional politics (reformers vs. hard-line conservatives) and of the evolution of Khomeini's Islamic thinking on the subject. His views have been employed by various political forces for granting women more rights as well as expecting women to uphold their traditional roles within the family.

In the 1960s Khomeini did not articulate equal political rights for women. However, in 1978 he offered a different vision for women: "In the Islamic system a woman is a human being who can be equally active as a man in the building of a new society."[20] While Khomeini did not argue for full equality in terms of political participation (women are not able to become Supreme Leader and have been rejected by the Guardian Council as candidates for president) he did offer women a limited space in the political realm, far greater than in some other countries in the Middle East. Despite some political rights, Iranian women have not enjoyed the same status as men and in many respects are second-class citizens in the Islamic Republic. Ganji has referred to the situation of Iranian women as "gender apartheid."[21] While the constitution guarantees the equal rights of women in Articles 3 and 20, there are also limiting clauses. Article 20 places this within the criteria of Islam:

> All citizens of the country, both men and women, equally enjoy the protection of the law and enjoy all human, political, economic, social, and cultural rights, in conformity with Islamic criteria.

When the revolution occurred in 1979 many women participated not only in street demonstrations but also in the referendum on Iran's political system. Since 1979 women have been encouraged—at times forced—to play the traditional role of nurturing mother and dutiful wife.[22] Women who were judges prior to the revolution were replaced by men and some women were dissuaded from practicing law.[23] Women are also segregated in many public places including in classrooms. Women in Iran do not enjoy equal treatment or equal status with their male counterparts. This inequality is translated into various laws and practices including the fact that a woman's testimony in a court of law is "valued at half that of a man's."[24]

In addition, women do not have the basic freedom to choose their attire. The veil is mandatory for all women in public regardless of their religious beliefs. Women are mandated to have their heads covered because it is considered to be a means to protect their chastity and purity.

Some Iranian women have been brave enough to confront what they view as their second-class citizenship status in Iran. The response from the government has often been violent and harsh.[25] In March of 2006 several women who were part of the One Million Signatures Campaign were arrested and later convicted of "acting against national security, disrupting public order, and refusing to follow police orders." Nasrin Afzali, Nahid Jafari, and Minoo Mortazi were given suspended sentences of lashings and prison time.[26] The sentences will not be carried out unless the women commit additional crimes. However, one of the defense lawyers, Zahra Arzani, has suggested that the suspended sentences were an effort to limit human rights activists in Iran. The One Million Signatures Campaign is a campaign to end gender discrimination in Iranian laws especially in the area of family law.[27]

III   Progress on Human Rights: Basic Needs and Health Care

In the 30 years since the revolution we have seen some significant improvements in second-generation rights although this has received far less attention from scholars discussing human rights. There has been a significant improvement by the government in providing for the basic needs of its citizens. This commitment to improving the lives of the poor can be linked to the goals and rhetoric of the revolution in 1979 when Khomeini promised to help the oppressed. Furthermore, it is not viewed as threatening to the ruling elite.

Since the revolution Iran has reduced poverty. In the 1990s poverty had decreased from 26 percent to 21 percent.[28] Furthermore, access to electricity and piped water in rural areas increased substantially since the revolution. Access to electricity was below 20 percent in 1977 and by 2004 it was over 95 percent. Similar improvements can be seen with access to water.[29]

Iran has continued to invest in its health services and the results are encouraging. In the 15-year period from 1991 to 2006 Iran has increased the social service complexes in urban areas (from 414 to 980) and in rural areas (from 1121 to 1495). These complexes assist Iranians with their health care needs as well as providing orphanages and day-care centers.[30] There has also been increased access to medical services. One result has been the decline in child mortality rates.[31] These results have been possible because of government support, including increased female literacy. It has been estimated that the government is spending close to $2 billion on subsidies for food and medicine. Furthermore, various charities that receive government funding also provide direct assistance to over 2 million Iranians.[32] In addition, there has been greater access to birth control. In the late 1980s, the government developed a policy called The National Birth Control Policy, which "provided free contraceptives (to married couples) through the primary health care system."[33] This policy was developed to help with family planning and to encourage women to have fewer children.

Improvements in Education

In addition to the improvements in access to health care, women have also enjoyed access to the education system. Literacy rates have improved dramatically since the revolution. For example, between 1976 and 1996 women's literacy doubled (in 1976, 36 percent of Iranian women were considered literate and by 1996 the figure rose to 72 percent). By 2006, the literacy rates for girls ten years and older was 80 percent.[34] Some have suggested that the segregation of gender helped socially conservative families to allow their daughters to go to school. That some of the classes were offered in mosques furthered female literacy.[35] Further, Nobel Prize winner Shirin Ebadi noted that close to 65 percent of the students in universities were women.[36]

These improvements helped Iranian women in the labor market as well. In the past 30 years women's participation in the workforce has increased (although there were some women who lost their jobs in the immediate aftermath of the revolution). This increase in the female work-force has not been limited to cheap jobs in manufacturing. Rather women have been increasingly moving into the service sector. In 1976, women made up 38.2 percent of the manufacturing force, 39.5 percent of education, health care, and social services, and 18.3 percent in social, personal, and financial services. By 2006, women in manufacturing had declined to 18.7 percent, while in education, health care, and social services the number had increased to 48.6 percent and in the social, personal, and financial services it was up to 28.2 percent.[37] This shows that women are moving into higher-paying jobs.[38]

Women's Political Rights

Despite some discriminatory practices enshrined in the legal system, women do enjoy some political rights in Iran. Since the revolution women have been given the right to vote and have participated in every election in the past 30 years. A few women have even been elected to the Majlis, although they "did not succeed in producing substantive and lasting changes to the status of women in Iranian society."[39] However, Iran has more female members elected to Parliament than some other countries in the Middle East.

Some Iranians have even suggested that Iran's treatment of women should be a model for other Muslim countries—going so far as to suggest that Iran is more progressive than other countries because women can vote, drive, and hold positions within the government.[40] When examining the issues of birth control and women's education we see that neither is viewed as a threat to the political elites. Ultimately, while women enjoy some rights and some limited progress has been made, women do not enjoy full equality in many areas.

In sum, we can also see many human rights violations occurring as a result of perceived threats to those who control the levers of power[41] and a narrow interpretation of Islam. The role of threats can also explain the improvement on some second-generation rights. The progress we see in the areas of health care and education is because they can be seen as non-threatening to the regime. Therefore beyond a commitment to Islamic purity, the self-interest of political leaders in Tehran and their desire to remain in control of the levers of power can explain many of the human rights violations in Iran over the past 30 years.

IV   SOCIALIZATION OF INTERNATIONAL HUMAN RIGHTS NORMS

Beyond the desirability of human rights lies the more pragmatic question: How does a state evolve from a flagrant abuser of human rights to one where the rule of law protects the basic human rights of its citizens? Risse and Sikkink have offered a five-phase spiral model as a process by which international human rights norms concerning personal integrity rights are socialized and ultimately protected.[42]

The first phase of the model begins with the repression by the government and the initial activity of a transnational network given the weakness of domestic opposition groups. In the next phase, international NGOs raise awareness about the human rights violations in the country and encourage Western states to put pressure on the government. The government typically denies the charges:

> "Denial" means that the norm violating government refuses to accept the validity of international norms themselves and it opposes the suggestion that its national practices in this area are subject to international jurisdiction.[43]

The third phase of the model, the targeted state will offer tactical concessions with a few minor, cosmetic changes. Thus the regime begins to "talk the talk" and uses the language of human rights. There may be further limited acts such as releasing prisoners or allowing some additional limited press freedoms. Risse and Sikkink note that at times the regime can become "entrapped" by its own rhetoric when it is later used against it.

In the fourth phase, the regime, which despite continuing human rights violations, is regularly invoking human rights norms no longer controversial, they are accepted by the regime as legitimate.[44] At this stage the government may sign international human rights conventions or establish institutions to protect human rights.

The last phase occurs when international human rights have become institutionalized and habitual through the rule of law. International human rights are no longer controversial instead they are regularly protected within the domestic political system. In sum, we see that the spiral model is important because it shows how international norms and pressure from Western actors can influence non-Western states. The model also acknowledges that for states that are more independent of the Western community the model will not be as effective.

V   Adjusting the Model: Threats

Since threats, perceived and real, are central to understanding the human rights violations in Iran, the role of threats must be incorporated into any model that seeks to explain progress on human rights. Risse and Sikkink note that states that are less dependent on the West will be less sensitive to pressure from Western states and NGOs. While Iran is not entirely independent of the West due to its dependence on oil (and the need to see it in foreign markets not to mention the issue of refinement), the Islamic Republic has managed to survive 30 years worth of sanctions. Thus under the model previously discussed international pressure from NGOs and Western states would only have some limited impact.[45] Thus limited changes must be made to the spiral model to incorporate some features unique to Iran.[46] Namely, that in addition to international norms a diminishing level of threats from the international community is necessary if we are to see improvement in the protection of human rights and the eventual institutionalization of human rights in Iran.

Modification to the Spiral Model

Phase 1	→ Phase 2 → Phase 3	→ Phase 4	→ Phase 5	→ Phase 6
Repression →	Denial → Threat	→ Tactical	→ Prescriptive →	Rule

Reduction → Concessions → Status   → Consistent

& Negotiated   & Domestic → Behavior

Transition   Pressure on

Islam

Decreasing threats (and perceived threats) from abroad, from specific foreign countries, can provide the space for the gradual improvement of human rights. Risse and Sikkink suggest that international pressure (Western states and NGOs) and potential sanctions can push a targeted state on the road to socialization and institutionalization of international human rights. However, in Iran's case, 30 years of sanctions have defused some of the pressure at work in the spiral model. Over the past 30 years various attempts to pressure Tehran have been viewed as threats from Western states, especially the United States. This is why there is a need for threat reduction. Reducing the threats prevents a rally around the flag effect from political elites. In Iran's case removing threats would include avoiding any rhetoric about regime change and discouraging the threat from Israel.[47] Further international cooperation on the nuclear issue including economic incentives would be helpful. Threat reduction can provide the opening for a negotiated gradual transition.

Phase four of the adjusted model would incorporate some tactical concessions of human rights in the context of a domestically negotiated transition. In order to see some significant improvements in civil and political rights, domestic elites (reformists, pragmatic conservatives) must be willing to allow hard-line conservatives to maintain financial benefits and control over some military forces (Revolutionary Guard) in return for a gradual power-sharing agreement. This power-sharing arrangement (as seen in Chile) would require hard-liners to release control of the presidency and parliament (specifically who is allowed to run and hold office) and eventually control over the judiciary as well in order to start making progress toward the rule of law.

Phase four gradually shifts to Phase five where more political power is shifted to elected bodies and away from unelected bodies (Guardian Council, Supreme Leader). In the fifth phase human rights would have prescriptive status. We further see greater domestic NGOs pressure especially concerning Islam. Domestic NGOs arguing for a reinterpretation of Islam in a more human rights–friendly manner can lead to progress on human rights while continuing to work within an Islamic context. Thus efforts by Soroush and others who work within an Islamic framework to improve human rights protections in Iran are instructive. This is less threatening than a Western approach because it incorporates elements that are consistent with the culture and history of the people.

The last phase would incorporate rule-consistent behavior—the institutionalization of human rights under new leaders. In order for this to occur you will need to see a gradual transition of power (perhaps similar to Pinochet in Chile). Iranian reformers and pragmatic conservatives will need to agree to guarantee the hard-liners that they will be protected financially and from judicial punishment in return for a gradual handover of power and then you will have the opening to make more progress on human rights. While this is occurring in the realm of civil and political rights, progress can still be made on human rights on issues such as education or health care because they are viewed to be not as threatening as political rights.

VI   IMPROVING HUMAN RIGHTS

In the past, Iranian leaders have denied the applicability and the worth of international human rights. However, in more recent years, we have seen various Iranian leaders, including hard-line conservatives using the language of international human rights. This section shows that linguistic transition.

The Discourse on Human Rights

For Khomeini, international human rights treaties were inferior to Islamic law. On February 19, 1978, Khomeini gave a speech in which he articulated the hypocrisy of the West and the Universal Declaration of Human Rights:

> All the miseries that we have suffered, still suffer, and are about to suffer soon are caused by the heads of those countries that have signed the Declaration of Human Rights, but that at all times have denied man his freedom. Freedom of the individual is the most important part of the Declaration of Human Rights . . . But we see the Iranian nation, together with many other suffering at the hands of those states that have signed and ratified the Declaration.[48]

Khomeini went on to add that "the Declaration of Human Rights exists only to deceive the nations; it is the opium of the masses."[49]

This hostility toward international human rights law was echoed by Supreme Leader Khamenei who said, "changing some absolute Islamic decrees to correspond to certain international conventions is quite wrong."[50] Thus some prominent leaders have denied the validity of international human rights law. However, the language of some political elites has evolved from a denial of the legitimacy of international human rights to a denial of wrongdoing.

More and more we see Iranian leaders using the language of human rights in recognition of the Iranian public's demand for human rights.

For example, in his remarks on June 19, 2009, Supreme Leader Khamenei said that the Islamic Republic is a strong supporter of human rights especially for the oppressed.[51] Of course the notion that Iran is flag bearer for international human rights is fanciful especially in light of the harsh crackdown after the presidential elections in 2009.

Other Iranian leaders have denied that their country systematically violates human rights. Some Iranians have suggested that much of the criticism from the United States and other Western countries is politically motivated. Ayatollah Shahroudi argued that "the international community uses human rights as a weapon against the Islamic world."[52]

While Iran has not compiled a perfect record of protecting international human rights at home, it has voiced concerns about human rights abroad. One of the most pressing concerns for many in Iran (both political elites and Iranian citizens) is Palestine. For the past three decades, the Iranian government has raised concerns about the Palestinians' lack of basic human rights including fundamental freedoms and political rights. Khomeini urged Muslims in February 1971 to help liberate "the Islamic land of Palestine from the grasp of Zionism."[53]

The language of the concern voiced for the Palestinians has evolved over the years to incorporate aspects of international human rights. In the early months of 2009 the president submitted an international war crimes bill to parliament. The bill seeks to prosecute individuals in any part of the world with crimes against humanity and war crimes. Specifically this includes denying a civilian population humanitarian assistance, attempts to exterminate a group of people, rape, as well as using toxic weapons.[54] This bill is aimed specifically at Israel and was drafted in response to the war in the Gaza Strip in 2008. Although politically motivated it is important to note that Iran is using the tools and language of the international human rights community. This can also be used against Iran itself.

Thus over the past 30 years we have seen changes in the language employed by various elites in Iran. Instead of denying the importance or validity of international human rights, some political leaders are simply denying that Iran is acting improperly. In other cases, elites are using the language of international human rights to criticize other countries. This suggests a change in the regime's relationship to internationally recognized human rights. International human rights went from being a product of the West and hence easily rejected to the current status of being accepted as legitimate. Now they claim that the West manipulates the discussion of human rights or that the country's human rights record is misunderstood.

Potential for Additional Improvements
Various dissidents and domestic NGOs have tried to improve the country's protection of human rights. Some have done so from a religious reference point arguing that Iranian leaders have misinterpreted

Islamic texts. Thus, if a more accurate understanding of the Qur'an and Sunnah were applied to laws, a more just and rights protective society could be realized in Iran. Efforts to strengthen human rights protections from within an Islamic framework have the greatest potential for success because these efforts use the cultural and religious tools of the society.[55] For example, some Islamic feminists or religiously oriented feminists in Iran have argued that women's rights can be protected in an Islamic state if a proper reading of the Qur'an is undertaken.

VII IMPLICATIONS FOR THE FUTURE

Given that there has been some progress made in areas such as education, should we expect to see further gains in the protections of human rights? The picture is somewhat mixed. The nuclear issue will hinder progress on human rights. The international community's main focus is preventing, either through persuasion or sanctions, the Islamic Republic from becoming a nuclear power with the ability to build a nuclear weapon. While Iran insists that it is developing a peaceful nuclear energy program, the rest of the world has not been convinced.

Although the nuclear issue is a hindrance to human rights, there are some other developments that offer hope for progress on human rights. To begin with, political leaders in Iran from various political leanings have used the language of human rights. They are "talking the talk." One example of this was the international war crimes bill discussed earlier. Even if selectively applied this still suggests a use of the language of international human rights which is a large step from Khomeini's rejection of human rights and a step toward the protection of human rights. In addition, when discussing the case of journalist Roxana Saberi, President Ahmadinejad's Chief of Staff Abdolreza Sheikholeslami wrote, "Take care that the defendants have all the legal freedoms and rights to defend themselves against the charges and none of their rights are violated."[56] This statement echoes the value of the rule of law. Furthermore, with President Obama now occupying the White House, there are less threats emanating from the Great Satan.

VIII CONCLUSION

This chapter has argued that many of the human rights violations committed by the government stem from two sources: a specific interpretation of Islam (as opposed to Islam itself) and real and perceived threats to the political elite. Limitations on political rights including freedom of expression occur to curtail political opposition to the regime and especially the hard-line conservatives in power. Human rights violations that occur in the name of Islam may offer more hope for progress. Since *ijtihad* (interpretation of religious texts/independent reasoning) allows for the reexamination of some Islamic doctrines and ideas, this may provide an avenue for improving the human rights record in Iran. But we should also note the limitation to using Islam to promote human rights. Islam will only go so far when the political elites feel they are threatened.

Iran's political system is far from a mature, liberal democracy that guarantees all its citizens basic internationally recognized human rights. Various human rights including freedom of speech, press, assembly, the right to a fair trial, due process, and bodily integrity are often violated due to perceived threats to those in power. However we have also seen some limited progress on second generation rights such as improved health care and education. Since real and perceived threats account for some of the human rights violations in Iran, removing threats will be essential to improving human rights protection in the future. The spiral model with some modifications offers a blueprint (although not a teleological guarantee) for greater protection of human rights in the future. While the road is not guaranteed, the less threatened the regime feels the greater chance there is for improved human rights protections in Iran.

NOTES

1. Thomas Risse and Kathryn Sikkink, "The Socialization of International Human Rights Norms into Domestic Practices: Introduction," in *The Power of Human Rights: International Norms and Domestic Change*, edited by Thomas Risse, Stephen C. Ropp, and Kathryn Sikkink (Cambridge: Cambridge University Press, 1999), 1.

2. I cannot cover all of the rights articulated in the Universal Declaration of Human Rights, so I have selected some specific civil and political rights that are representative of the situation of human rights in Iran.

3. Akbar Ganji, *The Road to Democracy in Iran* (Cambridge, MA: MIT Press, 2008), 21–22.

4. The five years from 1992 to 1997 saw a deterioration in rights according to Freedom House: 6 and 7. Between 1998 and 2007 the number has remained relatively stable at 6.

5. Worldwide Governance indicators for 2009 (1996–2008). Percentile Rank: Voice and Accountability 8.2; Political Stability 14.4; Government Effectiveness 24.6; Regulatory Quality 2.9; Rule of Law 23.0; Control of Corruption 28.5; All of these statistics have deteriorated since 2003. infor.worldbank.org/governance. Accessed on August 5, 2011.

6. http://www.state.gov/g/drl/rls/hrrpt/2008/nea/119115.htm.

7. Robin Wright, *In the Name of God* (New York: Simon and Schuster, 1989), 98.

8. Ibid., 100–101.

9. Ibid., 107.

10. Zarah Ghahramani with Robert Hillman, *My Life as a Traitor* (New York: Farrar, Straus, and Giroux, 2008).

11. Scott Shane and Michael R Gordon, "Dissident's Tale of Epic Escape from Iran's Vise," *New York Times*, July 13, 2008. www.nytimes.com/2008/07/13/world/middleeast/13dissident.html.

12. In September 2008 President Ahmadinejad said, "Everyone is free to express what he or she wants whether for or against the government and there are in fact hundreds of opinions that in fact speak in favor of our policies." The interview can be found at www.nytimes.com/2008/09/26/world/middleeast/26iran-transcript.html?ref=world&...

13. John Esposito and John Voll, *Islam and Democracy* (Oxford: Oxford University Press, 1996), 66.

14. Khomeini, *Islam and Revolution: Writings and Declarations of Iman Khomeini*, translated and annotated by Hamid Algar (Berkeley, CA: Mizan Press, 1981), 113.

15. Mahmoud Sadri and Ahmad Sadri, "Introduction," in *Reason, Freedom, and Democracy in Islam: Essential Writings of Abdolkarim Soroush*, ed. Sadri and Sadri (New York: Oxford University Press, 2000), xi.

16. Quoted in Robin Wright, *The Last Great Revolution: Turmoil and Transformation in Iran* (New York: Knopf, 2000), 42.

17. Molavi, *The Soul of Iran*, (New York: Norton, 2002), 201–202.

18. Nazila Fathi "Iran's Top Leader Dashes Hopes for a Compromise"," the *New York Times*, June 20, 2009, www.nytimes.com/2009/06/20/world/middleeast/20iran.html?hp=&pa...

19. Ibid.

20. Vanessa Martin, *Creating an Islamic State: Khomeini and the Making of a New Iran* (New York: I. B. Tauris, 2000), 155.

21. Ganji, *Road to Democracy in Iran*, 33.

22. Azar Nafisi, *Reading Lolita in Tehran*, (New York: Random House, 2003). The legal age for girls to marry was raised from 9 to 13 Rebecca Barlow and Shahram Akbarzadeh, "Prospects for Feminism in the Islamic Republic of Iran," *Human Rights Quarterly* 30 (2008), 21–40 at 27.

23. Valentine M. Moghadam, "Islamic Feminism and Its Discontents: Towards a Resolution of the Debate," *Signs*, Vol. 27, No. 4 (Summer 2002), pp. 1135–1171.

24. Barlow and Akbarzadeh, "Prospects for Feminism in the Islamic Republic of Iran," 23.

25. Barbara Ann Rieffer-Flanagan, "Improving Democracy in Religious Nation-States: Norms of Moderation and Cooperation in Ireland and Iran," *Muslim World Journal of Human Rights*, Vol. 4, No. 2 (2007); Human Rights Watch, "Iran: Women on Trial for Peaceful Demonstration: Activists Arrested for Protesting Discriminatory Laws," February 27, 2007; Kasra Naji, *Ahmadinejad: The Secret History of Iran's Radical Leader* (Berkley, CA: University of California Press, 2008), 252.

26. Payvand, "Iran: Women's Rights Activists Get Suspended Lashing Sentences," April 24, 2008.

27. Ibid.

28. World Bank, "Poverty in Iran: Trends and Structure, 1986–1998," Middle East and North Africa Region, Washington, D.C.

29. Electricity: 16.2 percent (1977) to 98.3 percent (2004); Piped Water: 11.7 percent (1977) to 89.0 percent (2004). Statistical Center of Iran, 1984–2005 Household Income and Expenditure Surveys.

30. *Iran Statistical Yearbook 1385 (2006–7)* www.sci.org.ir.

31. In 1960 there were 281 deaths per 1,000 births versus 42 deaths per 1,000 births in 2001. World Bank, "World Development Indicators," 2003, Washington, D.C.

32. Djavad Salehi-Isfahani, "Oil Wealth and Economic Growth in Iran," in *Contemporary Iran: Economy, Society, Politics*, edited by Ali Gheissari (Oxford: Oxford University Press, 2009), 15.

33. Pardis Mahdavi, "Who Will Catch Me If I Fall? Health and the Infrastructure of Risk for Urban Young Iranians," in Ali Gheissari edition, at page 165.

34. Statistical Center of Iran, www.sci.org.

35. Roksana Bahramitash and Hadi Salehi Esfahani, "Nimble Fingers No Longer! Women's Employment in Iran," in Ali Gheissari edition, at page 92.

36. Barlow and Akbarzadeh, "Prospects for Feminism in the Islamic Republic of Iran," 24.

37. Statistical Center of Iran.

38. As Bahramitash and Saleshi Esfahani note this is contrary to the female workforce in other parts of the global south, at page 79.

39. Barlow and Akbarzadeh, "Prospects for Feminism in the Islamic Republic of Iran," 28.

40. Hassan Hanizadeh, "Women's Rights in Iran," *Tehran Times*, July 8, 2007.

41. This is consistent with Davenport's findings on threat perception and an increase in repression. Christian Davenport, "Multi-Dimensional Threat Perception and State Repression: An Inquiry into Why States Apply Negative Sanctions," *American Journal of Political Science*, Vol. 38, No. 3 (1995), 683–713.

42. The description of the five-phase spiral model can be found on pages 22–35.

43. Risse and Sikkink, "Socialization of International Human Rights Norms," 23.

44. Ibid., 29.

45. Note criticisms of Iran by various international NGOs discussed earlier in the chapter.

46. It is also worth noting that none of the countries discussed in *The Power of Human Rights* were oil producing states that were also making progress on the nuclear front.

47. While the United States does not control Israeli foreign policy, Washington can apply pressure on Tel Aviv to avoid threats to Tehran and especially a threat of strike on Iranian territory.

48. Khomeini, *Islam and Revolution*, 213.

49. Ibid., 214.

50. *Tehran Times*, "Leader: No Conflict between Women's Social and Family Roles," July 5, 2007.

51. His remarks can be found at http://www.leader.ir/langs/en/?p=content
Show&id=5618.

52. State Department Report, February 25, 2009.

53. Khomeini, *Islam and Revolution*, 195.

54. *Tehran Times*, "Ahmadinejad submits International War Crimes Bill,"
February 23, 2009, at www.tehrantimes.com.

55. Abdullahi Ahmed An-Na'im has argued for both an internal dialogue
within Islam and a cross-cultural dialogue between the Islamic world
and the West that would alleviate any conflicts between Islam and international human rights. "Shari'a and Islamic Family Law: Transition and
Transformation," *Ahfad Journal* (December 2006), Vol. 23, No. 2,
pp. 2–30, at p. 5.

56. Nazila Fathi, "Iran Judge Asks for Review Case of Jailed Journalist,"
New York Times, April 12, 2009, at www.nytimes.com/2009/04/21/
world/middleeast/2/iran.html.

CHAPTER 7

FROM OMISSION TO RELUCTANT RECOGNITION: POLITICAL PARTIES' APPROACH TO WOMEN'S RIGHTS IN TURKEY

Zehra F. Kabasakal Arat

INTRODUCTION[1]

Subordination of women in Muslim communities and states has been problematized by many, ranging from Muslim Feminists who focus on sociohistorical factors to Orientalists who essentialize religion and berate Islam. However, the secularist and republican regime of the predominantly Muslim-populated Turkey has been treated as an exceptional case. Although some improvements in the status of women in Turkey is undeniable, the country is far from granting equal rights to women and approaching gender equality (Arat 1994 and 1998). Major political actors have subscribed to traditional gender notions, and women face all forms of discrimination and human rights violations.

In this chapter, I focus on the gender approach of political parties in Turkey, as expressed in party programs issued between 1920 and 2007. First, I present that the political parties' approach developed from a complete omission of women to gradually recognizing them as citizens, acknowledging their presence in economic life—with a concern about balancing their family responsibilities with work—and finally accepting a range of women's rights. I also show that left-wing parties have been more responsive to women's needs and more willing to employ a feminist discourse in time. However, considering that the overall change toward addressing women's needs and rights has to be related to events that affect the whole country, I contend that domestic factors, especially socioeconomic changes and women's movements, have been critical for the overall shifts in party positions. By stressing the relevance and significance of domestic politics, I also intend to offer a corrective to the prevalent human rights models, which tend to focus on international relations and attribute improvements in human rights practices in developing countries to the external pressures asserted by Western states and international human rights organizations (Krasner 1993; Keck and Sikkink 1998; Risse, Ropp, and Sikkink 1999; Landman 2005).

WHY POLITICAL PARTIES?

Political parties are important political machinery that became indispensable in representative democracies. Although theoretically conceivable, politics without political parties constitute a dismal possibility in modern times. In all regimes, including one-party rules, parties fulfill numerous important functions. They serve as mediators and communication channels between the state apparatus and the public at large (Schattschneider 1942:124; Lipson 1959: 12–13; Epstein 1967: 31–45; Johnston 2005). In most societies they act as the main vehicle of political participation (Stokes 1999, 250). Among their overlapping functions, we can list: political socialization; interest articulation and aggregation (Almond and Powell 1966); political recruitment; debating and formulating policies and policy frameworks; and implementing or monitoring government policies.

Emphasizing their role in the policy formulation process, Anthony Downs argues that in multiparty systems political parties do not win elections in order to formulate policies but they formulate policies to win elections (1957: 54), and others note that "[p]ostwar democratic theory often asserts that political parties transmit popular preferences into policy" (Stokes 1999: 250). Although the extent to which parties' policy positions reflect those of the electorate or parties implement their programs upon assuming power has not been settled (Rose 1969; Budge and Hofferbert 1990; Hofferbert and Budge 1992; King et al. 1993; van Biezen 2004; Stokes 1999), analysts agree that political parties are important players in shaping the *political agenda* and *discourse* of the country in which they operate.

However, political parties are seldom studied for their approach to and impact on human rights, or in terms of their treatment and recruitment of women (Basu 2005: 1). Yet, trusting their political and policy influence, Amnesty International has recently called on "all political parties of Pakistan to honestly commit themselves to upholding respect for and protection of human rights" and issued a 12-point plan to be followed (Amnesty International 2008).

Political parties have been particularly important in Turkish politics. Fredrick Frey, assessing the political participation in Turkey as early as the 1950s, does not hesitate to assert that "Turkish politics are party politics," because within Turkey's power structure "the political party is the main unofficial link between the government and the larger, extra-governmental groups of people" (Frey 1965: 301–303).

Turkey started to experience party politics at the turn of the twentieth century, under the Ottoman rule (Tunaya 1998). Before the Republic of Turkey was established in October 1923, the Grand National Assembly, established by the nationalists in April 1920, was witnessing the emergence of groups developed around ideological and political rivalries. Mustafa Kemal and other founders of the Republic turned their group into a political party and established Halk Fırkası (HF) in September 1923. The event marked the beginning of the one-party regime, which lasted until 1945, when the multiparty electoral system was adopted. However, Turkey's democratic development has not been smooth and was interrupted by four military interventions (in 1960, 1971, 1980, and 1997). Although the military interventions and frequent Constitutional Court decisions led to closing parties and barring their leaders from politics, politicians and parties in Turkey proved to be successful at regrouping and emerging as a new party that carried a different name but the message of the then "extinct" party.[2] Most of these effectively conveyed their claims, and the core constituencies, if not the entire public, understood the link and saw the new party as the continuation or an offspring of the old one.[3]

Political parties in Turkey have played important roles in agenda-setting and framing issues, though at varying degrees at different junctures. Election times have been particularly important, even during the one-party era. Party programs and platforms were presented to the public in campaign speeches and publications. Even when broadcasting was a state monopoly, political parties enjoyed allocated times on radio and TV to convey their messages. After the transition to the multiparty/competitive electoral system in 1945, political parties enjoyed not only more legitimacy and visibility but also more freedom, compared to the past and to other civic organizations. Thus, how political parties address human rights in their programs can be taken as a barometer of the significance attributed to human rights in general and the relative importance of specific human rights. As such, political party programs at least partially reveal the *political elite discourse* on human rights.

I contend that since political parties try to win elections, they would employ certain language and agenda that are deemed appealing to the electorate and addressing their concerns and preferences. Thus, we can expect political parties to be more responsive to domestic politics and pressures than to the international ones. Although their susceptibility to external pressures may increase once they win elections and become the governing party.

PARTIES AND WOMEN'S RIGHTS IN TURKEY

The information on political party discourse on women's rights was gathered through 97 political programs issued during the 88-year period between 1920 and 2007, by employing manifest and latent content analyses. The study includes all political parties that have been represented in the parliament, as well as a few others that failed to secure representation but enjoyed considerable attention and media coverage. (See Table 7.1, for a list of parties included.)

Table 7.1   The list of political parties and programs included in the study

Party Name and Acronym	Program Date	Party Name and Acronym	Program Date
ACF—Ahali Cumhuriyet Fırkası	1930	LCİÇF—Lâyik Cumhuriyetçi İşçi ve Çiftçi Fırkası	1931
AKP—Adalet ve Kalkınma Partisi	2002	LDP—Liberal Demokrat Parti	1946
ANAP—Anavatan Partisi	1983; 2002	MÇP—Milliyetçi Çalışma Partisi	1986; 1988
AP—Adalet Partisi	1961 1964; 1969; 1974	MDP—Milliyetçi Demokrasi Partisi	1983
BBP—Büyük Birlik Partisi	1993; 1999; 2002	MHP—Milliyetçi Hareket Partisi	1969; 1973; 1993; 2000
BP—Birlik Partisi	1967	MKP—Milli Kalkınma Partisi	1945
CGP—Cumhuriyetçi Güven Partisi	1971	MNP—Milli Nizam Partisi	1970
CHF—Cumhuriyet Halk Fırkası	1927; 1931	MP—Millet Partisi	1948; 1967
CHP—Cumhuriyet Halk Partisi	1935; 1939; 1943; 1947; 1953; 1954; 1959; 1976; 1993; 1994; 2002; 2006	MSP—Milli Selamet Partisi	1973
CKMP—Cumhuriyetçi Köylü Millet Partisi	1961; 1965	MTSP—Müstakil Türk Sosyalist Partisi	1948
CMP—Cumhuriyetçi Millet Partisi	1954	MP—Muhafazakar Parti	1983
DEHAP— Demokratik Halk Partisi	1997; 2003	ÖDP—Özgürlük ve Dayanışma Partisi	1996; 2006
DEP—Demokrasi Partisi	1993	RP—Refah Partisi	1983

(Continued)

Table 7.1   Continued

Party Name and Acronym	Program Date	Party Name and Acronym	Program Date
DİP—Demokrat İşçi Partisi	1950	SCF—Serbes Cumhuriyet Fırkası	1930
DP—Demokrat Parti	1946; 1951; 1998	SHP—Sosyaldemokrat Halk Partisi	2002
DSP—Demokratik Sol Parti	1985; 2003; 2007	SHP—Sosyal Demokrat Halkçı Parti	1985; 1993
DP—Demokratik Parti	1970	SODEP—Sosyal Demokrat Parti	1983
DTP—Demokrat Türkiye Partisi	1997	SP—Saadet Partisi	2001
DTP—Demokratik Toplum Partisi	2006	TBP—Türkiye Birlik Partisi	1972; 1980
DYP—Doğru Yol Partisi	1983; 1998	TCAÇP—Türk Cumhuriyet Amele ve Çiftçi Partisi	1930
FP—Fazilet Partisi	1997	TCF—Terakkiperver Cumhuriyet Fırkası	1924
GP—Genç Parti	2002	TİÇP—Türkiye İşçi ve Çiftçi Partisi	1946
GP—Güven Partisi	1967	TİP—Türkiye İşçi Partisi	1964; 1975
HADEP—Halkın Demokrasi Partisi	1994	TKP—Türkiye Köylü Partisi	1952
HEP—Halkın Emek Partisi	1990; 1992	TSDP—Türk Sosyal Demokrat Partisi	1946
HF—Halk Fırkası	1923	TSEKP—Türk Sosyalist Emekçi ve Köylü Partisi	1946
HP—Halkçı Parti	1956	TSİP—Türkiye Sosyalist İşçi Partisi	1976
HP—Hürriyet Partisi	1983	TSP—Türkiye Sosyalist Partisi	1946
HYP—Halkın Yükseliş Partisi	2005	YTP—Yeni Türkiye Partisi	1961
İDP—İslâm Demokrat Partisi	1952	YTP—Yeni Türkiye Partisi	2002
İkinci Grup	1923	YVİP—Yalnız Vatan İçin Partisi	1946

For the manifest content analysis, the term "women's rights" is designated as the key word and the number of times it is mentioned in a program is tallied. The findings of this quantitative approach show that, overall, parties have been reluctant to employ the term in their programs. In 97 programs examined, the term appears only in 30 programs for a total of 49 times. Multiple references appear in later years, as the tendency to mention women's rights increases over time, starting in the 1960s and gaining momentum after 2000. As observed elsewhere, left-wing political parties are more inclined to address women's rights (Jacquette 1997; Basu 2005; Sacchet 2005), and more frequent references are made by smaller left-wing parties that lacked representation in the parliament.

However, some party programs promote women's rights without mentioning the term. The latent content analysis allows us to examine the overall gender approach of parties, which cannot be captured by a few key words. The section that follows reports the finding of the latent content analysis and shows both the overall pattern of change and the variation in the gender approach of ideologically distinct political parties.

The Pattern of Change

The political history of modern Turkey is typically examined by dividing it into three major time periods: (1) The one-party rule, 1920–1945; (2) the multiparty era, 1945–1980; and (3) the post-1980. I employ the same basic chronological approach and summarize the gender discourse of political parties accordingly.

The One-Party Era

Until 1945, the political regime in Turkey was a one-party rule by Cumhuriyet Halk Partisi (CHP).[4] However, although limited both in number and power, other parties were established during this period, and a few received considerable public attention and press coverage.

Until the 1930s, we do not see any references to women in political party programs. This is not a surprising finding, since women had no place in political life. In fact, the word "woman" enters into party programs for the first time in 1930, in reference to promoting women's political rights. The program of Serbes Cumhuriyet Fırkası (SCF) notes that the Party "will advocate the expansion of political rights to women as well" (Art. 11).[5] The governing party CHF, which had extended suffrage to women for the municipal elections in 1930, recognized women's political rights in its program after the fact in 1931:

> Our Party observes citizens' political rights without any distinction to sex. In fact, our Party, aware that our women have supported the unity from every corner of domestic life throughout the glorious and profound history

of the Turkish nation, considers its duty to prepare the conditions necessary for women to exercise their political rights in parliamentary elections, as it has been the case in municipal elections. The Party trusts that only then it would be invigorating our [nation's] historical and honorable life with its character appropriate to the new convention (Art. I.4).

The 1935 program of CHP includes a section on "Civic Rights," which introduces the equality principle: "The Party does not make a male-female distinction in assigning citizens [their] rights and duties" (Art. 4-B). The promise to ensure "equality in rights and duties" for both sexes becomes a common occurrence in party programs, especially after women were granted the right to vote in municipal elections (1930) and national election (1934). However, the principle of "equality in rights and duties" appears to apply to only a few rights, such as the right to vote, since the party programs tend to enshrine family and display a gendered discourse that recognizes and values women for their reproductive function, childcare, and household responsibilities.[6] The 1931 program of the CHP notes that "[t]he privacy of family is the principle element in Turkish domestic life" (VI.1),[7] promises to take measures that would stimulate population increase, and continues as follows: "The Party is particularly attentive to the lives of children. There will be an effort to increase the number of centers for child delivery. In work areas, the establishment and proliferation of institutions that take care of children when female laborers are at work will continue" (VII.3).

Starting with this program, the CHP recognizes the fact that some women *have to work*. In its 1935 program, the party's goals include "[t]he protection of working mothers and their children" (Art. 56-C) and "opening nurseries in business areas for women who have the responsibility of earning a living" (Art. 58). The 1943 program contains new proposals that would encourage women's participation in public life and desegregation of sexes: "Technical training is considered to be the most important issue of a strong nation. Providing, renewing, and enhancing the knowledge of every citizen, man or woman, in an educational institution, now take place among the duties of the State" (Art. 9). Referring to the state-sponsored community centers that provided adult education and cultural programs, the program indicates that "no Halkevi or Halkodasi can be established if it is lacking any of the main elements, including a meeting hall *for men and women to assemble together*, a library, and activities of fine arts" (Art. 9, emphasis added).

The Multiparty Era, 1945–1980

Although the inauguration of multiparty politics shows proliferation in the direct or implicit references to women's status and needs in party programs, *none* of the programs issued by Demokrat Parti (DP), which appeared as the main opposition party and then ruled the country through the 1950s, mentions "woman." However, they define "Turkish society" as one "that is based on family and the principle of [private] property" and place a special emphasis on the institution of family.

In fact, family is espoused and enshrined as the central unit of society and culture, practically in every party program issued in Turkey, including the most recent ones. Some programs issued in the 1940s and 1950s by right-wing political parties treat population increase as essential to economic development and take a pro-natalist position.[8] For example, the Liberal Demokrat Parti (LDP) states that "every citizen should consider raising a family as a national and sacred duty" (1946, Art. 19), and the 1952 program of the İslâm Demokrat Partisi (İDP) suggests imposing penalties for those who fail to meet a prerequisite of fulfilling that duty: "Marriage and birth are our national issues. We will facilitate both. For those who refrain from marriage, their taxes will be increased; and, if they are civil servants, they will be held back in promotions" (Art. 18). Since the workforce was mainly male, by imposing a penalty on men the program considers men's control over women as natural, legitimizes it, and expects it to be used by men to ensure that women continue to fulfill their "reproductive responsibility."

The pro-natalist approach resurfaces in the programs of Islamist and ultra-nationalist parties, which have promoted "Turkish-Islamic" synthesis, in the form of objections to birth control and abortion. The program of Milli Selamet Partisi (MSP), established in 1972, lacks explicit references to women but unequivocally states: "Our party opposes the idea of population planning. It will encourage the increase of our population" (1973, Art. 87).

As references to women in party programs increase in this period, we also see a common thread that recognizes women mainly as mothers and housewives. Consequently, any service promised to women is presented with an understanding that it will help women fulfill their domestic responsibilities better.

Adalet Partisi (AP), which dominated the politics between 1961 and 1980, either as the governing party or as the main opposition one, acknowledged women in its first program only in one article and simply in terms of domestic responsibilities: "The Party recognizes all rights in all areas held by men for women [as well], and it views the need to provide all forms of assistance to them, especially to facilitate [fulfilling] their duties in [sustaining] family health and social life" (961, Art. 23). Supposedly more progressive Cumhuriyetçi Güven Partisi (CGP) notes that "Turkish women have a distinguished and very important status within family and society in terms of the spirit and manners that will be conveyed to Turkish children who constitute the future of the nation" and defines raising "Turkish women as able to fully comprehend their duties and responsibilities within family and society and as able to fulfill the requirements of these with precision" as a "national need" (1971, 81–82).

The tendency to recognize and value women mainly for their reproductive and family responsibilities resurfaces in parties' treatment of women's employment and participation in the workforce. Programs that acknowledge that some women work usually express a concern about the accommodation of working women as mothers. Maternity leave and day care programs are promised frequently, but with an understanding that women's primary domain is home and childcare is women's responsibility. Designating certain occupations as inappropriate for women, some indicate that women, like children, should be spared from "harmful" work. As in the 1964 program of AP—which reads: "We consider it appropriate to have women and children among the working population to be protected by special provisions" (Art. 68)—often discussing women and children in the same section and tone, programs reveal parties' paternalistic approach toward women.

In addition to paternalism, the right-wing and far-right nationalist parties' programs display essentialism by proposing to devise jobs according to the "characteristics of men and women" or "appropriate to the citizen's age, strength and sex." For example, the programs issued by Cumhuriyetçi Köylü Millet Partisi (CKMP), which target "eliminating conditions that cause women's misery and enslavement" (1965 Art. 31), also include proposals that follow biological reductionism—e.g., differentiation of work according to the characteristics of men and women (1961, Art. 104), ensuring that characteristics of men and women will be considered in national education in a scientific manner (1965, Art. 56), and offering jobs as "appropriate to the age, strength, and sex of the citizen," and protecting "[c]hildren, the youth and women . . . from [dangerous and difficult] work conditions" (1965, Art. 242).

The same sentiments resurface in programs of Millet Partisi (MP) and Milliyetçi Hareket Partisi (MHP), which appeared as splinters and successors of CKMP. The MHP's program, issued in 1969, problematizes women's subordination, promises equality and fulfillment of women's already recognized rights (Art. 30), but then expresses the commitment to "ensure that *male and female characteristics are scientifically observed* in the national educational system"(Art. 56, emphasis added).

The left-wing parties of the 1960s and 1970s were not much different in their gender discourse. Although it adopted a Social Democratic outlook in the 1960s, CHP kept circulating its 1954 program, which addresses women only in one article that declares the party's mission as ensuring that "all Turks, men and women, freely apply their ability and reach an advanced and affluent living standard, as equals in rights and duties and as confident about their status and future" (Art. 1), for over two decades. The new program, issued in 1976, spares less than one page to women (p. 103) only to acknowledge that some women work and promise equal pay, healthy environment, childcare, increased participation in unions, and maternal leave.

Socialist parties could not escape gendering work and emphasizing mothering, either. The Türkiye Birlik Partisi (TBP) program, including a section entitled "Women's Rights," reads as follows:

> Women are equal to men in all respects. Women and men walk together in education, work, payment, and Türkiye Birlik Partisi *considers married women's work in occupations relevant to their skills as a social and economic necessity, and motherhood as a public service.* There should be special assistance to married women and women with little children, they should not be forced to work in hard and improper jobs because of low [family] income, and they should be able to have their vacations with their husbands. Women should have full legal equality, and their social and economic equality should not be eclipsed. Marriages should be facilitated, and both the man and woman should be able to initiate divorce.
>
> Although Türkiye Birlik Partisi recognizes women's right to develop her own individuality, it finds the protection of women from excessive work and fatigue as crucial to their ability to perform *their duties as mothers and home makers* (TBP 1972, 62, emphasis added).

Türkiye İşçi Partisi (TİP) was the only Socialist party that managed to acquire seats in the parliament (though only for a short period of time). TİP declared its opposition to all forms of discrimination, including discrimination based on sex, and became the first party that incorporated the "equal pay for equal work" principle into its program, in 1964. Although its 1972 program includes several progressive measures, it falls short of challenging the mentality that assigns childcare responsibilities to women:

> . . . [The Party] envisions the easing of work and living conditions for women through: removing the anti-democratic provisions in law; taking functional and effective measures to tackle *working women's difficulties related to motherhood*; meticulously implementing the principle of equal pay for equal work for female laborers; ensuring women's active role in [determining] the course of society by participating in every level of public affairs and social life, and rearranging the retirement age with a consideration of the abrasive impact of capitalist living conditions on women (emphasis added).

Women's education, if included in party programs issued during this era, was not treated as a "right" but as necessary for making them better mothers. The programs issued by Türkiye Köylü Partisi (TKP) not only note that its "goal is to provide for the education and advancement of our women in every respect, especially in regard to facilitating [the fulfillment of] their duties within the family heart" (1952, Art. 15) but also declares that it is the party's duty "to bring up Turkish women in a way that appreciates and teaches their duty and responsibilities in family and society" (1961, Art. 45). The same approach is evident in the program of one of the first Islamist parties, Milli Nizam Partisi (MNP):

> Our party, believing in the principle that everyone, man or woman, has the right to be learned, considers it necessary to equip our children, who are tomorrow's parents, with the necessary pedagogical knowledge, and to provide—especially for the future mothers, our daughters who are housewives—[instructions on] home economics and information on the physical, spiritual, moral and religious training of children (1970, Art. 24).

Since the 1980 Military Coup

The military coup of 1980 not only suspended party politics for three years but also revamped the political party system in Turkey. All political parties active before the coup were banned, and their leaders were barred from politics. During the transition to civilian rule, new parties were allowed to be established under the military government's watchful eyes, and only three of them were permitted to participate in the 1983 parliamentary elections: Anavatan Partisi (ANAP), Halkçı Parti (HP), and Milliyetçi Demokrasi Partisi (MDP). The screening of political parties and other measures taken by the military regime geared toward preventing the rise of class politics that characterized the 1960s and 1970s, and they were successful in squeezing the ideological spectrum of parties, at least until the late 1980s, when the ban on former party leaders was removed. The military repression was particularly harsh on the left-wing groups. But the suppression of class politics gave way to identity politics and allowed women to address their problems by focusing on gender oppression.

Although a few party programs of this time period fail to mention women (i.e., ANAP 1983 and 2002, MP 1983, RP 1983, and MÇP 1986), there is a noticeable increase in the number of references made to women and women's issues in the post-1980 era. Along with the increasing tendency to recognize women's needs and rights, party programs start to display considerable diversity in their gender approach.

In transition to the civilian rule in 1983, ANAP came to power with a landslide victory and ruled either alone or as a coalition partner for most of the 1980s and 1990s. However, it ignored women (not even mentioning the word) in both programs that it issued (1983 and 2002). MDP, which later merged with ANAP, demonstrated a traditionalist approach, defined family as the foundation of Turkish society, and pledged the protection of mothers, along with family and children (Art. 56). Its program, including a promise to "ensure that the *work conditions are appropriate for the age, sex and strength of the working person* and that *children, women and the mentally or physically disabled individuals* are under special protection" (Art. 44, emphasis added), displays both essentialism and paternalism. It acknowledges women's double burden and promises mitigation, but with an approach that treats women's participation in the workforce as undesirable and stemming out of need, (Art. 57).[9]

The program of the relatively more progressive Halkçı Parti (HP) also demonstrates a traditionalist and home-centered approach in addressing women's needs and promises to assist working women by providing childcare, part-time work, and maternal leave. The only program issued by the religious Refah Partisi (RP, 1983) fails to mention women; although it includes a nondiscrimination clause, indicating that the party "treats everyone as equals without distinction to religion, language, race or sect," it omits listing sex. The program of Fazilet Partisi (FP), which was established in 1997 by members of the Islamist RP after its closing by the Constitutional Court, also leaves sex out of its nondiscrimination statement but offers a brief statement in support of women: "We consider women to be the foundational pillar of the society. There will be special attention to women's education and training, in order to enable women to be more successful in economic and public life" (1997).

The break away from the traditionalist approach first appears in the program of Sosyal Demokrasi Partisi (SODEP), which treats women's emancipation and gender equality as prerequisites of social equality at large. Its section entitled "Women's Problems" addresses not only women's rights but also their freedom; it further implies that women may want to enter the workforce, as a choice, regardless of their financial need:

> The party is cognizant that *a free and egalitarian system can be realized only if all individuals in the society have free and equal rights* without any male-female distinction. There will be an emphasis on general and specific educational programs that enable a woman to be better cultivated and to claim her rights.
>
> The party considers it a duty to remove the obstacles faced by *women who desire to work*, [and plans to fulfill it] by opening childcare centers and nurseries, and taking similar measures (1983, 37–38, emphasis added).

SODEP's gender approach and proposals are repeated in the 1985 and 1993 programs issued by Sosyaldemokrat Halkçı Parti (SHP), which emerged in 1985, when SODEP and HP merged. The SHP program emphasizes the structural causes of discrimination by pointing out that "[w]omen's problems that stem from being a woman and have been sustained throughout history persist today, albeit in different forms, in our social structures and cultural conditioning" and considers removing "all obstacles placed before women for being women" as necessary

(1985, 46). Although it does not spare much space to women electorates, the 1985 program of the left-of-center Demokratik Sol Parti (DSP) also assumes a rather radical posture: "Women's active participation in party work will be encouraged in order to enhance the verity of male-female equality, to properly *appreciate women's approach to solving social problems,* and to start the *development of democratic culture at home*" (1985, 35, emphasis added).

Although pro-women and feminist discourses started to become increasingly common, especially since the 1990s, the importance assigned to family, emphasis placed on motherhood, and proposals to restrict women's employment opportunities to protect them—prevalent in the earlier periods—did not vanish. Most parties continued to display a dualistic approach, as exemplified by the pro-business Doğru Yol Partisi (DYP). The party's 1983 program does not address the female electorate directly, but promising "nurseries and daycare centers for working fathers and mothers," it presents a rather gender-neutral approach toward childcare. The 1998 program pledges to take action favorable to women on a number of issues, ranging from providing education and training opportunities to making legal arrangements that would secure women's property rights and increase penalties for domestic violence and sexual harassment in the workplace.

Arguing that "Women should gain their economic independence and be integrated into social life," the program calls for measures that involve "well-meaning discrimination" (1998, 14). On the other hand, justifying the need to address women's rights and problems by "their important place in our family structure," promising to make arrangements that would "allow women to work at home and get paid by unit," and "offering broad credit opportunities for the work that they do, or will do, at home by using their own labor and skills," the program reveals that women are still perceived as home-bound (1998, 14).

This dualism is more pronounced in programs issued by parties that emerged as successors to the far-right Turkish nationalist MHP,[10] which call for realizing women's rights recognized in law but also stress women's role within the family. The 1988 program of MÇP, later adopted by MHP (1993), includes a section entitled "FAMILY" that starts with the sentence declaring that "[f]amily is the main social unit of Turkish society" and continues as follows:

> . . . We also see the role of family in raising children, who are the guarantees of our future, as very important and believe in the necessity of supporting, protecting and fostering the Turkish family as immersed in our national and spiritual values. In an effort to mount family, which is the foundation of our nation, on healthy bases, the advancement of mothers will be assigned importance and all measures will be taken to ensure strengthening the

institution of family. The measures that are directed at the protection of the health of mothers and children will be emphasized.

We fiercely reject attacks directed at family and its social functions under the disguise of feminism. Nevertheless, we believe in the defense of women and women's rights, as well as the necessity of protecting women as respected beings along with men. (the bold font in the original)

They also object to abortion and artificial insemination, reject women's right to choose, and propose placing family planning under the state's control. However, this tone changes in MHP's 2000 program. Although women's issues and children are still addressed under the same subheadings and women are anchored in family, the new program drops the explicit rejection of feminism and pledges to remove "all actual and legal discrimination against women," and institute "equal pay for equal work." Noting that "Women's rate of literacy and participation in the labor force are low," the program promises to elevate "women's social status" by improving their "education level and ensuring their expanded participation in the development process, work life, and decision-making mechanisms."

In contrast, Büyük Birlik Partisi (BBP), which split from the MHP in 1993, adopted a more traditionalist approach. All of its programs (issued in 1993, 1999, and 2002) repeat the following: "Family is the foundation of society. The society and state take every measure to preserve the power of traditional Turkish-Islamic family. All forms of activities that would damage the order and health of family structure would be banned."

It should be noted that practically all parties continued to identify family as "the foundation of society" and promise its protection. Although in general they employ a progressive approach and seek gender equality, the programs of successive Kurdish nationalist parties also refer to "motherhood" as "a social and natural duty" and promise its protection (DEP 1993, 11; HADEP 1994, 12; DEHAP 1997, 14). Upholding motherhood appears to be more prominent in religious/Islamist parties' programs, although both Saadet Partisi (SP) and Adalet ve Kalkınma Partisi (AKP) appear to be more inclusive and progressive than FP, their predecessor. The SP and AKP programs, issued in 2001 and 2002, respectively, acknowledge women's low status and hardship and promise equal pay for equal work. However, the SP program addresses women's issues and rights only in a few sentences and with an emphasis on the protection of family. Recognizing that women are torn between their family and work, it notes that the cost of women's employment outside home should not be the neglect of children or family (2001, Section III.14 on family).

Compared to the SP, the AKP program takes a more comprehensive and progressive approach. It addresses a range of women's issues by including a subheading on women within the "Social Policies" Section and promises to improve women's education, employment opportunities, social security, work conditions, participation in public life, and involvement in the party and in politics at large. Also promised are measures to prevent violence against women and assisting those who have been subjected to violence. It further pledges to uphold "international standards on rights and freedoms regarding women, children and work life" and to implement all principles and requirements of the UN Convention on the Elimination of All Forms of Discrimination against Women (CEDAW). Yet, it also includes some stipulations that reveal the party's traditionalism. While the program recognizes women as "individuals," it justifies supporting women for "being the most effective [actors] in bringing up healthy generations." Thus, its pledge to create "new employment opportunities" for women is immediately qualified by another promise: "but the respect for [women's] work at home will be upheld." The program also notes that "[s]ocial security and work conditions will be improved with a consideration of women's work life and responsibilities regarding children and family."[11]

Most parties address women's work and work conditions and promise to help them, mostly by offering assistance for childcare. However, some programs, acknowledging that women are torn between their family and work, express a concern that women's participation in economic life may come at the expense of children's welfare (e.g., SP 2001). Nevertheless, the characterization of some work as not suitable for women, starts to disappear in later programs, with a few exceptions (e.g., MDP 1983 and BBP 1993).

Most programs issued after 1980 take working women as a given, but some start to make references to women's *right to work* and mention the need to ensure their equal access to employment, promotion, and pay. The principle of "equal pay for equal work," which is mentioned only in four political party programs issued in the 1960s and 1970s (TİP 1964 and 1974; MNP 1970; and TSİP 1976), becomes a common reference in programs adopted in the 1990s and later.[12] Moreover, economic freedom and independence enter into the lexicon of political parties, including some right-wing ones (e.g., DYP 1998; GP 2002).

Although they fall short of proposing concrete measures such as quotas for women, several programs acknowledge that the right to run for office does not guarantee women's equal representation. While the left-of-center DSP's programs promise that "women's active participation in party work will be encouraged in order to enhance the verity of male-female equality" (1985 and 2003), the right-of-center DP's 1998 program pledges to remove "[a]ll legal, administrative and traditional obstacles that prevent our women, who constitute half of our population and always have an important place in our society, from playing a more active role in all areas, but especially in politics and work life" (p. 42).

Statements such as "equality before law is not enough" (MHP 1993) or the need to employ a comprehensive approach to women's hardship and exclusion from public life become increasingly common in the 1990s and later. Although limited in number, some political party programs problematize women's extra burden and unequal status within family. For example, the short-lived YTP's program notes that "[w]omen do not share [the joys of] life; they carry the heaviest burdens of the family; they cannot benefit from family income or leisure time. . . . On this subject, we will support a change in mentality in every level" (2002, 7–8).

The most comprehensive approach to gender inequalities and women's rights are presented in programs issued by CHP in 1993, and later, by Özgürlük ve Dayanışma Partisi (ÖDP) and a couple of parties established by Kurdish nationalists (DEHAP 2003 and DTP 2006). In addition to addressing inequalities in the private domain, they challenge patriarchal norms and offer feminist analyses of women's lower status by employing feminist terminology, including "gender," "male-dominance," "male-dominant society," "sexism," "sexist," "patriarchy," and "feminism."[13] Beginning with the 1993 program, CHP programs note that "[w]omen's rights should be claimed, not only in law and economy," and promise them to be "positively secured" in the "new Turkey" that the party would create. They define "the main goal of the Turkey proposed by the CHP" as "having men and women share together both the benefits and burdens of life in family and society." The 1994 and 2006 programs include a section entitled "A Society in which Men and Women are Equals" that asserts party's commitment to "change the country from being a male-dominated society and transform it into a society of free individuals" (Section 1.4 B).

Under a subheading that reads "Freedom for Women!" the ÖDP programs provide a comprehensive list of feminist demands, including the elimination of discriminatory provisions in law, the sexist mentality in educational curricula, and "all forms of control over women's bodies"; and the recognition of "crimes against women" in law; the [public] acceptance of the notion that women should be "in charge of their lives"; and the establishment of government-financed counseling centers and shelters for women who face "male aggression in all public and private domains of life, at work, and at times of war," and putting them under women's management. Highlighting "[t]he goal being the elimination of male-domination" in all areas, the program affirms that "women should not be confined to house work, . . . work without pay or for low pay should be ended; women's right to be equal in all areas and right to work for equal pay should be warranted; and the principle of positive discrimination should be supported by law—in order to allow women's right to education and work to be sustained and deeply rooted" (1996 and 2006).

Similar issues and proposals are also included in DEHAP (2003) and DTP (2006) programs. DEHAP's program notes that "[i]n the twenty-first century, freedom of women will be important just like human rights. Contemporary democratic development distinguished itself by [placing emphasis on] human rights and human freedom." Three years later, DTP's program reintroduces the gender equality measures of the DEHAP program and mainstreams women's issues by discussing them as systemic problems connected to the hierarchical structure of social and state systems, militarism, capitalism, globalization, and patriarchy. On women's political representation, the DTP program sets a female quota of 40 percent within the party and proposes a 33 percent quota to be set by law for all political parties. Moreover, it suggests the expansion of the quota system for the executive boards of trade unions and associations.

The programs issued by CHP, ÖDP, DEHAP, and DTP since the 1990s stand out also for integrating the problem of gender inequality into the discussion of practically all issues. ÖDP and DTP take a more radical and comprehensive approach and appear to be the only parties that oppose discrimination based on one's sexual orientation.

The silence on gender-based violence, domestic violence, and sexual harassment is also broken in some programs issued in the 1990s and later, and several political parties take a stance against them.[14] A few of these programs also make explicit references to the CEDAW, and promise to uphold and implement its provisions (CHP 1994 and 2006; AKP 2002; DEHAP 2003; and DTP 2006).[15] Moreover, ensuring gender equality through positive discrimination is promised by a few parties.[16]

The analysis of references to women and women's rights in political party programs since the 1920s show a pattern of gradual change from no mention of women to explicit feminist analyses of women's subordination. Although the mid-1980s may appear to be a major turning point, the change has been neither linear nor unanimous. While the trend has been toward an acceptance of women's participation in economy and politics and the equality of sexes has started to be perceived as more than equality before law, several political parties, including the most powerful ones that have been forming governments, remain committed to preserving traditional family structures and a gendered division of labor.

WHAT CAUSES A CHANGE?

Although current human rights theories tend to attribute pro-human rights development in developing countries to international developments and pressure, I contend that international human rights developments have not had an immediate impact on the gender discourse of political parties in Turkey. Human rights declarations and treaties adopted by the United Nations (UN), the Council of Europe (CE), or the International Labour Organization (ILO) do not correspond to noted changes in political party discourse (or policies). In general, party programs do not incorporate the terminology of conventions adopted in international forums. Instead, they seem to be more responsive to domestic developments and their constituencies. They also appear to be reactive rather than proactive and respond to domestic pressure as well as to other parties' messages. The change in one party's discourse may be triggering change in others' that are competing for the support of similar constituencies.

The changes in political parties' gender discourse appear to have a stronger correlation with the rise of women's movements and socioeconomic changes in Turkey than with major international human rights events. For example, the recognition of women's political rights in Turkey, in 1930, both by political parties and by the government, preceded the recognition of these rights in international human rights documents. The move in Turkey can be partially explained by women's demands for the right to vote, which had been raised by the women's movement of the early twentieth century and had become the main goal of the Women's Union after the establishment of the Republic of Turkey (Arat 1998). While women's demands might have been informed by the international women's movement of the late nineteenth century, it would be hard to claim any sort of "foreign pressure" on the Turkish government to expand suffrage.

On the other hand, various international conventions that promoted nondiscrimination and women's rights seem to have been ignored by Turkish governments and were not incorporated into the political party discourse immediately. The ILO's Equal Remuneration Convention (no. 100) is a case in point. The convention, which institutes the "principle of equal remuneration for men and women workers for equal value" was adopted in 1951, but political parties in Turkey did not start to address the principle of "equal pay for equal work" until 1964, and only three rather small parties did so in the 1960s and 1970s. Political parties' references to the principle of equal pay for equal work, acknowledgment of working women's needs, and promises of day care centers began in the 1960s, and as likely responses to the changes in the country's economy, labor force, and intensified urbanization and unionization. As there is no evidence of external pressure, Turkey's ratification of the ILO Convention in July 1967 is likely to have been triggered also by these economic and social changes. Yet, it should be noted that women's rights that are related to work, employment opportunities, and equal pay appeared to be more common in party programs issued later, in the 1990s and 2000s, after the proliferation of women's organizations and a notable increase in feminist activism.

A similar pattern can be observed in relation to the country's adoption and ratification of UN declarations and conventions. Neither the

Universal Declaration of Human Rights (1948) nor the two major human rights covenants adopted by the UN General Assembly in 1966 seem to have made a significant impact on political party discourses on women's rights. More focused women's rights initiatives by the UN, such as the Convention on the Nationality of Married Women (1957), the Declaration on the Elimination of Discrimination against Women (1967), and the CEDAW (1979), or the designation of 1975 as the International Women's Year, have not resulted in an immediate change in the parties' approaches, either.

Starting with the 1994 program of the CHP, however, the CEDAW becomes a reference point in several party programs, but interestingly after the country had become a party to the convention in 1989. These references and the overall change in favor of a more progressive and inclusive gender discourse, again, seem to correspond to changes in domestic politics, particularly to the rise of women's activism. The CEDAW and other initiatives by the UN, such as the Declaration on Violence against Women (1993), and the Beijing World Conferences on Women (1995), have been embraced by the women's movement that took off in Turkey in the late 1980s (Ecevit 2007). This new wave of women's movement in Turkey deliberately avoided establishing a symbiotic relationship with any political party but employed different strategies, including protest demonstrations and petition campaigns, as well as sporadic collaboration with the state agencies and political parties (Ecevit 2007).

Turkey's candidature to the European Union (EU) is aptly considered as a catalyst, if not the cause, of several pro-human rights reforms undertaken in Turkey since the late 1990s. Some interactions that resemble the boomerang effect (Keck and Sikkink 1998; Risse, Ropp, and Sikkink 1999) could be detected between women rights/human rights organizations in Turkey, the Turkish state agencies, the EU agencies, and women's networks in Europe in this period.[17] However, it should be noted that the EU agencies started to pressure Turkey to improve its human rights practices relatively recently and did so selectively by focusing on physical integrity, due process, and minority rights (Arat and Smith, forthcoming). Even after the process of Turkey's accession to the EU gained momentum, the EU has not been particularly demanding on the issue of women's rights. In fact, the EU has been slow in addressing gender equality. Until the mid-1990s, European Commission's directives on gender equality were limited to the equal pay for equal work principle incorporated into its founding Rome Treaty of 1957 (Masselot 2007; Martinsen 2007; Pollack and Hafner-Burton 2000), and the EU approach and implementation of the principle has been criticized for following the market concerns and a neoliberal economic paradigm rather than women's rights (Lewis 2006; Martinsen 2007: 548–49).[18]

Gender equality and women's rights gained prominence in the EU agenda in relation to the UN's World Conference on women, held in Beijing in 1995, and were ultimately articulated in the Amsterdam Treaty of 1997.

I have been engaged in this research project to reveal the role of important domestic actors in the development of human rights norms and their implementation. The preliminary findings indicate that political parties are responsive to domestic changes and political pressures more than to the international ones. Further analysis of government discourse and policies and assessment of the extent to which political party discourses influence governments is needed to reveal the workings of domestic processes. Additional research on these lines, with attention to both domestic and international factors, would allow the development of more comprehensive models that explain shifts in human rights discourse and policies both in developing and developed countries.

Notes

1. The chapter reports partial findings of a broader research project that examines the human rights discourse and practices in Turkey since the 1920s and was sponsored by grants from the International Research and Exchanges Board (IREX), the National Endowment for the Humanities (NEH), and the United States Institute of Peace (USIP). I am grateful for their support but would like to note that views, findings, conclusions, or recommendations expressed here do not necessarily represent those of the IREX, NEH, or the USIP. I would also like to thank my assistant Alexandra Friedman, for her diligent work, and my son Hasan-Can for his critical reading and valuable comments. Earlier versions of this paper were presented at various professional conferences.

2. See Nicole F. Watt (1999) for an excellent review of what may be called a process of "reincarnation" for pro-Kurdish parties. On other parties, see Rubin and Heper, *Political Parties in Turkey*, 2000.

3. For debates on the institutionalization of political parties in Turkey, see Özbudun, "Turkey: How Far from Consolidation?" 1996 and Çarkoğlu, "The Turkish Party System in Transition," 1998. On political party organizations in Turkey, see Kabasakal, *Türkiye'de Siyasal Parti Örgütlenmesi 1908–1960*, 1991.

4. The CHP was previously called Halk Fırkası (HF) and Cumhuriyet Halk Fırkası (CHF).

5. The translation of all quotations from programs is mine.

6. The notion of equality expressed in these references falls short of meeting even the principle of "equality before law," since the laws and their interpretation by the courts and other state authorities were essentially biased and discriminated against women (Arat 1994).

7. A similar article appears in the party's 1927 program: "The privacy and stability of family is the principle that we support in regard to our domestic life."

8. This approach was recently demonstrated by Prime Minister Erdoğan, the leader of the ruling party AKP. Addressing women in the city of Uşak on the 2008 International Women's Day, he called every young woman to have three children to maintain a youthful Turkish population that would stimulate the economy. *Radikal*, March 8, 2008. http://www.radikal.com.tr/haber.php?haberno=249531, accessed on March 10, 2008. Despite protests from women's groups, he has been repeating the same call.

9. It reads: "On the one hand, as mothers and wives, they assume the care and service of their children and husbands, and on the other hand, they shoulder [the responsibility of maintaining] peace, order and management of their nest; with difficulties imposed by their biological and physiological characteristics, they work in the house, fields, factories and offices, in order to reduce the stress of the living conditions on the family."

10. MHP was closed down after the military coup of 1980, but reemerged as Muhafazakar Parti (MP) in 1983, which did not mention women in its program. In 1985, the MP adopted the name of Milliyetçi Çalışma Partisi (MÇP, Nationalist Labor Party). It went back to MHP in 1992, when it became possible to use the old party names again.

11. The party's policies, both at national and municipal levels, tend to follow the traditionalist discourse (Arat, "Women's Rights and Status," forthcoming; Ayata and Tütüncü, "Party Politics of the AKP," 2008).

12. CHP 1994 and 2006; ÖDP 1996 and 2006; MHP 2000; SP 2001; AKP 2002; YTP 2002; DEHAP 2003; and DTP 2006.

13. It should be noted that such terminology is sometimes employed to attack feminism, as seen in the 1993 MHP program.

14. Programs that address violence against women: CHP 1994 and 2006; ÖDP 1996 and 2006; DYP 1998; AKP 2002; YTP 2002; DEHAP 2003; and DTP 2006. Programs that problematize sexual harassment of women: CHP 1994 and 2006; DYP 1998; YTP 2002; DTP 2006; and ÖDP 2006.

15. It is important to note that HP's 1983 program alluded to the CEDAW, by promising that "[i]t will be ensured that our women's pre- and postnatal leaves are in compliance with the UN principles" (p. 28).

16. ÖDP 1996 and 2006, DYP 1998; YDP 2002, DEHAP 2003, and DTP 2006.

17. For example, women's objections to the AKP government's plan to include adultery in the new penal code as a public offense was supported by the EU and European women's groups, and the women's position prevailed in the 2004 legislation.

18. Subscription to the neoliberal economic paradigm has led the EU to undermine social and economic rights in general and push candidate states, including Turkey, to adapt policies that result in the deterioration of some rights, e.g., the right to social security (Arat and Smith, "The EU and Human Rights in Turkey," forthcoming).

References

Almond, Gabriel, and Bingham Powell Jr., *Comparative Politics: A Developmental Approach.* Boston: Little, Brown and Co., 1966.

Amnesty International, "Amnesty International's Call to Political Parties to Commit Themselves to Uphold a 12-Point Plan on Human Rights," February 14, 2008. http://www.amnesty.org/en/library/info/ASA33/006/2008 (accessed June 2, 2009).

Arat, Zehra F. K. "Kemalism and Turkish Women," *Women and Politics* 14, no. 4 (Fall 1994): 57–80.

———, ed. *Deconstructing Images of "The Turkish Woman."* New York: St. Martin's Press, 1998.

———. "Women's Rights and Status," in *Routledge Handbook of Modern Turkey*, ed. Metin Heper and Sabri Sayarı. Routledge (forthcoming 2011).

Arat, Zehra F. K., and Thomas Smith. "The EU and Human Rights in Turkey: Political Freedom without Social Welfare?" in *What Difference Does the EU Make for Democratization and Human Rights?* Ed. Henry Carey. London: Rowman and Littlefield (forthcoming 2011).

Ayata, Ayşe Güneş, and Fatma Tütüncü. "Party Politics of the AKP (2002–2007) and the Predicaments of Women at the Intersection of the Westernist, Islamist and Feminist Discourses in Turkey," *British Journal of Middle Eastern Studies* 35, no. 3 (2008): 363–384.

Basu, Amrita. *Women, Political Parties and Social Movements in South Asia.* Occasional Paper 5. United Nations Research Institute for Social Development (UNRISD). Geneva: UNRISD, July 2005.

Budge, Ian, and Richard Hofferbert. "Mandates and Policy Outputs: U.S. Party Platforms and Federal Expenditures," *American Political Science Review* 84 (1990): 111–132.

Çalı, Başak. "Human Rights Discourse in Turkey: A Study of the Domestic Human Rights NGOs," in *Human Rights in Turkey: Policies and Prospects*, ed. Zehra F. Kabasakal Arat. Philadelphia: University of Pennsylvania Press, 2007: 217–232.

Çarkoğlu, Ali. "The Turkish Party System in Transition: Party Performance and Agenda Change," *Political Studies* 46 (1998): 544–571.

Downs, Anthony. *An Economic Theory of Democracy.* New York: Harper and Row, 1957.

Ecevit, Yıldız. "Women's Rights, Women's Organizations and the State," in *Human Rights in Turkey: Policies and Prospects*, ed. Zehra F. Kabasakal Arat. Philadelphia: University of Pennsylvania Press, 2007: 187–201.

Epstein, Leon D. *Political Parties in Western Democracies.* New York: Praeger, 1967.

Frey, Frederick W. *The Turkish Political Elite.* Cambridge, MA: MIT Press, 1965.

Hofferbert, Richard, and Ian Budge. "The Party Mandate and the Westminster Model: Election Programmes and Government Spending in Britain 1948–85," *British Journal of Political Science* 22, no. 2 (April 1992): 151–182.

Jacquette, J. "Women in Power: From Tokenism to Critical Mass," *Foreign Policy* 108 (Fall 1997): 23–37.

Johnston, Michael. *Political Finance Policy, Parties, and Democratic Development. Political Parties and Democracy in Theoretical and Practical Perspectives.* Washington, D.C.: National Democratic Institute for International Affairs, 2005.

Kabasakal, Mehmet. *Türkiye'de Siyasal Parti Örgütlenmesi 1908–1960.* Ankara: Tekin Yayınevi, 1991.

Keck, Margaret E., and Kathryn Sikkink. *Activists beyond Boarders: Advocacy Networks in International Politics.* Ithaca, NY: Cornell University Press, 1998.

King, Gary, Michael Laver, Richard I. Hofferbert, Ian Budge, and Michael D. McDonald. "Party Platforms, Mandates and Government Spending—Comment/Reply," *American Political Science Review* 87, no. 3 (September 1993): 744–750.

Krasner, Stephen D. "Sovereignty, Regimes and Human Rights," in *Regime Theory and International Relations,* ed. V. Rittberger and P. Mayer. Oxford: Oxford University Press, 1993: 139–167.

Landman, Todd. *Protecting Human Rights: A Comparative Study.* Washington, D. C.: Georgetown University Press, 2005.

Lewis, Jane. "Work/Family Reconciliation, Equal Opportunities and Social Policies: The Interpretation of Policy Trajectories at the EU level and the Meaning of Gender Equality," *Journal of European Public Policy* 13, no. 3 (April 2006): 420–437.

Lipson, Leslie. "Party Systems in the United Kingdom and the Older Commonwealth: Causes, Resemblances and Variations," *Political Studies* 7 (February 1959): 12–31.

Martinsen, Dorte Sindbjerg. "The Europeanization of Gender Equality—Who Controls the Scope of Non-Discrimination?" *Journal of European Public Policy* 14, no. 4 (June 2007): 554–562.

Masselot, Annick. "The State of Gender Equality Law in the European Union," *European Law Journal* 13, no. 2 (March 2007): 152–168.

Özbudun, Ergun. "Turkey: How Far from Consolidation?" *Journal of Democracy* 7, no. 3 (1996): 123–138.

Pollack, Mark A., and Emilie Hafner-Burton. "Mainstreaming Gender in the European Union," *Journal of European Public Policy* 7, no. 3 (September 200): 432–456.

Risse, Thomas, Stephen Ropp, and Kathryn Sikkink, eds. *The Power of Human Rights: International Norms and Domestic Change.* Cambridge: Cambridge University Press, 1999.

Rose, Richard. "The Viability of Party Government: A Theoretical and Empirical Critique," *Political Studies* 17, no. 4 (December 1969): 413–445.

Rubin, Berry, and Metin Heper, eds. *Political Parties in Turkey.* London: Frank Cass, 2000.

Sacchet, Teresa. *Political Parties: When Do They Work for Women?* United Nations. EGM/EPWD/2005/EP.10. December 12, 2005.

Schattschneider, E. E. *Party Government.* New York: Holt, Rinehart, and Winston, 1942.

Stokes, S.C. "Political Parties and Democracy," *Annual Review of Political Science* 2, no. 1 (1999):243–267.

Tunaya, Tarık Zafer. *Türkiye'de Siyasi Partiler*, 3 volumes. Istanbul: İletişim Yayınları, 1998.

van Biezen, Ingrid. "How Political Parties Shape Democracy." Center for the Study of Democracy, University of California, Irvine, 2004. http://repositories. cdlib.org/csd/04-16/ (accessed May 20, 2009).

Watt, Nicole F. "Allies and Enemies: Pro-Kurdish Parties in Turkish Politics 1990–94," *International Journal of Middle East Studies* 31, no. 4 (November 1999): 631–656.

CHAPTER 8

MINORITIES AND MARGINALIZED COMMUNITIES IN THE MIDDLE EAST: THE CASE FOR INCLUSION

Mahmood Monshipouri and Jonathon Whooley

To better understand the history and the heritage of ethnic and sectarian divides in the Middle East, it is essential to grasp the unity and diversity of Islam, as well as the region's cultural mosaic. The issue of sectarian and ethnic divides lies at the heart of marginalized communities. Virtually all Middle Eastern countries have minority groups. Some are religious minorities; others are ethnic-linguistic minorities; and still others are a combination of both. Some minorities in the Middle East have aspired for a separate national home (the Kurds in Iran, Iraq, Syria, and Turkey), while others are content with grants of equal rights within a country (the Copts in Egypt, the Druze in Lebanon). That some minorities have been overrepresented in power hierarchies helps explain their support for the maintenance of the status quo (the Sunnis in Iraq prior to the 2003 U.S. invasion).[1] Although broadly speaking all groups are minorities no matter who rules, in some countries minorities rule, such as the Maronites in Lebanon and the Alewites in Syria.

The issue of possible linkage between human rights situation of religious minorities in the Middle East and the political and legal contexts merits particular attention. Historically, the status of the "People of the Book" has been secured by contractual obligations to protect non-Muslims. This legal obligation has guaranteed their life, body, property, freedom of movement, and religious practice. Protection had been extended against taxes of various kinds, including a head tax (*jizya*) and a property tax (*kharaj*). The traditional *Shari'a* notions of the minorities, critics note, should evolve into a coherent and humane principle of citizenship in the "territorial state." To equate citizenship solely with nationality at the expense of other forms of membership, especially ethnic or religious minorities, they argue, is fundamentally wrong.[2]

This chapter's core argument is that the minority issues in the Middle East are more heavily influenced by the political, legal, economic, social, and cultural circumstances than religious differences. In the sections that follow, we systematically examine such minorities as the Kurdish leaders, groups, and parties in Turkey, as well as the Druze population of Lebanon, and the Copts in Egypt. In virtually all cases—including the Copts in Egypt who are an economically better off, educated, and influential religious minority—participation in the political process may create a sustainable platform for advancing the causes of those minorities.

MINORITIES IN PERSPECTIVE

In the Middle East and North Africa (see table 8.1), 31 politically active minorities are found. Since the postwar period, they have engaged in considerable communal protest and rebellion. In the postwar period evidence in some Islamic states points to numerous incidents of mistreatment of minority groups, such as Ahmediyas (Pakistan), Baha'is (Iran and Tunisia), Berbers (Algeria and Libya), Coptic Christians (Egypt and Sudan), Jews (Syria), and Jews and Christians (Yemen). Some experts have found that minority groups in the Middle East are subject to the most severe political discrimination of any region in the world and are second only to Latin America in the severity of economic discrimination.[3]

Most written constitutions of Muslim states now confirm the principle of equality of all citizens irrespective of religion, sex, and race.[4] Today, in some countries (Lebanon, Jordan, or the Islamic Republic of Iran) non-Muslim and other minority groups are guaranteed a fixed share of seats in representative political bodies.[5] Some observers have emphasized the possibilities of a struggle for human rights from within a Muslim framework.[6] Others have attempted to decouple human rights and religion, arguing that Islamism, as a religious nationalist ideology, has had a markedly negative effect on human rights throughout the Muslim world.[7] They argue against privileging Islam such that human rights must be warranted in Islamic terms in order to be seen as relevant. Islam, Anthony Chase insists, "is neither responsible for rights violations nor the core basis for advancing rights."[8] In the sections that follow, we shall study the cases of the Copts in Egypt, Shiites and Druze in Lebanon, and Kurdish minorities in Turkey.

Table 8.1 Selected minority groups

Country	Group	Group Type
Algeria	Berbers	Indigenous
Bahrain	Shiites	religious sect
Cyprus	Turkish Cypriots	Ethnonationalist
Egypt	Copts	religious sect
Iran	Arabs	national minority
Iran	Azerbaijanis	national minority
Iran	Baha'is	religious sect
Iran	Bakhtiari	Indigenous
Iran	Baluchis	Indigenous
Iran	Christians	religious sect
Iran	Kurds	Ethnonationalist
Iran	Turkmen	national minority
Iraq	Kurds	Ethnonationalist
Iraq	Shiites	religious sect
Iraq	Sunnis	communal contender
Israel	Arabs	Ethnoclass
Israel	Palestinians	Ethnonationalist
Jordan	Palestinians	Ethnonationalist
Lebanon	Druze	communal contender
Lebanon	Maronite Christians	communal contender
Lebanon	Palestinians	Ethnonationalist
Lebanon	Shiites	communal contender
Lebanon	Sunnis	communal contender
Morocco	Berbers	Indigenous
Morocco	Saharawis	Ethnonationalist
Saudi Arabia	Shiites	religious sect
Syria	Alawi	communal contender
Syria	Kurds	Ethnonationalist
Turkey	Kurds	Ethnonationalist

Source: *Minorities at Risk Project*, available at http://www.cidcm.umd.edu/mar/assessments.
asp?regionId=5. Last visited on December 3, 2008.

The Copts in Egypt

Known as the Christians of Egypt or direct descendants of the original inhabitants of the country in the Hellenistic and Roman periods, the Copts were a majority in Egypt from the fourth to the seventh centuries. Although estimates vary widely, Copts represent approximately 8 percent of the Egyptian population (6.5 million), and some say 95 percent of them are Christians.[9] Historically, Copts have not constituted a cohesive political group, even as they have been well integrated into the fabric of the country's society.[10] Coptic is the ancient language of Christian Egypt and the Copts are an Arabic-speaking minority who only retain the Coptic language in their liturgies.[11]

The advent of the Crusades led to a deterioration of the position of the Copts, as the Crusaders scorned them as heretics, forbidding them from making their traditional pilgrimages to Jerusalem.[12] The Copts suffered persecution in Egypt after Chalcedon (Orthodoxy in the fifth and sixth centuries) by Christians—under Byzantine control—until the Islamic-Arab conquest of Egypt (640–642 CE). After that, they found themselves coexisting with their Muslim rulers, sometimes under an uneasy but peaceful armistice, and at others under attack.[13] The Islamic conquerors were interested in the civil and financial, but not religious affairs of the Copts.[14] When Alexandria was conquered by the Arabs in 641, the indigenous patriarch Benjamin, who was treated sympathetically by Muslims, emerged from hiding. He returned triumphantly from Upper Egypt and was greeted everywhere by the people. Amr ibn al-As (died 661 CE), the renowned Arab conqueror of Egypt, was impressed with him and paid his respects to him in Alexandria. Benjamin functioned as a representative of the church and of the people. The church buildings that had belonged to the Melchites (the Byzantine Christians), were turned over to the Copts.[15]

The Copts' *dhimmi* status was abrogated by Said Pasha (1822–1863) in 1856. Said's reign was a liberal one, involving many reforms for landownership, taxation, and the abolishment of the slave trade. Copts were exempted from paying the *jizya*, the head tax paid by non-Muslims in Egypt from the Muslim conquests until 1855.[16] In the twentieth century, especially during the 1940s and 1950s, the proportion of Copts in official posts exceeded their proportion of the population. Copts were among Egypt's large landowners, and many were leading members of the Wafd—Egypt's most popular political party before a military coup in 1952 toppled the monarchy. Copts have also figured prominently in the evolution of Egyptian and Arab arts, theater, and scholarship.[17]

In the 2011 revolt against then president Hosni Mubarak, many Copts took an active role in pro-democracy demonstrations, contributing to the downfall of Mubarak's regime. In rare displays of public defiance and unity, Copts and Muslims proclaimed their grievances, calling at once for change and freedom from fear and poverty. They waved signs of cross and crescent in Tahrir Square as responsible stakeholders and staunch defenders of the revolution. Although Islamic political parties and movements have denounced violence against Christians, many attacks against Copts have occurred since Hosni Mubarak's ouster. On May 8, 2011, Virgin Mary Church, in the impoverished Cairo neighborhood of

Imbaba, near the Tahrir Square, was a scene of devastation. Copts have been angered by the ruling military council's lenient response to this and other similar incidents of violence against them. While calling for protection from sectarian violence, many Copts fear that the army's cooperation with the Muslim Brotherhood—now and in the future—may result in further exclusionary politics, undermining the interests and the status of this minority religious group.[18]

Integration, Confrontation, and Retraction

Caught between the atmosphere of violence and that of integration, the Coptic Church leadership has steadily rejected a confrontational approach, arguing that while Christians have gone through hard times, they had faced harder times in the past. Father Aghaton, secretary to the Supreme religious leader of Egypt's Copts, Pope Shenouda III, has said: "We have gone through horrendous periods of oppression but here we are, strong, well-educated and present. The facts are that all the Copts can do is hunker down in bad times and wait until the oppression lifts."[19] During Jamal Abdul Nasser's tenure (1952–1970), a few Copts were nominated to the parliament, often in consultation with the Coptic patriarch, so as to maintain a formal Coptic representation in the political structure. The upshot was the gradual erosion of the influence of the Copts in political life and the surge in the role of religious institutions and church hierarchy.[20] The government's policy of minimizing this tension, as one expert noted, was no mean task, as it became increasingly harder to appease the Christians without antagonizing the Islamists.[21]

During the 1970s, Anwar al-Sadat's policies fostered Islamization programs in an attempt to undermine secular leftist opposition. The conversion from Islam to Christianity became illegal under Egypt's penal code when in 1977 the "law of apostasy" was announced. Reacting to this law, thousands of the Copts and church authorities participated in a voluntary "fast of protest."[22] This and similar policies led to the intensification of restrictions on the social and political activities of the Copts. Muslim militants plundered and burned Coptic shops and churches. Despite the guarantee of religious equality before the law contained in Article 40 of the Egyptian constitution, Copts continue to suffer discrimination, especially regarding the appointment to such key governmental positions as provincial governors, city managers, police commissioners, university presidents, and directors of educational districts.

Similarly, the Egyptian Family Status Law of 1955 (still in effect), which is considered part of the "civil" code of law, continues to have religious elements, referring to the *Shari'a* as a basis for Muslims and to the corresponding religious principles or regulations for non-Muslim communities. Courts often ignore the law and pass judgments according to *Shari'a*, which they regard as the basis of all legislation. This represents numerous problems for the Copts, as the Coptic community finds itself forced to submit to Islamic *Shari'a* regulations.[23]

It should be noted, however, that Copts in Egypt are often so completely integrated into Egyptian society that their religious identity has faded away into the national one. The same may be said of their Muslim compatriots.[24] President Hosni Mubarak declared January 7—Coptic Christmas—a national holiday. In some respects, the Copts have advanced within Egyptian society and in other spheres of life are subject to restrictions. They are economically advantaged and have engaged in commerce, medicine, law, and accountancy. They tend to be better educated than Muslims and are well represented in the bureaucracy—albeit not in the upper levels of government and the military.[25] Rarely are any Copts appointed to posts in the judicial system, police ranks, or army. Copts are underrepresented in the police, security forces, armed forces, and much of the civil service.[26] The People's Assembly or (*Majlis al-Sha'b*) has 454 seats, of which 444 are elected by popular vote and 10 are appointed by the president. Parliament deputies serve five-year terms. Copts are not proportionally represented in the People's Assembly; in 2005, only 2 out of 444 were Copts.[27]

Since the 1970s, the growth of Islamist politics and the flow of laborers to and from the conservative Arab countries of the Persian Gulf, where they have absorbed that region's conservative form of Islam, have enhanced the influence of orthodox Islam and made life more difficult for Christians. Violence between Muslims and Christians breaks out sporadically. Following the 2005 parliamentary elections, Abd al-Nur, the Wafdist politician who lost his parliamentary seat in those elections, noted: "It is a fact that we are marginalized. We have to try to understand why it is that way. Copts are less and less active not only on the political scene, but they have also retracted from a lot of public activities."[28] Likewise, Yusuf Sidhum, a secular-minded Copt who edits *Watani*, Egypt's only mainstream Coptic newspaper that is not an official church publication, argues that "Christians are withdrawing into churches and mixing less with Muslims."[29]

Several recent events have shown the intensity of Muslim-Christian relations in Egypt. In 2006, the Alexandria violence, which was caused by a Muslim entering the church of Mar Girgis (Saint George) and stabbing three parishioners who had gathered for a service and attacking worshippers at two other churches, led to three days of violence and spurred a lasting debate over the state of relations between Muslims and minority Coptic Christians in Egypt.[30] In the most dramatic confrontation, settled Arab Bedouins on May 31, 2008, attacked monks who had been reclaiming the 1,700-year-old monastery of Abu Fana from the desert in southern Egypt.[31] The Islamist bombing of a Coptic Christian church in Alexandria on January 1, 2011, sparked widespread outrage in Cairo. Copts accused the Egyptian government of refusing to acknowledge religious motivations as a key factor behind such attacks, often blaming such violent acts on other mundane factors. The growing Islamization of society, coupled with this perceived discrimination against Copts, has propelled many Copts to seek refuge in the church. The fault lines in church-government ties are likely to deepen in years to come—an ominous prospect for a regime that is in the process of preparing the ground for the arrival of a new leader on the political scene.[32]

Additionally, some Copts believe that they are treated as second-class citizens in Egypt, as they require governmental approval, for instance, for the construction of any church. Copts point out that state security services have little interest in safeguarding Christians.[33] It is also worth noting that Copts are underrepresented in both the teaching and research faculties at universities. There are few or no Copts in the highest-level university administrative positions.[34] Despite antidiscrimination laws, Copts are also subject to official and unofficial religious discrimination. This situation has provided an incentive for conversion. Some Copts, however, have done well. Under the British rule, one Copt—the original Boutros-Ghali—attained the position of premiership in 1908. But he was later denounced as too pro-British and was assassinated in 1910. The Boutros-Ghali family has produced the former Acting Foreign Minister and later United Nations Secretary General Boutros Boutros-Ghali, as well as the present minister of the Economy and Foreign Trade, Dr. Youssef Boutros-Ghali. The other Coptic member of the Cabinet was the Minister of State for Environmental Affairs, Dr. Nadia Makram 'Ebeid.[35]

The government strictly enforces an 1856 law that renders it illegal to build or repair a church without presidential approval. In January 1998, President Hosni Mubarak delegated authority to provincial governors to approve such permits. Since then, it has become much easier to get permission for building and renovating churches. There is no Coptic political party or movement, however.[36] Coptic activists have articulated several demands in recent years. Some of their demands include more representation in the political system; greater equality in promotions in academia, the public sector, and the state bureaucracy—especially the police and the military; removal of religious identification from government-issued documents where religion is irrelevant; and easier licensing procedures for church construction.[37] In the aftermath of 2011 revolution, Copts are likely to add yet another demand to this list: to participate equally alongside their Muslim compatriots in decisions on how to govern society.

The Druze in Lebanon: Religious Characteristics and Demographics

Powerful culturally and religiously homogenous, and militarily renowned, the Druze of Lebanon have made for themselves an immense impact for such a small, relatively isolated, religious/ethnic minority. While much of the political attention and acrimony is normally focused upon the oft-publicized Sunni-Shia-Maronite cycle of grievance and violence, the Druze population keeps mainly to its own interests in support of its own localities. Their population numbers only about 350,000 and is sequestered mainly in the Shouf, Metn, Aley, and Mount Lebanon regions. While their religious and political impact is perhaps felt most sharply within the Lebanese territories, and will be the distinctive focus of this analysis, it is worth noting that the Druze also have significant populations in Israel (100,000, concentrated in the Galilee and Golan) and Syria (500,000, concentrated in the Jabal Druze mountains).[38]

The Religious Nature of the Druze

While Druzism may take some of its flavor (secrecy, isolation, belief in vanished imams as divine) from Shiite religious practices, its own pursuits are fundamentally different.[39] First and foremost there is no proselytization among the Druze. Much like the Yazidis and Allawis, the Druze believe that the number of their souls was fixed at Creation. Accordingly, when a Druze dies, the individual soul is passed into another Druze body (*tansukh* in Arabic). By this logic with the closing of the da'wa, or spreading of the faith, in 1043, there has been no new Druze created outside of rebirth or metempsychosis since.[40] The most important religious aspect of their movement results from the unique political nature of the Druze in Lebanon, and most specifically the relationship of the Druze population to their non-Druze peers.

In Druze scripture a strict religious hierarchical order is observed regarding relations with outsiders. First, as stated above, strict secrecy is required for all non-Druze; this holds both for their religious tenets and their cultural practices. Second, contemporary Druze tradition maintains that "the Shi'a deserve fifty curses, the Sunnis forty, the Christians thirty and the Jews twenty."[41] This intense acrimony for all outsiders more than likely stems from their relatively small numbers, intense cultural homogeneity, and persecution in their exodus from Egypt under the Fatimid Empire.[42] The Druze preference for Jews, as the least cursed, may help to describe the generally positive relations that to this day the Druze of the Galilee and Golan share with the modern Israeli government, often providing regional security, and fighting in the Israeli Defense Force (IDF).[43] It is worth noting that their political character, as described below, is always fluid and supportive of those in position of power.

The Political Characteristics of the Druze: The Civil War (1975–1976), the March 14 Coalition, and Beyond

An examination of Lebanon's civil war years does much to define the effective and powerful political characteristics of the Druze.[44] Through the fall of 1975 to early winter 1976, the Progressive Socialist Party (PSP) cut a deal with the Lebanese National Movement (LNM) and the Palestinian Liberation Organization (PLO). All the while Kamal Jumblatt was also battling to gain the attention and support of foreign backers, namely, Syria. While Hafez al-Assad and Kamal Jumblatt had no great affection for each other, a political marriage of their ideals would be highly fortuitous for the relatively small PSP-LNM-PLO faction. With Syrian backing and Pierre Gemayel's right-wing Keta'eb Christian coalition temporarily on the run, the Druze and their Muslim allies seemed to be on the verge of a genuine political takeover of Lebanon.[45]

While brokering deals with Syria, the LNM, and the PLO to ensure a possible reversal of 30 years of inequitable treatment, Kamal Jumblatt and his PSP party somehow lost sight of the prize, when on March 31, 1976, the Syrians intervened in Lebanon on behalf of the Maronite Christian community. This politically sagacious move by Assad, seen by some as a way to guarantee a Syrian presence in Lebanon without requiring an Israeli one, cemented a Syrian presence in Lebanon until April of 2005. These casualties of politics and war, as well as the personal loss of Kamal Jumblatt on March 16, 1977, were a deep and lasting setback for the Druze community.

With the death of Kamal, continuous bloodshed and sectarian violence through 1991, one might wonder at the political plight of a small exogenous group like the Druze. Their role in Lebanese politics is as it always was. Jumblatt broadly supported a reduced role of confessional politics, still powerful, tenacious, and adaptive despite its small size and relative disconnectedness from either Christian or Muslim social, cultural, or religious practice. The actions in and around the death of Prime Minister Rafik Hariri and its aftermath best characterize the current political climate of Lebanon and the extant abilities of the Druze to achieve what they have always accomplished: to fight marginalization and survive. Recent Lebanese politics is instructive on this chord as well.

On February 14, 2005, an explosive equivalent to 1,000 kg of TNT exploded underneath the vehicle carrying Prime Minister Rafik Hariri as he passed the St. George Hotel in downtown Beirut.[46] This violent death of a beloved public figure, philanthropist, and what many would describe as the benefactor of modern Lebanon was a catalyst that drove the unlikeliest of former enemies to make both common causes in opposition, and move for reforms in modern politics. Two rallies divided sharply the Lebanese political makeup; the first on March 8,

2005, drew thousands, was composed primarily of Hassan Nasrallah's Hizbullah organization, and broadly supportive of Syria; and a second denounced Syria as being a likely sponsor for the attack. Both factions, and indeed both rallies, were an open expression of bewilderment, anger, and anguish over the death of Hariri. However, the March 8 and the March 14 alliances identified the new political fault lines in Lebanese politics until recently.

The most recent state of Druze affairs comes in the context of the Arab Spring uprisings, the silence of the Lebanese in the midst of region-wide protests; the events of this past January represent the recent tectonic shift of Druze attentions away from its traditional allies in Saad Harriri's political establishment. The Druze leadership negotiated an entente toward its long supposed enemies in Syria and its position to its domestic rival the Shi'a faction Hezbollah. As has been recently reported Walid Jumblatt engaged in recent talks with the now maligned Syrian president Bashar Al-Assad.[47] It can be argued that this owes to the political acro-batics of the Druze in that they have pulled a 180 degree shift in their political support. Gone are the condemnations of violence and oppres-sion that led to the Syrian withdrawal in 2005, and the manifest rejection of the Hariri assassination as a reprehensible act of political bloodshed, quite to the contrary in their place is the overt support of the Druze leadership toward the latest significant power grab; for Jumblatt it is time to "turn the page."[48]

On January 12, 2011, Hezbollah successfully maneuvered a walkout on the Lebanese *majles* displacing the governing March 14 coalition and establishing Najib Mikati, a Hezbollah supporter, on January 24, as the new prime minister.[49] What the Druze gained by this action, a place of power and a defining role in the new political arrangements, owes to nothing less than a complete reversal of their potentially despondent political fortunes; by backing Hizbullah over their former allies they have kept for themselves at least a portion of power amid a changing land-scape. What this demonstrates to the observer is the pragmatic, kinetic, and opportunistic nature of Druze political life, they will achieve what they can, when they can, and exploit any opportunity to retain relevancy and relative power within their environment.

THE KURDS IN TURKEY

The Kurds are an Indo-European people who are estimated to be 25–30 million and live in a mountainous area straddling the borders of Iraq, Iran, Syria, and Turkey. They are a large and distinct ethnic minority who are mainly Sunni Muslim tribal people with their own language and customs. There are as many as 800 separate Kurdish tribes in Kurdistan. Kurdish history has been one of failed attempts at achieving independence. In the twentieth century alone, Kurdish rebellions in Turkey in 1925, 1930, 1937, and 1984 only resulted in additional defeats, death, and destruction.[50] Resistance against Iraq during the Iran-Iraq War (1980–1988) brought about the wrath of Saddam Hussein who, in 1988, launched poison gas attacks on Kurdish village of Halabje, causing the death of several thousand people. In the 1991 Persian Gulf War, Iraq's Kurds revolted against Saddam Hussein but were crushed by the Iraqi army, forcing many of hundreds of thousands of them to flee to Turkey.[51]

Turkey's 15 million Kurds are spread throughout the country, especially on the outskirts of major cities such as Istanbul. Mustafa Kemal, also known as Atatürk, who laid the foundation for the modern and secular Turkey, enacted a constitution in 1923 that denied the existence of distinct cultural and ethnic groups in Turkey. The rise of Kurdish nationalism since 1970 has resulted largely from the economic deprivation and marginalization of the southeastern region. In 1984, the conflict between the Kurdish desire to form cultural and political autonomy and the Turkish state efforts to prevent that autonomy reached a new level of intensity with the launching of a widespread Kurdish insurrection that was met by Turkish military repression. This insurrection was organized by a militant organization within the Kurdish nationalist movement, the Kurdistan Workers' Party (PKK). The PKK's main objective was to achieve the recognition of Kurdish political and cultural autonomy within the framework and boundaries of the Turkish state.[52]

To achieve its goals, the PKK resorted to terrorist operations as a legitimate tactic, engaging in a campaign of assassination and destruction that rendered normal life in the Kurdish provinces impossible. Throughout the 1980s and 1990s, successive Turkish governments placed most of the Kurdish regions under a state of emergency and gave the military a free hand to undertake whatever policies and measures it takes to subdue the local insurgency. By the late 1990s, according to one study, the armed forces had destroyed more than 2,300 Kurdish villages and more than 2 million Kurds had fled or been forcibly relocated.[53]

Until the mid-1990s, the existence of Kurdish people and identity was officially denied and the people of the southeastern Turkey were called "mountain Turks."[54] Since the early 1990s, Turkish people and officials had begun to recognize the cultural rights of the Kurds, legalizing the use of the Kurdish language in the process.[55] These changes in law and mainstream views on the Kurdish issue have pointed to a desecuritization process transpiring in Turkey, a process that would not have been possible without the external legitimization provided by the European Union.[56] In the meantime, Kurdish nationalism has grown in strength, even as it has been legally regarded as separatism and thus grounds for imprisonment.

The Turkish government has consistently thwarted attempts by the Kurds to organize politically. Its counterinsurgency campaign against the outlawed PKK in most of Kurdish southeastern Turkey has resulted in many deaths since it began in the early 1980s. In the aftermath of the 1991 Gulf War, there have been numerous instances of forced repatriation of Kurdish refugees to Iraq, caused in many instances by threats from Turkish authorities and by the brutal conditions of imprisonment. The PKK has also resorted to violent tactics in confronting the Turkish military. More recently, the leaders of the pro-Kurdish People's Democracy Party were sentenced to several years' prison terms for allegedly having ties with the outlawed PKK guerillas. The state prosecutors' evidence consisted largely of press releases found in the People's Democratic Party offices from a news agency close to the PKK.

Since the U.S. invasion of Iraq, the tensions between Turkey and the Kurds in northern Iraq have intensified. Ankara fears that as Iraq's Kurds push for their autonomy in Iraq, their own agitated Kurdish population will likely drive toward independence and act as a magnet for Kurdish nationalists in Turkey. In response, Turkey's parliament has repeatedly extended the military's year-old mandate to launch cross border strikes against the PKK in northern Iraq. Immediately after the October 3, 2007, attack in which 17 Turkish soldiers were killed, the Kurdistan Regional Government (KRG), the local body that administers northern Iraq, condemned its fellow Kurds in the PKK. Massoud Barzani, the head of the Kurdish government insisted that such attacks be stopped.[57]

In recent decades, some progress has been made. Consider, for example, the increase in the literacy rate. The 1992 literacy rate in Mardin Province (48 percent) was considerably lower than the national standard (77 percent).[58] By 2007, the literacy rate in the Mardin Province had increased to 71 percent compared to the nation's 87.4 percent.[59] Starting in 2005, Turkey's prime minister Recep Tayyib Erdogan encouraged several steps to ease bans on Kurdish broadcasting and educational systems. As a result, vast sums of money were poured into Kurdish regions to subsidize education for the poor, especially for girls. These measures, some observers noted, helped the Justice and Development Party (AKP) to defeat the pro-Kurdish Democratic Society Party (DTP) in much of the southeastern Turkey in the July 2007 elections.[60] The results of these elections, many experts concur, persuaded Turkish policymakers that the challenge of Kurdish nationalist movements in Turkey could be effectively met by economic measures.[61] As Shiite and Sunni opposition to Kurdish policies on the share of oil and the final status of Kirkuk has increased, and as the U.S. military has found it imperative to work with both Shiites and Arab Sunnis in an attempt to assure the success of the so-called surge strategy, the idea of an independent Kurdistan has become increasingly discredited.[62]

Views differ over how the Kurdish issue can be resolved. Some experts have noted that an integrationist approach toward both the Iraqi and Turkey's Kurds has helped pave the way for the solution of the Kurdish question.[63] Others have insisted that both the AKP and the Turkish Armed Forces (TAF) had accepted the strategy of managing the challenge of the Kurdish nationalism in Turkey by simply crushing the PKK in Iraq.[64] Still others have argued that the Kurdish moderates' demand for freedom to speak and learn their mother tongue as well as to establish Kurdish-oriented political parties and foundations may not necessarily conflict with Turkey's national interests.[65]

CONCLUSION

The study of minorities in the Middle East is directly linked to the root causes of marginalization. In cases of the Copts in Egypt and the Kurds in Turkey, it appears an integrationist approach toward socioeconomic and cultural inclusion and recognition of the rights of minorities has proven a positive step toward the reasonable resolution of the problems. Caught between the atmosphere of violence and integration, the Egyptian Christian Copts have in recent years, navigated between apathy and engagement. But after the 2011 Revolution, many Copts seek new possibilities and opportunities. All Egyptians have the potential to build a civil society and construct a new constitution that accords the full citizenship rights to its myriad sects and groups, including Christians. Two key questions persist: What role will the Copts play in the new Egyptian political system and whether they will be invited to play a positive role in shaping the country's new constitution and bright future.

In Lebanon, the old fault lines that have made the tensions among Shiites, Sunnis, the Druze, and the Maronite Christians so intractable show signs of submerging, perhaps precisely because of the potential transformation of Hizbullah from a military to a political force. In Turkey, the Kurds' participation in the political process is likely to create a sustainable base for improving the living conditions of such a marginalized community.

Finally, it should be noted that the framing of these minority issues in terms of threats to national security and political stability—not in terms of cultural and political inclusion—has prolonged the plight of these groups at both local and regional levels. Desecuritization of the minority threats, as well as appropriate external pressure (the EU in the case of Turkey), have enabled national policymakers to pursue reformist agenda, while engaging the minority groups and their legitimate demands. The main lesson to draw is that in virtually all societies it is vitally important to end marginalization if a peaceful coexistence among people of different ethnic, religious, sectarian, and racial backgrounds is to be achieved.

The key to shoring up minorities' desire to remain loyal to a nation-state in which they live—rather than leaning toward building up new forms of political community—is to frontally address the issue of marginality.

NOTES

1. David S. Sorenson, *An introduction to the Middle East: History, Religion, Political Economy, Politics,* Boulder, CO: Westview Press, 2008, p. 111.
2. Abdullahi Ahmed An-Na'im, *Islam and the Secular State: Negotiating the Future of Shari'a,* Cambridge, MA: Harvard University Press, 2008, pp. 32–33.
3. Ted Robert Gurr, *Minorities at Risk: A Global View of Ethnopolitical Conflicts.* Washington, D.C.: United States Institute of Peace Press, 1993, p. 67.
4. Gudrun Kramer, "Minorities in Muslim Societies," in *The Oxford Encyclopedia of the Modern Islamic World,* Vol. 3, ed. John L. Esposito. New York: Oxford University Press, 1995, pp. 108–111; see pp. 108–110.
5. Ibid., p. 110.
6. Nazila Ghanea, "Human Rights of Religious Minorities and Of Women in the Middle East," *Human Rights Quarterly,* Vol. 26, 2004, pp. 705–729; see pp. 722.
7. Anthony Chase and Amr Hamzawy, ed., *Human Rights in the Arab World: Independent Voices.* Philadelphia, University of Pennsylvania, 2006, p. 24.
8. Ibid., p. 21.
9. Donald Spanel, "Copts," in *Encyclopedia of the Modern Middle East and North Africa,* Vol. 1, 2nd ed., ed. Philip Mattar, New York: Thompson/Gale, 2004, pp. 638–642; see 639.
10. Monte Palmer, *Comparative Politics: Political Economy, Political Culture, and Political Independence,* Belmont, CA: Thomson Higher Education, 2006, p. 502.
11. John H. Watson, *Among the Copts,* Portland, OR: Sussex Academic Press, 2000, p. 9.
12. Marlis J. Saleh, "Copts," in *Medieval Islamic Civilization: An Encyclopedia,* Vol. 1, ed. Josef W. Meri, New York: Routledge, 2006, pp. 173–175; see p. 175.
13. David S. Soreson, *Introduction to the Middle East,* p. 69.
14. Antonie Wessels, *Arab and Christian? Christians in the Middle East.* Kampen, the Netherlands: Pharos, 1995, pp. 130–131.
15. Ibid., p. 131.
16. Issandr El Amrani, "The Emergence of a 'Coptic Question' in Egypt," *Middle East Report Online,* April 28, 2006, available at http://www.merip.org/mero/mro042806.html. Last visited on October 13, 2008.
17. Youssef M. Ibrahim, "Muslims Fury Falls on Egypt's Christians," the *New York Times,* March 15, 1993, available at http://query.nytimes.com/gst/fullpage.htm? Last visited on October 14, 2008.

18. Yasmine El Rashidi, "Egypt: The Victorious Islamists," *The New York Review of Books*, Vol. 58, No. 12, July 14, 2011, pp. 23–24.
19. Ibid.
20. Danald Spanel, "Copts," p. 641.
21. Ami Ayalon, "Egypt's Coptic Pandora's Box," in *Minorities and the State in the Arab World*, ed. Ofra Bengio and Gabriel Ben-Dor, Boulder, CO: Lynne Rienner Publishers, 1999, pp. 53–71; see p. 68.
22. Antonie Wessels, *Arab and Christian?*, p. 140.
23. Adel Guindy, "Family Status Issues Among Egypt's Copts: A Brief Overview," *The Middle East Review of International Affairs*, Vol. 11, No. 3, September 2007, available at http://media.idc.ac.il/journal/2007/issue3/iv11no3aa.html. Last visited on October 13, 2008.
24. John H. Watson, *Among the Copts*, p. 11.
25. Jonathan Fox, "The Copts in Egypt: A Christian Minority in an Islamic Society," in *Peoples Versus States: Minorities at Risk in the New Century*, ed. Ted Robert Gurr, Washington, D.C.: U.S. Institute of Peace, 2000, pp. 138–142; see p. 139.
26. Issandr El Amrani, "The Emergence of a 'Coptic Question' in Egypt," *Middle East Report Online*, April 28, 2006, available at http://www.merip.org/mero/mro042806.html. Last visited on October 13, 2008.
27. Donald Spanel, "Copts," p. 642.
28. Issandr El Amrani, "The Emergence of a 'Coptic Question' in Egypt," *Middle East Report Online*, April 28, 2006, available at http://www.merip.org/mero/mro042806.html. Last visited on October 13, 2008.
29. Ibid.
30. Ibid.
31. Ellen Knickmeyer, "Egypt's Coptic Christians Choose Isolation," the *Washington Post*, July 7, 2008, p. A08; also available at http://www.washingtonpost.com/wp-dyn/content/article/2008/07/06/AR2008070602283_2.html. Last visited on September 20, 2008.
32. Kristen Chick, "Egypt's Troubled Christians," *The Christian Science Monitor*, January 17, 2011, pp. 8–9.
33. Ibid.
34. Jonathan Fox, "The Copts in Egypt," p. 139.
35. "Egypt's Copts after Kosheh: Part I, a Sensitive Coexistence," *The Estimate: Political and Security Intelligence Analysis of the Islamic World and Its Neighbors*, Vol. 12, No. 2, January 2000; available at http://www.theestimate.com/public/01282000a.html. Last visited on September 22, 2008.
36. Jonathan Fox, "The Copts in Egypt," pp. 140–141.
37. Khairi Abaza and Mark Nakhla, "The Copts and Their Political Implications in Egypt," October 25, 2005, *Policy Watch/PeaceWatch*, The Washington Institute for Near East Policy, available at http://www.washingtoninstitute.org/templateC05.php?CID=2386. Last visited on September 22, 2008.
38. Nissam Dana, *The Druze in the Middle East: Their Faith, Leadership, and Status*, London: Sussex Academic Press, 2003, p. 99.

39. Robert Brenton Bretts, *The Druze*, New York: Yale University Press, 1988, p. 6.
40. Ralph Crow, "Religious Sectarianism in Lebanese Politics," *The Journal of Politics*, Vol. 24, No. 3, August 1962, pp. 489–520.
41. Arthur John Arberry, *Religion in the Middle East: Three Religions Concord and Conflict*, Vol. 2. Cambridge, MA: Cambridge University Press, 1st ed., 2008, p. 338.
42. Robert Brenton Bretts, *The Druze*, New York: Yale University Press, 1988, p. 21.
43. Ruth K. Westheimer and Gil Sedan, *The Olive and the Tree: The Secret Strength of the Druzes*. New York: Lantern Books, 2007, p. 45.
44. David C. Gordon, *The Republic of Lebanon: Nation in Jeopardy*. Boulder, CO: Westview Press, 1983, p. 85.
45. Theodor Hanf, *Coexistence in Wartime Lebanon: Decline of a State and Rise of a Nation*. London: I. B. Tauris, 1993, pp. 217–221.
46. Susan Sachs, "Rafik Hariri, Ex-Premier of Lebanon, Dies at 60," *New York Times*, February 15, 2005. Accessed through the Internet: http://www.nytimes.com/2005/02/15/international/middleeast/15hariri.html, March 27, 2011.
47. "Al-Assad Receives Ex-Foe Jumblatt: Lebanese Druze Leader Holds Talks with Bashar al-Assad Following Five-Year Rift," *Al Jazeera.com*, March 14, 2011. Accessed through the Internet: http://english.aljazeera.net/news/middleeast/2010/03/2010331151628717408.html, March 27, 2011.
48. "Jumblatt Apologises to al-Assad Lebanese MP Regrets Past Criticism of Syrian President and Seeks New Beginning." *Al Jazeera.com*, March 14, 2011. Accessed through the Internet: http://english.aljazeera.net/news/middleeast/2010/03/2010314111023700949.html; March 27, 2011.
49. Mariam Karouny, "Hezbollah-Backed Mikati Set to Lead Lebanon Government," *Reuters.com*, January 24, 2011. Accessed through the Internet: http://www.reuters.com/article/2011/01/24/us-lebanon-government-idUSTRE70N33820110124, March 27, 2011.
50. Richard W. Mansbach and Kristen L. Rafferty, *Introduction to Global Politics*, New York: Routledge, 2008, p. 717.
51. Ibid., p. 718.
52. William L. Cleveland, *A History of the Middle East*, 3rd ed., Boulder, CO: Westview Press, 2004, p. 525.
53. Ibid., pp. 526–527.
54. Rabia Karakaya Polat, "The Kurdish Issue: Can the AK Party Escape Securitization?" *Insight Turkey*, Vol. 10, No. 3, 2008, pp. 75–86; see p. 76.
55. Ibid., p. 80.
56. Ibid., pp. 84–85.
57. Mark MacKinnon, "A Bitter War Has Kurds Divided among Themselves: The PKK Risks Losing Popular Support as Its Increasingly Bloody Conflict with Turkey Threatens the Stability of Iraqi Kurdistan," *The Global*

and Mail, October 27, 2008; available at http://www.30cycles.com/monsh/II/ABitterWar.pdf. Last visited on November 14, 2008.

58. Mahmood Monshipouri, *Islamism, Secularism, and Human Rights in the Middle East*. Boulder, CO: Lynn Rienner Publishers, 1998, p. 125.

59. See Republic of Turkey, Mardin Governorship, available at http://www.mardin.gov.tr/english/tarihi/nufus.asp. Last visited on November 15, 2008. Also see Human Development Report 2007, NY: UNDP, 2008.

60. "Terror in the Mountains: Turkey and the Kurds," *The Economist*, October 18, 2008.

61. Robert Olson, "Turkish-Kurdish Relations: A Year of Significant Developments," *Insight Turkey*, Vol. 10, No. 3, 2008, pp. 23–51; see p. 28.

62. Tarik Oguzlu, "Turkey's Northern Iraq Policy: Competing Perspectives," *Insight Turkey*, Vol. 10, No. 3, 2008, pp. 5–22; see p. 19.

63. Ibid., p. 20.

64. Robert Olson, "Turkish-Kurdish Relations," p. 38.

65. Ertan Efegil, "Turkey's New Approaches toward the PKK, Iraqi Kurds and the Kurdish Question," *Insight Turkey*, Vol. 10, No. 3, 2008, pp. 53–73; see p. 70.

CHAPTER 9

LESSONS FROM MOVEMENTS FOR RIGHTS REGARDING SEXUAL ORIENTATION IN THE ARAB WORLD

Anthony Tirado Chase

Controversies over rights regarding sexual orientation have been particularly contentious in the Arab world. But, while sexual orientation has been a flashpoint garnering media and academic attention, in fact such controversies reproduce political and intellectual debates over the legitimacy of a broad range of human rights that have taken place both globally and in the Arab world. These debates are particularly important in the wake of the Arab Spring, which has moved to center stage both movements for human rights in the Arab world and the political and intellectual backlash against such movements. In that context, questions regarding the source of human rights legitimacy have become particularly acute. Reflecting on controversies over sexual orientation, thus, gives a point of entry to thinking not just about the legitimacy of rights in that specific regard but, as well, the legitimacy of human rights writ large.

I will argue in this respect against both relativist and universalist claims regarding human rights. Relativist critiques (particularly in contemporary structuralist form) that see human rights as reflections of either cultural specificities or hegemonic power interests underplay human agency. That agency informs engagements with the transnational normative currents that have been a key impulse behind the rights regime's global expansion. This does not mean, however, that human rights have an extrapolitical, philosophical, or legal foundation that is universally relevant.[1] Such "universality" implies an authoritative, static foundational source for human rights that is mythical. To the contrary, the reasons behind human rights' global resonance are varied and multiple rather than being based on an all-encompassing moral or legal principle.[2]

An explanation is required beyond either philosophic universalism or legal pragmatism for the dynamic that has pushed human rights into international law, politics, and institutions as a global language for those seeking justice. This dynamic comes from the degree to which the rights regime can absorb, represent, and structure claims made by populations previously excluded from conversations that inform global politics. In other words, human rights are too often conceptualized as being about universal law or morality on top and social movements at the bottom, and the uneasy interaction between those elite and popular levels. To the contrary, human rights are grounded in law (domestic and international), political processes, institutions (local, international, and transnational), and normative currents. These groundings are not in a hierarchical relationship in which one of them is the ultimate foundation. They are, instead, in a circular relationship in which the rights regime is vibrant (or not) to the degree these groundings mutually inform and permeate each other.

The source of human rights' continued resonance in this reading—its only real origin—is its ability to be part of dynamic transnational conversations such as those initiated by movements that make claims for rights regarding sexual orientation—conversations that take place at legal, political, institutional, and normative levels. These circular connections among the elements in which human rights are grounded are essential to the maintenance and expansion of its global resonance. Responding to assertions of rights regarding sexual orientation, therefore, is to engage in and reflect transnational discourse and its normative agents in societies around the world, allowing the human rights regime to be transformed just as it was transformed (and continues to be transformed) via mutual engagement with the other normative networks, such as the global women's movement to give just one example.[3] These claims will, by definition, be "difficult." But addressing such claims is what gives the human rights regime the ability to sustain itself in global politics.

BACKGROUND

Sexual orientation has to various degrees increasingly come to be taken as constitutive of public identity rather than a private matter in many societies around the world.[4] In response, there have been virulent reactions against assertions of a space in the public sphere for those with alternative sexual orientations or gender identity. From Jamaica to the United States to Iran and elsewhere, nationalist-patriarchal credentials have been advanced by demonizing and violating the rights of those whose sexual orientation or gender identity challenge traditional norms. This has, in turn, made the rights claims of those who are subject to such violence all the more urgent.

While one can argue that broad human rights language in core treaties about nondiscrimination could be read as inclusive of sexual orientation and gender identity, there is no evidence that early human rights instruments were elaborated with such groups in mind. Indeed, for many years human rights protections were not acknowledged to be applicable to sexual orientation or gender identity, whether by Geneva-based treaty monitoring bodies or by international human rights NGOs such as Human Rights Watch.

In recent years new readings and new instruments have brought these topics into international human rights law. This is not because international law already contained these protections, but rather because new readings and new law flowed out of transnational normative conversations pushed by activist groups.[5] In other words, as with many other evolutions of the human rights regime, it came out of a process of continuous reinterpretation in the context of grassroots normative movements and political processes. As Gruskin and Ferguson note, "prior to 1994 sexual orientation was not in any way recognized as a protected 'other status.'"[6] The Human Rights Committee's 1994 holding in the Toonen case was the first expansion of rights in this domain as it rejected Australian law that criminalized sodomy.[7]

Under the impact of lobbying from transnational normative networks and underlying shifts in normative constructs as to what rights are, in 2000 and 2009 the Committee on Economic, Social and Cultural Rights issued General Comments 14 and 20 that deemed discrimination in access to health services based on sexual orientation and gender identity as unacceptable.[8] In this they gave legal grounding to a reconceptualization that had been bubbling up over previous decades. Even now, however, making the rights' regime inclusive toward sexual orientation remains contentious and on the margins of the work of dominant human rights institutions.

Nonetheless, many mainstream human rights practitioners and theorists see rights regarding sexual orientation as too contentious to be advanced. In the Arab world, for example, those arrested in the 2001 Queen Boat case in Egypt and accused of "debauchery" had difficulty finding representation from human rights groups. One arrested person was told that "human rights matters in Egypt have 'more serious' issues and they don't want to lose their credibility with the people if they take on this case."[9] The understandable fear is that pushing such cutting-edge issues goes too far, and risks discrediting the human rights regime by reinforcing an image of it as overly focused on the rights of those who affront putatively local cultural identities. Examining rights movements regarding sexual orientation and critical responses to those movements, thus, provides a nuanced context to the basic question: On what basis does one legitimately advance human rights?

CASE STUDY: SEXUAL ORIENTATION IN THE ARAB WORLD

Tension regarding rights and sexual orientation has been notably acute in parts of the Arab world in which there are ongoing debates that pit contrasting ideas of "Islam" and "the West" or "local" and "global" against each other.[10] Notions of rights regarding sexual orientation have been particularly discomfiting insofar as they might reinforce such monolithic categories, i.e., that rights are about a "Western" identity or project, rather than claims that legitimately reflect "authentic" Arab identity. Negar Azimi summarizes political dynamics over recent years in this regard in the Arab world:

> The politics of homosexuality is changing fast in the Arab world. For many years, corners of the region have been known for their rich gay subcultures. . . . But sexuality in general and homosexuality in particular are increasingly becoming concerns of the modern Arab state. Politicians, the police, government officials, and much of the press are making homosexuality an "issue": a way to display nationalist bona fides . . . The policing of homosexuality has become part of what sometimes seems like a general moral panic.[11]

Revolutionary movements coursed through the Arab world in 2010–11. The degree to which such movements are sustainable remains to be seen, but they certainly overturned commonly held intellectual assumptions (particularly common to academics) that human rights have little place in the Arab world. The political-moral "panic" to which Azimi refers had, in fact, long existed simultaneous to churning on-the-ground social movements, especially among the region's youth. Indeed, it is these changing social realities that nationalists demonized as a way of reinforcing the status quo. In that context, among various sexual orientations in the Arab world, it is gay men who have been most prominent as subjects claiming a (limited) public space, objects of reprisal, and (again, in a limited though expanding manner) moving toward making rights claims.[12] Two possible conclusions can result. One, that such articulations of public identities and rights claims reflect political-cultural dynamism and social-individual agency. Or, two, that articulations of rights' claims imply fellow-traveling with the West in a way that reflects political and cultural imperialism deserving of political repression and social stigma.

Debates in this regard have taken place regarding virtually all pushes for human rights in nearly all parts of the world. In the Arab world, they are by now a form of Kabuki theater in which new topics are shadowed by previously rehearsed roles and arguments. Sexuality and gender, however, are particularly intense intersections of the personal, cultural, and political, so the emotion and fear they arouse are unsurprising. The intensity of these debates is also behind the fear that sexual orientation and gender rights risk being constructed in a way that reinforces notions of a binary split between the "West" and the "Arab world," reifying ideological views that endanger *any* articulation of rights in the Arab world—hence the understandable fear that such rights are too difficult. This comes to a head in Massad's dismissal of Arabs making rights claims, most specifically claims regarding sexual orientation.

Joseph Massad and the Gay International Critique

The question of the foundation for human rights has always been charged, subject to critiques from relativist influenced scholars as uncritically universalizing Western norms. Rights regarding sexual orientation, more specifically, have been subject to particularly harsh critiques as illegitimate "Western" exports. Joseph Massad's work has connected these two critiques with his assertion that Arab gay male identity is an illegitimate import and that its emergence is part of the illegitimate spread of human rights across the globe. Examining Massad's argument is important as it raises, in a difficult context, the question of human rights' justification for working globally.

Massad's arguments are problematic, but do raise the issue of how unsatisfying standard justifications for human rights are. Examining controversies over sexual orientation in the Arab world, thus, gives context and indicates the urgency of the basic questions being addressed: Is there an authoritative foundation to human rights? Is it possible to think of human rights from an antifoundational perspective that avoids either, on the one hand, a naïve notion of universal foundations or, on the other hand, an insular separation from the normative and political currents that impel rights claims? And, if so, does that allow an answer to those who question working on difficult human rights issues who have been subject to (rather violently emotional) attacks such as Massad's that rights claims are foreign imports?

Massad poses the issue of rights regarding sexual orientation in binary terms. Using language that calls to mind a Huntingtonian clash of civilizations worldview, he speaks firmly from the camp that rights for gay men are part of an imperialist project. He argues that activism supporting rights regarding sexual orientation around this issue is, adopting Foucauldian language, "an incitement to discourse"—in his terms, gay missionaries have "created" gay men where none existed in the Arab world.[13] Massad argues that rights regarding sexual orientation are a "Western" identity project that does not come out of claims that could legitimately reflect an identity authentic to Arabs. The implicit idea in this concept is that gay Arab men can only be explained due to the imposition of an outside force rather than their own agency.

Massad's underlying assumption reflects a basic notion in structuralist critiques of human rights: that human rights are about creating global citizens and, as such, are a leveling project that serves the purpose of global capital and global hegemony by leading powers. This assumption endorses a static notion of human rights bound to the culture and location of their supposed origins. The irony is that this antiuniversalist position is analogous to naïve universalisms in its monolithic notion of political culture. Each assert a static, totalizing construct of the world, the only difference being whether that construct is of one or of multiple monoliths.

There are overlapping and mutual constitutive theoretical and empirical issues in Massad's argument. There are, specifically, three problematic aspects to Massad's argument:

1. It deprives agency to Arabs. Massad says that Arab gay men are "created" by "gay missionaries whose aim is to defend the very people their intervention is creating."[14] There is no more stark statement of a point-of-view that sees Arabs as child-like and incapable of agency or, in other words, incapable of moving outside social-cultural borders predetermined by an assumed uniform and static Arab society and culture.

2. It assumes that normative currents are necessarily nefarious impositions rather than currents with which Arabs can (and, inevitably, do) engage, contest, and contribute. Massad's conceptualization of identity formation ignores that sexual and gender identities are defined in a space that, for better or worse, moves us beyond an insular conception of the local and is, instead, informed by the transnational flows of norms, networks, media, diasporas et cetera that define life in the Arab world and elsewhere.

3. It essentializes culture and freezes movements for change. Denial of evolving identity construction and transnational currents in such cases does not just deny reality, it denies a culture's inherent pluralism and changeability. Per points 1 and 2, this negates agency and ignores the transnational currents that inform daily life. In so doing, it gives a deeply distorted view of the realities of how peoples have engaged with human rights, understating political and social dynamism in the Arab world and globally.

A rejoinder to Massad's polemic must note the vibrancy of individual and group agency, the inevitability of transnational normative connections, and how these inform conceptualizations in which political societies are not essentialized as static, but rather open to changes based on fluid identity constructions and social pluralism. The issue, thus, is not *if* gay Arab men can or should exist, but what to do *when* Arab gay men (and others) are demanding their rights. On a purely academic level, one can bloodlessly observe that such voices exist and are making their voices heard. That empirical reality must be recognized and integrated into theoretical frames, a project of which this chapter is a part. Indeed, this empirical reality is what is missing from the sort of academic literature that smugly dismisses those making rights claims as "created."

Beyond this, it is worth noting that Massad's work is in the well trod cultural nationalist tradition of emphasizing static cultural purity in such debates. To borrow a phrase from Arjun Appadurai and apply it in a somewhat different context,[15] it is a clear expression of "fear of small numbers" (i.e., the anxiety felt by politically and culturally dominant groups when faced with assertions of difference) that so often leads to explosions of violence targeting minorities. In Appadurai's terms, this "remind[s] these majorities of the small gap which lies between their condition as majorities and the horizon of an unsullied national whole, a pure and untainted national ethnos."[16]

The essential issue at the nexus of the theoretical and the empirical/ political is that Massad's work on gay Arab men encapsulates a discourse of violence that often faces those with identities that challenge the status quo—the "small numbers" that challenge, as Appadurai says, the pure whole. Again, this extends beyond sexuality into nationalist discourse on minorities in other categories, part of what Appadurai describes as "an emerging repertoire of efforts to produce previously unrequired levels of certainty about social identity, values, survival, and dignity."[17]

This reproduces the repression of a vulnerable and marginalized group and turns their victimizers in regimes such as Egypt's Mubarak into seeming heroes for defending Arab integrity against cultural traitors. Egypt's February 2011 revolution would seem to be a move toward rejecting precisely such stultifying social straightjackets. Indeed, the essential is to recognize agency and how agency is defined in the context of changing social configurations structured by local, transnational, and global interactions. Multiple sexual and gender identities are defined in a space that, for better or worse, moves us beyond the global and the local and is informed by all pluralistic flows of power, information, and meaning that move across various cultural locations.[18]

Of course, sexuality raises intense fears and insecurities. So it is no surprise claims that emphasize the fluidity of sexual and gender identity will see a severe backlash against assertions of sexual and gender identities that challenge embedded structures of surveillance and control. This backlash makes clear the urgency of responding to the questions I raised at the start of this chapter: Why have human rights resonated globally and what is the legitimacy of such global resonance when faced with Massad-like backlashes?

MOVING TOWARD ANTIFOUNDATIONAL
UNDERSTANDINGS OF HUMAN RIGHTS

There are two interconnected ways in which human rights are commonly distorted: by being invoked as a singular philosophical abstraction or as a static, unchanging entity. In either mode (or in both, as quite often they overlap), human rights are taken to have been invented in one philosophical or legal moment and to have remained fundamentally defined by that moment. Both universalists in their enthusiasm and relativists in their skepticism make that assumption their point of departure in conceptualizing human rights. It is, however, a futile quest to seek out human rights' foundation as a way to understand what human rights are today.[19] This notion that we know what human rights are and merely have to apply them is deeply unsatisfying in its implication that human rights are a static thing that simply need to be protected by some sort of benevolent power that will oversee human rights. This plays into a savior vision of human rights in which they are a predetermined entity that those with power can provide. To the contrary, human rights are objects of struggle that can be seized from below and, in that process, redefined.

Two elements give the human rights regime tangible substance: one, the obligations it imposes and, two, its ability to be redefined in order to change how existing obligations are understood and to be open to evolving new obligations. Regarding the former, rights take on relevance at the level of the very real obligations they impose on states to respect a panoply of rights. To the degree such rights resonate with the political, economic, and social needs of groups within a state—and, especially, give a basis for legal and political claims to those structurally disadvantaged within a society—human rights will be relevant. This anchor gives essential structure and solidity to the rights regime.

The second element combines with the first to move into the core of my argument. It is simplistic to think of human rights as an unchanging entity defined in treaty tablets that evolved out of philosophical abstractions or disconnected legal consent. Continued reconfigurations of human rights—such as its increased emphasis on the interdependency of economic and political rights or the emergence of rights regarding sexual orientation—epitomize how they have often been reconstructed on a grassroots level, in a transnational context. Human rights' dynamism has come from transnational conversations that can be (and have been to some, perhaps overly limited, degree) two-way streets. This back and forth is essential if human rights are to remain relevant as something other than a distant, Geneva-based legal entity or a culturally particular imposition. This is an argument that goes deeper into why it is a dangerous mistake to turn away from even the most difficult, contentious issues: doing so is to also turn away from permitting the potential redefinition of the rights' regime in a way that can keep it vibrant.

So where to begin regarding a more complex reading of human rights' origins, and toward an antifoundationalist position? Addressing such origins can be based less on a broad universalism and more on an understanding of human rights that sees its expanding resonance as lying in its engagement with emerging normative movements. I will make this argument in four steps. The first of these steps is the importance of agency, the second the implicit cosmopolitanism[20] —albeit not universalism—in any notion of human rights, the third the structures of contemporary global society that are marked most significantly by the globalization of the state and by the growing expanse of transnational currents and networks that bypass the state, and, last, a "chemical reaction" model of human rights evolution borrowed from Samuel Moyn that indicates how groundings in law, politics, institutions, and norms inform human rights in a circular manner, rather than human rights resting on one foundation. This dynamic is illustrated in how the global women's movement helped transform the human rights regime and was, in turn, transformed by its integration into the human rights regime. The push for rights regarding sexual orientation shows potential for a similar dynamic.

Michael Ignatieff's argument that rights are fundamentally about giving space for agency give a basis for the first step toward this antifoundationalist argument. To Ignatieff, human rights are not necessarily about the good nor the ethical, but rather about the minimum necessary to guarantee human agency – the right to be different, the right to dissent, and the right to engage in the politics, economics, society, and culture within a state without discrimination. Ignatieff summarizes a notion of agency as fundamental to the human rights regime in the following way:

> Such grounding as modern human rights requires, I would argue, is based on what history tells us: that human beings are at risk of their lives if they lack a basic measure of free agency; that agency itself requires protection through internationally agreed standards; that these standards should entitle individuals to oppose and resist unjust laws and orders within their own states; and, finally, that when all other remedies have been exhausted, these individuals have the right to appeal to other peoples, nations, international organizations for assistance in defending their rights.[21]

This emphasis on bottom-up agency connects to the idea that there is no singular foundation for human rights, but rather various impulses that reflect the agency of diverse individuals and human societies. Rather than viewing the global resonance of human rights as the imposition of powerful Western hegemony onto agentless subjects, its resonance is instead indicative of the power of individual agency to engage and transform transnational normative currents. The question remains: how to take these "various impulses" and integrate them into a compelling justification for transnational human rights.

A second step in this direction is that there is often some notion, articulated or not, of cosmopolitanism at the heart of any justification for human rights—that is, an idea of a connected humanity that binds us in an ethical community, rather than the sorts of particularisms grounded in religion, race, or nationality that limit an ethical commitment only to a specific community.[22] Part of the grounding of such a cosmopolitan worldview is philosophical (with variants, including the "thick" or "thin" cosmopolitanisms that Walzer and others discuss), but such a philosophical cosmopolitanism's ability to globally underpin human rights is limited. As Donnelly argues, human rights have an "overlapping universality" functionally grounded in the politics and law of contemporary global society but, on the other hand, have, at best, a weak conceptual or ontological universality.[23] There is, as the UDHR's drafters seem to have understood, little basis to assert a unitary philosophic foundation to human rights. To the contrary, human rights are open to various justifications that move beyond both cultural particularism and singular universality.

So agency and an implicit cosmopolitanism may be key building blocks, but as an ultimate justification are not as globally convincing as some might hope. Is there a way to push agency and "overlapping universality" into a holistic but not universalizing, top-down theory of human rights? It may be useful, in this regard, to focus on why human rights are relevant—that is, an "origin" may not be located in a historical or philosophical moment, but rather in our understanding of the dynamics of contemporary global society. This would combine agency and cosmopolitanism with a third step toward antifoundationalism: recognition of the structural factors that have made human rights globally relevant.

This third step is put into focus via a transnationally grounded perspective that can lead us toward recognizing how human rights have evolved in the context of the particular structures of contemporary global society—both transnationally and state-based. The global movement of peoples, goods, technologies, media, social networking, and norms has exploded any notion of a "local" community, making assumptions about the impermeability of domestic sovereignties and solidarities questionable.[24] Domestic politics do not exist in an insular vacuum blissfully separate from transnational currents, but are rather informed by those currents. Structurally, beyond general transnational currents, post-WWII decolonization brought with it the globalization of the modern state system structure and the rise of international organizations that have come to be both a focal point in global politics and an inescapable presence in many parts of the developing world. On that basis, human rights can be seen to be based less on a philosophic worldview and more as flowing out of the dynamics of the globe's transnational political, economic, social, and normative networks.

It is no surprise, in short, that a globalized human rights discourse has flowed out of contemporary normative and political structures rather than cultural or philosophical abstractions. Human rights discourses have global relevance in the context of the unprecedented power of the globalized modern state over individuals and social groups in all parts of the world; international organizations and transnational networks that open up paths around the state's powerfully intrusive ability to dominate political and social life; and transnational norms that can connect peoples to the relevance of human rights protections to their local politics. It makes no sense to naively break the world into discrete, distinct communities— as Massad does in his understanding that "gay" is an acceptable public identity in some parts of the world but not others—when the structures that define politics around the globe are so interconnected. Human rights' relevance or irrelevance comes from the degree to which it responds to those structures and, specifically, how states, international organizations, transnational networks, and, especially, grassroots political movements have come to insist—in varying degrees and in contradictory ways—on the bearing of specific rights to the political, economic, social, and cultural realities and power relations they confront. This is the most salient "origin" of human rights' integration into contemporary law, politics, norms, and institutions.

Disembodied intellectual disputes about a foundation risk ignoring the empirical fact that the human rights regime is a shifting and transnationally defined entity that is often rearticulated and redeployed in different contexts, making the search for a foundation misleading. Ultimately, the relevance of rights is due to how it has enmeshed states in a human rights web (one partly of their own making), how extensive human rights programming by international organizations and donor agencies has reinforced human rights movements on the ground, and how civil society groupings in virtually all parts of the world have seized on human rights law and norms as a basis to advance their work. This is not a singular idea of human rights foundations. But, by being pluralistic, this anti-foundationalist justification does coherently account for the multitude of political and normative movements that have grasped onto human rights and, in so doing, both informed the rights regime with their energy and, in turn, have constituted human rights.

A fourth step toward conceptualizing this circular dynamic at the heart of human rights is to note how human rights' permutations do (or do not, to the degree the rights regime is static) respond to and flow out of the needs of peoples around the globe. As Samuel Moyn puts it, "human rights in their specific contemporary connotations are an invention of recent date, which drew on prior languages and practices the way a chemical reaction depends on having various elements around from different sources, some of them older than others."[25] The incentives behind this activity may share, in some sense, a cosmopolitan worldview and certainly engage rather than deny a transnationalized world, but we need to go further if we are to understand how the rights' regime has evolved under the impact of numerous impulses. Emerging movements for rights regarding sexual orientation, for example, have been at the cutting edge of change in both the Arab world and the international human rights regime. This epitomizes a "chemical reaction" model of how the human rights regime has been able to invent and reinvent itself in ways that maintain its global relevance, rather than by virtue of some eternally powerful point of origin. The emergence, resonance, and continuous evolution of sexual identity speak to the fluidity of human identity. In order for the human rights regime to remain relevant, it must adapt and evolve with such fluid currents. The "origin," in short, is in the way that movements—such as those for rights regarding sexual orientation—can take rights as a tool to advance their own interests and norms. In this they are taking part in the dynamism that has given human rights an entry point into the power relations of a heterogeneous, changing world.

The global women's movement has been at the forefront of pushing the rights regime to define itself in more expansive terms that emphasize the indivisibility of rights and the need to not just respect but also protect and fulfill rights.[26] The "women's rights are human rights" movement and how it transformed international human rights is a classic example of antifoundationalism, epitomizing the diverse forces that impact on how the rights regime shifts and changes. Human rights as we now understand them were redefined from the bottom up rather than according to the regime's "founding" principles. Global women's rights' advocates insisted that human rights could not simply be a matter of passively respecting the rights of those who are subject to political or civil violations. Rather it took as just as important the protection and fulfillment of a spectrum of rights in ways that require positive actions by the state. This means taking into account how violations are systemically built into political, economic, social, and cultural structures and, most importantly, that a state's obligations include taking all viable measures possible to address those structural bases of rights violations. This has had a transformative and lasting impact on how human rights have come to be understood.

Subsequently, movements for rights regarding sexual orientation are pushing even harder in a direction that emphasizes that "negative" respect for rights is inseparable from "positive" fulfillment of rights, be those rights in the economic, political, civil, cultural, or social categories. Sexual and gender rights have challenged traditionally narrow notions of what constitutes a protected status against discrimination, emphasizing that respect for rights based on a singular identity risks creating a straightjacket that denies the fluidity of identity.[27] Movements for rights regarding sexual orientation have been distinctive in their insistence on how identities are multiple and overlapping. This move away from simple identity politics in which sexuality is just one more identity to be protected is perhaps the distinctive contribution of movements for rights regarding sexual orientation. If breaking down monolithic identities becomes normalized as part of how the human rights regime is understood, it will be as transformative and as important as the transformation pushed by the global women's movement in preceding decades. Both theocratic and secular authoritarianisms share a fondness for controlling women and repressing sexuality. This is not a coincidence or a side issue, but indicates the threat human agency is to political power founded in the narrow straightjacket of social control and exclusivist identity politics. The alternative to repression lies less in changing a particular policy and more in opening space for fluid, multiple identities that break down authoritarianisms justified in essentialized constructs of politics, society, and culture.

And, to my argument, if this continues to progress it will be another example of how the rights' regime can be reconstituted in ways that are about grassroots political action and transnational normative movements just as much as international legal treaties and institutions. Those scattered impulses are the opposite of a permanent foundation, and yet are the concrete basis of human rights increasing global relevance. Without an openness to these pushes from the bottom-up, the human rights regime will be lifeless. In other words, a longer way of phrasing antifoundationalism is that having an openness to cutting-edge normative movements is, paradoxically, the "foundation" of the human rights regime's ability to sustain its global relevance. It is for this reason that conceptualizing the human rights regime in all of its complexity is so important, as that complexity is a rebuke to the notion that it is defined eternally by one foundation. Human rights are constantly renewed, in part by intersections with transnational political and normative currents, not by recourse to some sort of creation myth.

CONCLUSION

An antifoundational reading of human rights does not mean that human rights have no groundings. The interplay between the legal, political, normative, and institutional groundings of human rights is essential, as I have argued. Indeed, to break down these groundings further, there is an ongoing dialectic between laws and institutions (domestic and international) that give permanent structure to human rights and the political processes and normative currents that, if they penetrate laws and institutions, renew this regime and give it life.

As important as all these groundings are, however, the primary impulse flows out of something Claude Lefort identifies: that human rights are the product of past struggles and the object of new ones.[28] While there is no ultimate foundation for human rights, the chaotic impulses that keep human rights relevant most often come from people on the ground in different political, economic, social, and cultural locations around the globe. Hence the theoretical understanding of human rights I have sketched out that sees its continued relevance and expanded resonance as dependent on engagement with emerging normative movements, not a turning away from them.

The global women's movement and movements for rights regarding sexual orientation and gender identity also show how this must be a two-way street. For the human rights regime to maintain its relevance it is dependent on continuously evolving in response to normative currents. Rights rely for their relevance on an ability to be (re)constituted by those making claims in the emancipatory language of rights that is evolving and multisourced rather than singular and static.

It is intellectually impoverished to conceptualize human rights as eternally defined by one historic moment that has since progressed in a linear fashion.[29] While created by states and embedded in domestic law, pushed by grassroots and transnational normative movements, overseen by domestic and international organizations, and anchored in international law, the human rights regime only takes shape from the circular back-and-forth among these elements. Normative movements and political processes continually inform and redefine the rights regime at the legal and institutional level, just as law and institutions give solidity to human rights' place in global politics. The rights' regime is not a matter of top-down bequests or a universal foundation.[30]

This returns us to the question posed at the start of this chapter: how to deal with difficult rights in contentious circumstances, such as rights for gay men in the Arab world. By the logic of my argument, even though I am entirely sympathetic to the political difficulty claims for such rights pose, there is really no choice. All rights are, by definition, difficult. The essence of the rights' regime is to take on claims from vulnerable groups that are articulated in the language and structure of the rights' regime. To the degree it has done so, the rights' regime has, remarkably, thrived. To the degree it has not, it has been static and elitist.

In short, claims for difficult rights in contentious circumstances are, indeed, problematic. Their difficulty, however, speaks directly to the essence of the human rights project. Taking up such difficult challenges has been and remains essential to the maintenance and expansion of its global resonance. To ignore such claims from Arabs because some say their source is "Western" is to impose an Orientalist-like notion that Arabs (and "Westerners") have unchanging mentalities and, specifically, unchanging sexual and gender constructs that do not permit rights' claims to be made. To the contrary, the Arab world is not and never has been an insular backwater; peoples from within its diverse communities have always been a part of transnational currents affecting changing social constructs. To ignore rights' claims that come from within that dynamic sphere is to both reinforce monolithic notions of identity and unchanging community and, most importantly, to narrow the sources that define what human rights can become.

A response to the questions regarding the source and legitimacy of human rights I posed at the beginning of this chapter, therefore, flows out of the arguments I have been making. The source for human rights regime's global resonance is the way in which it is fluidly informed by impulses and claims that come from numerous sources—sources that have no reason to be seen as geographically or culturally bordered. Regarding legitimacy, such sources shift the issue away from whether or not a defined human rights corpus should be applied from "on high" to resistant parts of the world. Rights are not static moral principles that need to be protected by the globe's most powerful actors the way a baby is protected by a parent. Instead, in all parts of the world human rights are an object of struggle, and their legitimacy depends not on geography or ethnic identity, but rather on the degree to which they respond to those struggles.

NOTES

1. For an example of a "universalist" approach with much to recommend it, see William Talbott, *Which Rights Should Be Universal?* (New York: Oxford University Press, 2005).

2. For an excellent example of a "moral" argument for human rights, see Michael J. Perry, *The Idea of Human Rights: Four Inquiries* (New York: Oxford University Press, 1998).

3. Arvonne Fraser, "Becoming Human: The Origins and Development of Women's Human Rights," *Human Rights Quarterly*, vol. 21, no. 4 (November 1999). See also Arvonne Fraser and Irene Tinker, *How Women Transformed International Development* (New York: Feminist Press, 2004).

4. Sexuality and Human Rights: Discussion Paper (Versoix, Switzerland: International Council on Human Rights Policy, 2009); Arvind Narrain, "Human Rights and Sexual Minorities: Global and Local Contexts," *Law, Social Justice and Human Development*, no. 2 (2001); Alice Miller, "Sexuality, Violence against Women and Human Rights: Women Make

Demands, and Ladies Get Protection," *Health and Human Rights* 7, no. 2 (Winter 2004); Ignacio Saiz, "Bracketing Sexuality: Human Rights and Sexual Orientation—A Decade of Development and Denial at the U.N.," *Health and Human Rights* 7, no. 2 (Winter 2004).

5. For a "gatekeeper" theory for the emergence of such rights, see Julie Mertus, "Applying the Gatekeeper Model of Human Rights Activism: The U.S.-Based Movement for LGBT Rights," in *The International Struggle for New Human Rights*, ed. Clifford Bob (Philadelphia: University of Pennsylvania Press, 2009).

6. Sofia Gruskin and Laura Ferguson, "Government Regulation of Sex and Sexuality: In Their Own Words," *Reproductive Health Matters* 17, no. 34, p. 2.

7. For further details, see International Commission of Jurists, *Sexual Orientation, Gender Identity, and International Human Rights Law* (Geneva: ICJ, 2009) or Douglas Sanders, "Sexual and Gender Identity," in *Encyclopedia of Human Rights*, vol. 4., ed. Forsythe, pp. 433–445.

8. General Comments being the definitive treaty monitoring body interpretations of the rights in the treaties they oversee.

9. Maher Sabry interview with David Khalili, "Exposing Oppression in Egypt," National Sexual Resource Center, June 18, 2008, http://nsrc.sfsu. edu/article/homophobia_oppression_egypt_film_queen_boat, accessed October 1, 2009.

10. In general, see *Deconstructing Sexuality in the Middle East*, ed. Pinar Ilkkaracan (Aldershot: Ashgate, 2008).

11. Negar Azimi, "Prisoners of Sex," *New York Times*, December 3, 2006. Azimi adds that "[p]ublic regulation of morality is an area in which [Egypt's] secular regime—often through its mouthpiece religious institution, Al Azhar—is in harmony with the Islamists." It's also interesting that Azimi notes police reports often justify arrests for homosexuality as the arrested threaten to harm "the country's reputation at the international level" (Azimi is quoting from a police report)—as noted, transnational currents work in many different directions.

12. Indeed, the focus in this chapter on gay Arab males is quite limiting. Sexuality is a set of undefined erotic practices mediated by social norms, economic structures, and political situations. The subjectivities that flow out of this are multiple, not reducible to the standard categories of heterosexual or homosexual.

13. Joseph Massad, "Re-Orienting Desire: The Gay International and the Arab World," *Public Culture* 1, no. 2 (Spring 2002), and Joseph Massad, *Desiring Arabs* (Chicago: University of Chicago Press, 2007).

14. Massad, *Desiring Arabs*, p. 41.

15. Appadurai is discussing ethnic minorities, not sexual or gender minorities. His concepts, however, illuminate their structurally similar position.

16. Appadurai, *Fear of Small Numbers*, p. 8.

17. Ibid., p. 7.

18. Evelyn Blackwood, "Transnational Sexualities in One Place: Indonesian Readings," *Gender & Society* (April 2005).

19. Lynn Hunt, *Inventing Human Rights: A History* (New York: Norton, 2007).

20. "Critical cosmopolitanism" is the term used, usefully, by Gerard Delanty and that informs some of my thoughts on this topic. Gerard Delanty, "The Cosmopolitan Imagination: Critical Cosmopolitanism and Social Theory," *The British Journal of Sociology* 57, no. 1 (2006).

21. Michael Ignatieff, *Human Rights as Politics and Idolatry* (Princeton, NJ: Princeton University Press, 2001), p. 55.

22. In addition to Delanty, see, for a more classic example of cosmopolitanism that nonetheless avoids simplistic universalism, Kwame Anthony Appiah, *Cosmopolitanism: Ethics in a World of Strangers* (New York: Norton, 2006).

23. Jack Donnelly, "The Relative Universality of Rights," *Human Rights Quarterly* 29, no. 2 (2007).

24. Christian Reus-Smit, "Human Rights and the Social Construction of Sovereignty," *Review of International Studies* 27 (2001).

25. Samuel Moyn, "On the Genealogy of Morals," *The Nation*, April 16, 2007.

26. On the "Respect, Protect, Fulfill" paradigm, see Gruskin and Tarantola, "Health and Human Rights," in *Perspectives on Health and Human Rights*, ed. Gruskin, Grodin, Annas, and Marks (New York: Routledge, 2005). My own take on "Respect, Protect, Fulfill" is in Chase and Alaug, "Health, Human Rights, and Islam: A Focus on Yemen," *Health and Human Rights: An International Journal* 8, no. 1 (2005).

27. Scott Long, "When Doctors Torture: The Anus and the State in Egypt and Beyond," *Health and Human Rights: An International Journal* 7, no. 2 (2004).

28. Claude Lefort, *Writing: The Political Test* (Durham and London: Duke University Press, 2000).

29. For an elegant examination of this and related questions, see Reza Afshari, "On Historiography of Human Rights," *Human Rights Quarterly* 29, no. 1 (2007).

30. See Ingram, "What Is a 'Right to Have Rights?'".

PART III

INTRODUCTION III: STRATEGIES

In some ways, protecting and promoting human rights and responding to human rights abuses are struggles that are typically fought on national turfs, yet they are not necessarily beyond the influence of international forces and actors. It is important to frame human rights issues in terms of the interplay between international and local factors. As the recent uprisings in Tunisia, Egypt, Libya, Jordan, and Yemen have demonstrated, while the triggering factors are local, the language of protest is couched largely in terms of universal or inalienable human rights. These struggles against poverty, unemployment, corruption, and repression must be placed in a broad context that compels a depth of description. The Western world's support—or lack thereof—for such popular movements may prove crucial in shaping things to come. The same can be said of socioeconomic and political situations in Honduras, Ivory Coast, Peru, Kenya, and Colombia, where issues are local but outside actors can play an important role in influencing the outcome. The largest recipient of U.S. military aid outside the Middle East is Colombia, and this may be a crucial indicator of the extent to which the United States can influence developments there. These and other cases are a testament to the fact that the Middle East is not unique in facing such challenges.

Contributors to this section introduce a wide variety of strategies for improving human rights. Some suggest sanctions, boycotts, and divestment in the case of the Israeli-Palestinian conflict. Others suggest engagement of legitimate Islamist groups in the processes of political participation and the introduction of a broader discourse on human rights. Still others admonish us against democracy promotion project, considering it a complicated and long-term adventure that entails enormous risks. They argue that we should instead focus narrowly on protecting certain basic human rights by setting limits to political repression. Regarding the rights of migrant workers, many observers espouse the strategy of prevention and intervention in the form of government control over markets. Without such regulations, migrant workers' rights cannot be upheld in the long term.

In the context of the 2011 uprisings in North Africa and the Middle East, Bahey eldin Hassan argues that it is premature to proclaim the victory of democracy and human rights in the region. The conflict between democratic and entrenched authoritarian forces in Tunisia and Egypt—where their peoples managed to remove the heads of the police states—and political youth forces that only began to find their way to politics in recent years rages on. There was a virtual consensus among academics, experts, and policymakers that the Arab world is one of the most resistant regions to democratization and human rights today. According to Freedom House, not one country in the region can be classified as "free" or as having a free press. Torture is widespread in most nations, along with arbitrary arrest, whether sanctioned by some form of emergency law or not. The judiciary lacks even a modicum of independence, and the freedom of expression and assembly are severely restricted.

Yet, the 2011 uprisings sweeping across the region have upended the assumption about the Arab people's regressive views about their national politics and have further exposed the problematic nature of the assumed separation of the ordinary people from politics. As far as the Western world is concerned, these leaderless and spontaneous uprisings have rendered working with the old, local autocrats unpredictable and costly. As regards the outcomes of these uprisings, great battles lie ahead. Whether the Egyptian army will initiate as well as sustain the drive toward fundamental reforms and political openings remains a proposition in search of a proof. The youth organizations are bound to face mounting challenges from traditional politics and groups.

In Chapter 11, Mahmood Monshipouri and Shadi Mokhtari demonstrate that the pursuit of the so-called war on terror invariably generates extremely difficult choices for societies espousing liberal values and identities. A choice must be made at the outset of the campaign between the approach to and form of counterterrorism policies on the one hand, and the adherence to stated values and practices of the liberal order on the other. Many dilemmas arise out of the policy choices faced by liberal societies in responding to terrorism. The choice of insulation, repression, and the potential for creating egalitarian societies requires the fundamental compromising of liberal economic and political values. The fact remains that the United States cannot defend its core values while simultaneously resorting to the excesses and hysteria of securitization. Rethinking what is practical and desirable in the Middle East has perpetually brought paradoxical and contradictory policies into the open. Despite the Arab revolts, U.S. foreign policy has followed the all-too-familiar zigzag pattern of supporting democratic change in some countries (Egypt, Tunisia, and Libya) while at the same time acquiescing to the status quo in others (Bahrain and Jordan).

In the ensuing chapter, Mahmood Monshipouri and Ali Assareh turn to the plight of migrant workers in the Persian Gulf region, focusing more specifically on the case of the United Arab Emirates (UAE). Monshipouri and Assareh assert that today's Dubai, built over decades by migrant labors, stands out as the center of the Arabian Peninsula's finance and reexport business. Ironically, these same workers are identified as the human collateral damage of the global financial crisis that has paralyzed Dubai's booming housing and construction industry since 2008. When combined with food insecurity resulting from the 2008 global food crisis, the agony of migrant labor working in the UAE becomes striking.

While some nationals have come to view migrant workers as a threat to the cultural integrity of their nation, others have cautioned against such skepticism, arguing that large-scale migration regulations must be put in place to direct and fortify the national economy. The UAE government, Monshipouri and Assareh insist, needs to do a balancing job of determining the level of imported labors with that of its local needs, while at the same time maintaining a reasonable capacity to defuse potential social unrest. The case for government intervention has never been more essential. The pervasive abuse of the rights of workers has led to mounting pressure for direct government involvement. A strategy that seeks to improve standards and augment regulations is the best place to start. This means seeking more federal control over markets as well as pursuing mechanisms to provide for the most basic of amenities and living conditions.

Jess Ghannam examines the relationship between basic health requirements and human rights in the context of the occupied territories of the Palestinians, arguing that the occupation and colonization of Palestine stands out as an egregious example of how health rights are denied with devastating consequences for the Palestinians. Ghannam describes the current context of human rights violations in Palestine and their impact on health rights, especially since the siege and invasion of Gaza and its aftermath. What is more troubling is the continuing Israeli impunity and the failure of international entities—nation-states, NGOs, international judicial bodies—to hold Israel accountable. Ghannam offers the so-called boycott, divestment, and sanctions (BDS) paradigm as one strategy for bringing justice to Palestine. An international grassroots movement is emerging for the academic and cultural boycott of Israel (ACBI) as a method of peaceful resistance to the occupation of Palestine.

CHAPTER 10

A PROSPECT OF DEMOCRATIC
UPRISINGS IN THE ARAB WORLD

Bahey eldin Hassan

Throughout December 2010 and January 2011, political protest movements and uprisings shook the Arab world. The revolts began in Tunisia on December 17, 2010, when Mohammed Bouazizi committed suicide by setting himself on fire, in protest against unemployment and the violation of his dignity. Before a month had passed, on January 14, 2011, the Tunisian people had forced President Zine el-Abidine Ben Ali out of the country. On January 25, the Egyptian uprising began; within 18 days, on February 11, President Hosni Mubarak was compelled to relinquish power. And a mere six days later, the uprising of the Libyan people erupted. In the meantime, the Yemenis had risen up demanding that President Ali Abdullah Saleh leave, and in Bahrain political protestors sought to transform the existing autocratic monarchy into a constitutional monarchy. This same period saw successive political protests in Syria, Algeria, Morocco, Jordan, and Saudi Arabia, and to a lesser extent in Sudan and Oman.

It is still too early to proclaim the victory of democracy and human rights in the region. As I write this, the conflict continues between entrenched authoritarian forces in Tunisia and Egypt—where its peoples managed to remove the heads of the police states—and political youth forces that only began to find their way to politics in recent years.

There was a virtual consensus among academics, political analysts, and international, regional, and local human rights groups that the Arab world is one of the most resistant regions to democratization and human rights today. According to Freedom House, not a single country in the region can be classified as "free" or as having a free press.[1] Torture is widespread in most nations, along with arbitrary arrest, whether sanctioned by some form of emergency law or not. The judiciary lacks even a modicum of independence, and freedom of expression and assembly are severely restricted. Even solidarity protests with the Palestinian people are not immune to suppression.[2]

Poor scores on indicators for the region are not limited to the fields of human rights and democracy, but extend to areas such as corruption, academic research, dissemination of information, education, and poverty (the oil-rich countries are an exception to the poverty factor).[3]

The three major, global waves of democratization failed to breach the walls protecting Arab dictatorships; one might even say that a fourth wave failed as well—the international initiatives for political reform in the Arab world led by the United States and the EU following the September 11, 2001, attacks. Indeed, the opposite has occurred. Arab states have gone on the counteroffensive at home and on the international stage, with concerted action in the UN Human Rights Council to undermine instruments for the international protection of human rights in cooperation with other dictatorships, starting with member countries of the Organization of the Islamic Conference.[4] After a long struggle to liberate themselves from foreign occupation, involving great sacrifice, most people of the region successfully achieved independence from foreign rule during the 1950s. Nevertheless, they have failed, abjectly and persistently, to become free people.

The people of the region rid themselves of foreign tyranny only to fall under various "national" tyrannies. Both types of tyranny were and are grounded in one basic principle: that these peoples are unqualified to rule themselves except after some ill-defined transitional period, the end of which no one seems to know. Both systems believe local people need an overlord; they just differ as to whether this master should be of foreign or local origin.

But the people in the Arab world have not yielded to national tyranny. As the joy of national liberation faded, they quickly embarked on a struggle for a second independence.[5] This struggle reached its peak in 2003–2006, when, for the first time since national independence, the indigenous desire for democracy coincided with a reconsideration by Europe and the United States of their unconditional support for autocracies in the Arab world. Prompted by the attacks of 9/11, the latter sponsored several initiatives to support democratization. This chapter seeks to explain the root causes of the recent democratic uprisings in the Middle East and North Africa, as well as to explore the prospects for democratic change in the region.

I   Political Systems and Human Rights

The deplorable human rights conditions in the region are in large part a product of the hegemony of systems that are wholly unaccountable to the people they rule. Although they run the gamut from monarchy to republic, at heart they embody authoritarianism and autocracy. They employ virtually the same tactical maneuvers at home with their people as they do abroad in the international community, using the same self-justifying political lexicon and public discourse.[6]

It should be noted in this context that all the monarchies in the region are absolute monarchies—none are constitutional monarchies; similarly, most of the republics are based on the absolute dominance of the executive authority at the expense of the judiciary and legislature, if any exists at all. Most are fixed as a one-man rule where the president enjoys prerogatives no less absolute than those of a king.[7] The majority of presidents of these nations are unelected, with no term limits. They may be subject to a public referendum as the sole candidate, as was the case in Syria, Iraq under Saddam Hussein, and Egypt until 2005, but this is largely a charade. Republican leaders in the Arab world remain in the seat of power for much longer than their peers in other regions—even longer than Arab kings themselves. President Muammar al-Qaddafi has ruled Libya since 1969, while President Ali Abdullah Saleh has ruled Yemen since 1978. The list goes on: President Mohammed Hosni Mubarak in Egypt since 1981, President Zine el-Abidine Ben Ali in Tunisia since 1987, and President Omar al-Bashir in Sudan since 1989.

It is remarkable that some of these presidents have remained in power for long stretches without being compelled to stand in elections or even receive approval by a popular referendum without competitors (as in the cases of President al-Qaddafi and President al-Bashir). Some countries have developed electoral systems that are, at root, mere referendums: elections are organized for the eternal president and uncrowned king while other candidates are mere extras chosen by the ruling party, directly or indirectly, as part of a stage performance with constitutional or legislative trimmings serving as the costumes (Tunisia, Algeria, and Egypt since 2005).

Since 2000, the Arab world has seen the removal of the major obstacles remaining to a complete merging of monarchy and republicanism as sons have been groomed to assume their fathers' presidencies. It began in Syria when Bashar al-Assad followed his father, Hafez al-Assad, as president. Saddam Hussein was preparing one of his sons, Uday or Qusay, to succeed him, and presidential sons or relatives are already standing in line in Egypt, Libya, and Yemen.[8]

Of course there are differences among the monarchies of the region, particularly in their degree of authoritarianism. There are also a few exceptions to the general nature of political systems and the structure of political authority in Arab republics. For example, this description does not apply to Sudan in its democratic period, before the military coup of 1989. Similarly, the sectarian political system of Lebanon does not allow for such maladies, but it does create other problems that are no less serious while also holding out the possibility of civil war at a moment's notice. The Palestinian Authority is a temporary exception, but it still embodies the major problems of rule in the Arab world, with a "secular" face in the West Bank and an "Islamic" face in the Gaza Strip. The new political regime in Iraq is an exception, too, but for how long?

The common authoritarian nature of political systems in the Arab world—and the fact that the prevailing political and religious culture mimics this authoritarianism—has led to the spread of similar policies and similarly grave human rights abuses throughout the region. The common element among most of these systems, with the exception of Lebanon and more recently Iraq, is the lack of any semblance of balance between the three state government branches due to the dominance of the executive branch over the legislative and judicial branches, usually headed by a king or an absolutist president. In all cases, the security apparatus enjoys enormous influence within the executive branch, such that many of the simplest administrative decisions cannot be made without first consulting the security authorities. These apparatuses may differ in their compositional nature between military (Syria, Algeria, Yemen, and Iraq under Saddam Hussein) and police (Tunisia and Egypt before their 2011 revolution), but they are ultimately alike in the central role they place in decision making and in their nature as "security." This includes the way these forces impact the development of the structure and composition of the ruling elite in these countries.[9]

II STATE OF HUMAN RIGHTS

The dominant role of the executive branch—and the security apparatuses at the heart of it—has led to a chronic failure to build a nation of rights and laws. Institutions and mechanisms that are meant to protect the individual and society from autocracy are used to legitimize a systematic assault on the liberties and rights of the individual and society, all the while methodically destroying independent expression and organization in civil society, which was created in some countries such as Egypt, Syria, and Iraq during the periods of relative liberalism in the first half of the twentieth century.

Thus the constitution, legislative process, courts, parliament, and religious establishments have been used to legitimize methodical assaults on the rights of individuals and society. These tools have been used to institutionalize and normalize such assaults, including the whole or partial nullification of all means of protection and resistance, such as political parties, trade and labor unions, NGOs, and independent media. The cruellest, most extreme forms of violence are used to repress dissenters and intimidate society as a whole: arrest, torture, extrajudicial killing, death sentences issued by sham courts, forced disappearance, exile, denial of passports after exiting the country or denial of citizenship to those at home, restrictions on freedom of movement, disruption of televised, electronic, and mail communication, severance of the means to a livelihood through dismissal and bans on future employment, financial strangulation of nonstate workers through the intimidation of their clients and coworkers, character assassination in the media, fraudulent and trumped-up charges, kangaroo courts that hand down the desired verdict and punishment, and much more.[10]

Main Patterns of Human Rights Violations

Structural Imbalance

Ruling elites in the region tend to use the constitution and legislation as a tool to systematize the undermining or assault on human rights: constitutions in the Arab world, when they exist, do not recognize a proper balance or separation of powers, but instead entrench the hegemony of the executive over the legislative and judicial authorities, granting absolute authority to the king or president.

This chronic structural imbalance is the primary avenue through which human rights abuses are introduced in each country, to varying degrees. When real judicial and legislative oversight is absent, it allows the executive branch to act without accountability in all fields, and the harm it creates goes beyond human rights per se—for example, the enduring failure of these states to engage in the sound management of human, material, and cultural resources in general.

Turning to those articles related to human rights in Arab constitutions, we find that some (in Egypt and Syria, for example) are very benevolent and guarantee several basic rights. Nevertheless, these constitutional guarantees have no relation to practice; indeed, they are diametrically opposed to the reality of human rights in these countries and are often described as "dead" articles.

This reality is attributable to the lack of political will to comply with these articles. Although legislation should draw and expound on the letter and spirit of the constitution, it often acts to restrict the constitutional article itself—that is, a right enshrined in the constitution.[11] In the same context, it is remarkable the ease with which states of emergency are declared without any objective justification, as well as the scope of covering the entire country for an indefinite period of time. Additionally, declarations of emergency in Arab countries are accompanied by emergency laws that do not meet international standards and suspend vital constitutional guarantees.

Lack of Judicial Oversight

In most Arab nations, the judicial authority enjoys no independence from the executive authority. The exception—and it is a very limited exception—is Egypt, where the judicial system still has some degree of independence preserved from the semi-liberal period in the country's history despite coming under successive waves of assault that have gradually diminished it since the 1952 revolution.[12]

The lack or severe weakness of an oversight role for the judiciary strips citizens of the last line of defence in the face of arbitrary authority, rendering them unable to achieve justice if one or several of their rights are violated. The ways in which the executive authority encroaches on the judiciary vary from one country to the next, but the method is similar in all cases. The most prominent types of assault on judicial independence are:

1. The formation of exceptional legal or court systems that operate parallel to the normal judicial system. The most widespread of these exceptional systems is the military justice system, which is subservient to military hierarchy and military obedience and discipline. Citizens are referred to such courts when a "speedy" trial is sought in cases involving harm to "state security."

2. The normal judiciary is placed under the control of the Ministry of Justice, turning judges into government employees who often follow the directives of the minister of justice, either explicitly or indirectly. Cases that are sensitive for the government or influential figures are assigned to particular judges who will issue the required ruling, whether it is a heavy sentence or an acquittal.[13]

3. The public prosecutor is wholly or partially placed under the control of the security apparatus, whether directly or through the Ministry of Justice. This dependence makes the interior minister or his representative the de facto chief prosecutor in all cases, particularly in sensitive cases involving so-called state security. This means that the prosecutor's office may be prohibited from investigating "secondary" matters linked to the case, such as defendants' complaints of arbitrary arrest or torture. In all cases, even those not defined as matters of national security, the prosecutor's office does not follow up complaints about the conduct of the security apparatus.[14]

4. The executive authority does not comply with or implement judicial rulings it does not like (even final, compulsory rulings), and there

is no instrument to force compliance given the overwhelming dominance of the executive and the weakness of civil society and public opinion.[15]

Lack of Freedom of Expression

The lack of independent means of expression of political parties, trade and labor unions, NGOs, and written, visual, aural, and electronic media, as well as the right to strike and assemble, may be wholly or partially confiscated, or they may be arbitrarily restricted in ways that do not serve the public interest of individuals or society. This is achieved through constitutional articles, legislation, trials lacking all semblance of due process, or security repression at various levels.

Religious sentiment may be exploited to legitimize some of these restrictions by using the pretext of protection of religions (either the protection of Islam alone, or the Islamic confession predominant in a particular country). Intellectuals, academics, and artists pay a heavy price for these restrictions, and the coercion may sometimes be life endangering.[16] The imposition of arbitrary restrictions on freedom of opinion, thought, and belief may be prompted by political or religious considerations, but in most cases religious sentiment is used to justify restrictions that are politically motivated.

Religious and Ethnic Persecution

The Arab world is familiar with the rule of a minority over the majority of the population, as was the case in Iraq for several decades when the regime was based on Sunni rule and discriminated against and persecuted a majority of citizens (Shiites), in addition to Kurds, an ethnic minority still belonging to the Sunni confession. A similar situation prevails in Syria and Bahrain today.

Persecution takes different forms from country to country, including bans on the practice of some or all religious rites and the establishment of houses of worship, bars to entrance to senior government positions, restrictions on the right to change one's religion (if it means abandoning the religion of the majority), and restrictions on freedom of expression. The persecution may also involve violent repression of the minority, including arbitrary arrest and unfair trials. In exceptional cases, the persecution is likely to become genocidal, as was the case of Iraqi Kurds under Saddam Hussein.

The Practice of Torture

Widespread use of torture and mistreatment are an endemic problem in the region. This may take place in police stations or unofficial and unrecognized detention facilities. At times, the fiercest forms of torture are employed that cause irreparable harm, partial or total incapacitation, or even death. The victims may then disappear, their bodies not even returned to their families.[17] Ending police abuse and emergency laws, which have for a long time enabled a culture of impunity for security forces, was a major motivation behind the 2011 revolutions in North Africa.

III   PREVALENT CULTURE OR POLITICAL WILL?

There are numerous explanations for the exceptional situation transpiring across the entire region and prompt concerns for good governance and respect for human rights. The most common explanation attributes the situation to the prevalent culture in the Arab world, particularly the religious component of culture, given that this is, objectively, the common link among all residents of the region. This explanation is not just widespread among political analysts and academics; ironically, some officials in Arab governments and the governing elite adopt this "explanation" as well, for it gives them an excuse for their abject failure to respect human rights;[18] it is the people's fault, they aver.[19] It is they who resist advancement and change, whether because of the adoption of conservative and Salafi religious thought or due to long-standing social customs that require much time to overcome.

This analysis, however, fails to explain why advancement or improvement happens in the Arab world in fields that run directly counter to conservative religious thought or deeply rooted social traditions—even in Saudi Arabia, in the areas of women and child rights, for example. Likewise, this view falls short of explaining why there is no improvement in human rights violations that do not conflict with the prevailing religious culture or social mores, including torture.[20]

The other explanation relates to the political will of the ruling elite, which promotes some improvements—however limited or partial—to women's rights under the patronage of the wives of presidents and kings in the Arab world as long as they do not subtract from the absolute political authority of the ruling elite.

IV   THE FOURTH WAVE OF DEMOCRATIZATION

In the wake of the 9/11 terrorist attacks, the U.S. administration concluded that the lack of democracy in the Arab world had fueled the growth of terrorism and led to its export to the Western world. As such, several initiatives were formulated—American, European, and international—that sought to democratize the region, with a focus on Egypt and Saudi Arabia, the countries from which the majority of the 9/11 hijackers hailed. These initiatives included the Broader Middle East and North Africa Initiative (BMENA), the G8 Greater Middle East Initiative (GMEI), and the European Neighbourhood and Partnership Instrument (ENPI).

In effect, these initiatives gave political support for the democracy movement and fostered respect for human rights in the region, contributing to the growing political ferment in Egypt, Syria, Saudi Arabia, Tunisia, and Lebanon. This moment could even be called the fourth wave of democratization. However, this wave soon subsided because from the very moment these successive international initiatives for reform in the Arab world were announced, they lacked the necessary political will to drive them resolutely to achieve their goals. They were more like declarations of political intent than an accurate diagnosis accompanied by practical plans.

On the internal level, and despite the fact that the forces of reform in the Arab world have had no respite in calling for reform for four decades (at least since the military defeat of June 1967), and despite the fact that one of the main obstacles before these forces was the external support offered to authoritarian regimes, it has to be admitted that the basic conditions for the internal interaction with the fourth wave of democratization have been lacking. This is due to the absence of the elements that would constitute a social basis for reform.

The ruling regimes in the Arab countries lacked the necessary will to embark on political reform, and hence all their efforts during 2004–2005 were spent on trying to relieve and absorb external and internal pressures. Much of these efforts also went into exacerbating the internal contradictions in the other fronts and making an alliance with "the devil" to forestall reform. The outstanding adroitness with which the Arab ruling regimes, under the leadership of Egypt, managed this decisive crisis deserves to be an object lesson in the study of crisis management. If only these regimes had been managing their societies and providing for its needs with a mere 5 percent of such adeptness, they might not have needed any reform.[21]

1   The Main Features of the Stratagems of the Arab Regimes

- Claiming that they have changed their skin, and have decided to respond positively to the calls of reform. Examples include the Arab Summit convened in Tunis in May 2004, which included on its agenda for the first time in the history of Arab Summits the issue of reform and democracy.[22] They also include the Sanaa[23] and Alexandria[24] conferences for Arab Reform organized by the governments of Yemen and Egypt, respectively, in January and March 2004. The two conferences adopted certain documents that were discarded into the dustbin by the Arab governments after they fulfilled their function, namely, pacifying and absorbing the pressures of civil society.

- Responding favourably to international programs that offer financial assistance in the field of democracy, and facilitating the convening of conferences, workshops, and seminars with the participation of elements from the government, especially in the Gulf States, Jordan, and Egypt. This latter, however, obstructed the opening of offices of international organizations, but did not stop the U.S. organizations already in existence in Egypt from receiving funding for democracy training.

- Raising the slogan of "cultural specificity" of Arab societies, and that reform comes only "from within," with the aim of checking the momentum of the international community's calls for reform from "outside." The result was the rejection of all calls for reform whether from within or elsewhere.

- Raising the slogan of gradualism, and arguing that the democratization process took hundreds of years in European societies. In practice, this did not lead to taking a single step forward, but rather several steps back in such countries as Egypt, Syria, and Bahrain.

- Trying to undermine the international consensus on the importance of reform in the Arab world and the methods of bringing it about, by seeking to widen the gap between the different positions within U.S. political circles and between the EU and the United States.[25] Offering Europe and the United States more attractive options for servicing their security interests in the region, especially given the rise of new regional security challenges in light of the evident failure of the American project in Iraq, Hamas reaching power in Palestine, the rise of Iran as a regional power, and the exacerbation of the threat of exporting terrorism. Still, such offers did not involve any serious contribution to putting an end to any conflict. For the common strategy of the Arab regimes has always been to keep regional conflicts brewing, in order to stir up the national security concerns at all times at home. They employ such concern with their peoples and their political, cultural elites in order to keep their attention focused on the "external threat," and thus indirectly support the legitimacy of their continued existence without change. This strategy, however, stops short of letting these conflicts heat up to the extent of threatening the interests of these regimes.

- The skilful use of the Islamists as a scarecrow to dampen the enthusiasm of the calls for reform, whether by the international community or the local political class—liberals, leftists, secularists, and nationalists. Egypt offers the most astute example: the parliamentary election in 2005 took place for the first time without any member of the Muslim Brothers in prison. They had been all released several days before the elections to enjoy, during the first stage and the first round of the second stage, the best political and security atmosphere in any elections in the past 25 years. This had direct results, as the Muslim Brothers were able to hold 20 percent of parliamentary seats. It was an excellent tactical win for the Islamists, yet it turned into a strategic win for the Egyptian regime,[26] and other Arab regimes, as it helped settle the debate about the European and American priorities to the benefit of regional security interests while at the expense of democratic reform in the Arab world.

- Coordinating with the powerful Israeli lobby in the American Congress on the grounds of common interests against political reform, especially since the rise of the Islamists (the common enemy of those regimes and of Israel's) in the Egyptian and Palestinian elections.
- Stoking religious sentiments against the "crusading" West, including seizing the opportunity of the Danish cartoon incident to fan the flames of a wide political, media, and popular mobilization campaign. Arab governments did not even refrain from facilitating attacks on embassies and setting them on fire, all in an attempt to distract attention from local contradictions and direct it toward the foreign threats that "target" Islam.[27]
- Raising the flying colors of "women's rights" and organizing a huge number of meetings and conferences, with the presence of the "first ladies" of the Arab countries, typically under the auspices of the Arab League. Making concessions in this regard does not reflect directly on the political system and the balance of power. Such concessions also help reduce the international pressures toward political reform, as they seem to be getting something at the very least.
- Finally, all forms of repression (security, legislative, media, and administrative) continued unabated during the two years of "reform" (2004–2005).

2   What Went Wrong with the Arab Political Mobility?

In addition to the astute efforts of regimes in the Arab world, the nonruling elites in this region were not ready to lead the process of reform. They have suffered from systematic and organized repression for several consecutive decades, with the assistance or collusion of the international community. This has caused them to be quite limited in number, fragile, fissured, and always easy to manipulate politically or through security services.

Democratic reform has never been a solid priority for any significant sector of these elites. They have been concerned with other priorities, in particular Palestine, Lebanon, and Iraq, or the conflict with the West in general. Hence, it is not a complete surprise to find that certain active sectors of these elites stand in the frontline of the confrontation with their own local regimes and ruling forces (on issues of democracy and human rights). All the while they support the anti-reform regimes and parties in Syria, Lebanon, Sudan, and other nations, and hold funerals in several Arab capitals to honor the mass-murdering "martyr" Saddam Hussein.

The conduct of significant sections of these elites has been morally abhorrent. They shed tears for the absence of democracy in their countries while stabbing it in the back in broad daylight in other countries. They cry in grief for the violated human rights in their countries while glorifying mass murderers in others, even raising them to the level of historic heroes. They appealed for the help of the international community to put an end to collective rape of Muslim women in Bosnia while still found it deplorable that the world rallied to help the Muslim women who were being raped in Darfur. These views are contradictory, hypocritical, and lacking in any moral appeal, and stand as one of the biggest obstacles to the possibility of enlarging the social base for reform.

One of the main weaknesses in the constitution of these elites is the frailty of the human rights component in the outlook of some of their sectors. This has led some of them to slide into embracing some forms of the governmental anti-human rights discourse, or to refuse to include in their platforms a number of vital human rights issues such as the issues of religious and ethnic minorities, women's rights, the freedoms of thought, beliefs, and literary and artistic creativity, which, in turn, has had a negative effect on their ability to widen their bases of social support. An interesting irony in this regard is the "Kefaya" movement in Egypt. This movement steered clear of including the legitimate and vital demands of the Copts in their platform. The choice of a Copt at its head (a development the likes of which Egypt has never known) did not succeed in bridging this gap or attracting the support of Copts.

The chronic failure of these elites to reach a consensual and creative solution for the issue of the relation between religion and state played an important role in making democracy seem in the view of some sections of these elites a danger no less menacing than the persistence of the current despotic regimes. More so even, given that democracy could actually bring the Islamists to power. An example of this is the position taken by sections of the leftist, secular, and liberal elites in Algeria, Tunisia, and Egypt (we can add the Copts as a group from the latter). They have come to fear the consequences of "democracy" more than those of the continuation of despotism.[28]

This pattern of contradictions and paradoxes has always made it possible for the ruling regimes to manipulate, politically and through security services, vital sections of these elites, in order to set them against each other to create a confidence gap between them. This lack of trust has made it impossible for them to forge a strategic consensus that is able to endure for even a short period of time. In fact, the ruling elite have always been able to form tactical short-term alliances with one section or another of the nonruling elite to go against the others.

Because of this weak stand on human rights, political and intellectual fragility, and political splintering, there has been no momentum toward democracy from within. Instead, there has only been romantic yearning for democracy expressed loudly and boisterously, yet without the willingness to offer the necessary price and sacrifice. It would be a mistake to reduce this to the individual readiness to sacrifice one's life or security; it is rather gauged as the willingness to pay the political price. That is, to sacrifice for the profound belief in the priority of reform any other local, regional, or international considerations, and exert the willingness to make mutual concessions between the nonruling elites in order to be able to form a viable and useful number in the political equations that would be able to break from the status quo, however limited, to cause a crack in the ruling elite's monopoly of power and wealth.

The young generation and their political organizations are fully aware of this. Their movements were formed outside the orbit of traditional political elites—indeed, in opposition to them—taking a critical, radical posture toward the traditional opposition parties from the outset, both in terms of their ideologies and their methods of action. Opposition parties themselves (in those countries where parties are permitted) also assumed a stance toward these groups early on, fluctuating between condescension and outright political hostility. In Egypt in particular, some opposition parties were more openly critical of youth groups than of the regime and its media. Nevertheless, it is a mistake to reduce this political conflict to a generational conflict. Youth groups were in agreement with and even maintained alliances with small parties that took a serious critical stance toward regimes. This same alliance was seen between these groups and human rights organizations.

Youth political groups successfully engendered a different political discourse, slogans capable of mobilizing and attracting the solidarity of a massive number of citizens, and methods of action that fully incorporated the advances of this era. These are the primary reasons they outmatched not only regimes, but also traditional opposition parties, including those with whom they have ideological affinities.

V   Democratic Transformation Process

The two most widely cited central features of human rights conditions in the Arab world before the 2011 revolutions were: (1) authoritarian systems shored up by strong security apparatuses that were unaccountable before the law, and (2) a fragile, distorted civil society with no room for advancement that systematically crushed emerging democratic tendencies over the long term. While the Tunisian and Egyptian people did succeed in removing regime heads and a great many of their supporters, this does not mean that the deeply rooted elements that fostered and entrenched a classic police state in both nations will be eliminated in the near future. The fact that neither "revolution" was based on well-established political movements or parties with deep roots in society raises questions about the current horizon for change. Are we moving toward a genuine democracy? Or will this end in merely a corrective "revolution," with the regime shedding its most corrupt leaders or those incapable of evolving, along with a few "extreme" practices that only served to increase the number of discontents across societies? For now, this remains an open question.

CONCLUSION

The spread of modernity and modernizing forces in a society is an important factor. It is likely to push a country toward the first possibility—that is, a gradual democratic transition. This seems more likely in Tunisia, particularly since the Tunisian army has no experience with politics and it will be some time before Islamists are able to recover their dynamism. Egypt, by contrast, may be headed toward the second possibility. Modern forces are weak there; the military establishment has been the main prop of the regime since July 1952, and organized Islamist groups alternate between support for democracy and human rights and a conservative, hard-lined, and hostile stance.

Moreover, the past 60-year history of Egypt indicates that Islamist groups possess an infinite readiness to make deals with regimes at the expense of basic democratic principles. To be sure, both countries may suffer a setback as the balance of power tips toward traditional forces and the nascent youth forces that carried out the "revolution" may prove unable to completely uproot their now impotent regimes to enable revolutionary forces to take power.

NOTES

1. Freedom House, "Freedom of the Press," 2009 annual report. http://www.freedomhouse.org/uploads/fop09/FoP2009_Regional_Rankings.pdf. Last accessed on 20 March 2011. See also Freedom House, "Freedom in the World 2010: Erosion of Freedom Intensifies," pp. 7–12. http://www.freedomhouse.org/uploads/fiw10/FIW_2010_Tables_and_Graphs.pdf. Last accessed on 21 March 2011.
2. "Bastion of Impunity, Mirage of Reform," Human Rights in the Arab World, 2009 annual report, Cairo Institute for Human Rights Studies, December 2009, pp. 36–46. http://www.cihrs.org/Images/ArticleFiles/Original/485.pdf. Last accessed on 21 March 2011.
3. "Overcoming Barriers: Human Mobility and Development," Human Development Report 2009, United Nations Development Programme (UNDP), 2009, pp. 213–217. http://hdr.undp.org/en/media/HDR_2009_EN_Complete.pdf. Last accessed on 2 March 2011.

4. Bahey eldin Hassan, "The Dilemma of Human Rights between a Lack of Political Will and the Emerging Forms of Resistance," in *From Exporting Terrorism to Exporting Repression*, the First Annual Report on the state of human rights in the Arab Region, Cairo Institute for Human Rights Studies, 2008, p. 22. http://www.cihrs.org/Images/ArticleFiles/Original/382.pdf. Last accessed on 23 March 2011.

5. The "second independence" is an expression used by some African movements calling for democracy in the late 1980s and the early 1990s. Afterwards, it was used by a Tunisian thinker as a title for one of his books on the significance of democracy in the Arab world. See "*The Second Independence: Towards an Initiative for Political Reform in the Arab World*," adopted by The First Civil Forum and organized by the Cairo Institute for Human Rights Studies (CIHRS) in Beirut, in cooperation with the Association for Defending Rights and Freedoms (ADL) and the Palestinian Human Rights Organization (Rights). (2004). http://www.cihrs.org/Images/ArticleFiles/Original/520.pdf. Last accessed on 25 March 2011.

6. Ibid.

7. For Egypt as an example, see Bahey eldin Hassan, "The Human Rights Dilemma in Egypt: Political Will or Islam?" in *Beitraege zum Islamischen Recht* [Contributions to Islamic Law] *Focusing on Human Rights and Islam*, ed. Hatem Elliesie. Bern, Berlin, Bruxelles, Frankfurt am Main, New York, Oxford, Wien: Peter Lang Publishing Group, 2010.

8. Political observers in Tunisia thought that Zein el-Abidin Ben Ali, who was elected to a fifth term in 2009, was preparing his son-in-law to succeed him, given the young age of his own four-year-old son. In Algeria, the president's brother is the main political candidate to succeed the ailing president Boutaflica.

9. As the revolutions of the two countries are uncompleted and there is ongoing internal struggle between the old and new forces, it is too early to make a concrete judgment at the moment of writing this chapter.

10. Report Summary: General State of Human Rights in the Arab Region, "Roots of Unrest," Human Rights in the Arab World, 2010 annual report, Cairo Institute for Human Rights Studies, March 2011.

11. Bahey eldin Hassan, "Political Civil War," in *A Nation without Citizens*, Cairo Institute for Human Rights Studies, 2007. http://www.cihrs.org/Arabic/NewsSystem/Articles/28.aspx. Last accessed on 23 March 2011.

12. Nabil Abdel-Fattah, "State, the Judiciary and Political Reform," in *Judges and Political Reform*, ed. Nabil Abdel-Fattah, Cairo Institute for Human Rights Studies, 2006, p. 15. http://www.cihrs.org/Arabic/NewsSystem/Articles/46.aspx.

13. Mahmoud Reda Khudayri, "How the Act No. 46 of 1972 Legalizes Attacking the Judicial Independence", in *Judges and Political Reform*, ed. Nabil Abdel-Fattah. Cairo Institute for Human Rights Studies, 2006. pp. 111–112.

14. Abdullah Khalil, "The Public Prosecution: An Attorney Acting for Society or a Subordinate to the Executive Authority?" in *Judges and Political Reform*, ed. Nabil Abdel-Fattah. Cairo Institute for Human

Rights Studies, 2006, pp. 45–46, 54–64. See also first Annual Report of the National Council for Human Rights 2004–2005, 2005, pp. 242. http://nchregypt.org/en/images/files/1st%20Annual%20Report.pdf. Last accessed on 23 March 2011.

15. Negad Bur'ai Bur'ai, "Justice Despised: The Government Does Not Comply with Judicial Rulings," in *Judges and Political Reform*, ed. Nabil Abdel-Fattah. Cairo Institute for Human Rights Studies, 2006, Motives and Results," *Judges, and Political Reform*, pp. 222–224.

16. For Egypt as an example, Kareem A'mer: Blogger; sentenced to four years in prison for defaming the President of Egypt and inciting hate to the Islamic religion. ("Bastion of Impunity, Mirage of Reform," p. 9.) Last accessed on 26 March 2011.

17. A Joint Report by the Coalition of Egyptian Human Rights Non-Governmental Organizations (NGOs) on the Universal Periodic Review (UPR) of Egypt. http://afteegypt.org/en/index.php?newsid=28. Last accessed on 26 March 2011.

18. See the report of the Egyptian Government to the United Nations, National report submitted in accordance with paragraph 15(a) of the annex to Human Rights Council resolution 5/1–"Egypt," 8–19 February 2009. See also comments by the Coalition of Egyptian Human Rights Non-Governmental Organizations (NGOs) on the Universal Periodic Review (UPR) of Egypt, "Human Rights in Egypt: A History of Oppression, Prevarication and Duplicity," Cairo Institute for Human Rights Studies, pp. 43–52.

19. For more details, see Universal Periodic Review–Egypt. http://www.ohchr.org/EN/HRBodies/UPR/PAGES/EGSession7.aspx. Last accessed on 27 March 2011.

20. "When the Oppressed Are Used as Shields: Women's Rights Up for Negotiation," *Bastion of Impunity, Mirage of Reform*, pp. 193–205.

21. Bahey eldin Hassan, "Political Civil War," in *Nation without Citizens*, pp. 7–10.

22. Tunisia Declaration of the 16th Arab Summit, May 22–23, 2004. http://www.arabsummit.tn/ar/declaration.htm. Last accessed on 26 March 2011.

23. Sana'a Declaration on Democracy, Human Rights and the Role of the International Criminal Court, January 10–12, 2004. http://www.pogar.org/publications/reforms/documents/sanaa-declaration04.pdf. Last accessed on 26 March 2011.

24. Alexandria Statement, "Arab Reform Issues: Vision and Implementation," March 13–14, 2004. http://www.pogar.org/themes/reforms/documents/alexandria.pdf. Last accessed on 26 March 2011.

25. See, for example, President Mubarak's speech at Arab Reform: Vision and Implementation, Alexandra Conference, March 2004. http://www.arabicnews.com/ansub/Daily/Day/040313/2004031330.html. Last accessed on 27 March 2011.

26. The author surmised that the Muslim Brothers' win of 20 percent of the seats in parliament was a plan hatched by the regime upon realizing "its overriding interest in having the group by its side—the most threatening

and only alternative left after all other alternatives had been crushed, the latest being presidential candidate Ayman Nour" (see Bahey eldin Hassan, "Political Civil War," p. 11). Yet, Mehdi Akef, the general guide of the Muslim Brothers during the 2005 parliamentary elections later revealed that this concession to the Muslim Brothers came as part of a deal with the regime. See Al Masry Al Youm, Interview with Mehdi Akef, October 24, 2009. http://www.almasry-alyoum.com/article2.aspx?ArticleID= 230596&IssueID=1568. Last accessed on 27 March 2011.

27. The cartoons were published in August of 2006 but the first popular protest took place in January 2007.

28. Bahey eldin Hassan,"Political Civil War," *A Nation without Citizens*, pp. 13–15.

CHAPTER 11

COUNTERTERRORISM, NATION-BUILDING, AND HUMAN RIGHTS IN THE MIDDLE EAST: COMPLEMENTARY OR COMPETING INTERESTS?

Mahmood Monshipouri and Shadi Mokhtari

Nation-building has been a steady and conspicuous feature of U.S. foreign policy since the end of World War II, but since 9/11, it has become directly linked to the so-called war on terror. While the language of nation-building has been embraced by some policymakers who view it as an effective measure to fight terrorism, it has by now become abundantly clear that the imposition of altering alien political and legal structures is a problematic process at best that may yield an undesirable outcome. This is especially true regarding countries that are unwilling to easily accept the whims of foreign governments as their own. There has emerged a fundamental question about whether nation-building has become the ideology and tool of dominant political players. Similarly, invoking the use of force in the name of democracy promotion has become just as controversial.

The United States faces a crisis of international legitimacy that is adversely affecting the successful outcome of its foreign policy. Promoting democracy and security interests can often be contradictory objectives. At the same time, wars generally come at tremendous human cost and can hardly be considered a foolproof method of producing democratic regimes. This is largely due to the simple fact that the logic of force and occupation runs counter to the process and tenor of democratization. For one, the logic of force is foreign and, at least at the outset, (often justifiably) treated as exogenous and suspect. For another, democratization should nominally manifest the will of the people within a given polity. For a foreign occupier to appreciate and take into account the tenor of the population, they must first pay some attention to the ambitions of the conquered population. As in Afghanistan and Iraq, the first goal of any broad political salience may be to remove the occupiers. The wisdom of military intervention and the promotion of democracy continue to be at odds.

Beyond the exigencies of "humanitarian intervention," and "the responsibility to protect," moral and ethical justifications for military intervention under the rubric of nation-building have fallen by the wayside. It may be the case that investing in nation-building and peace-building is an effective way to combat terrorism, but postconflict societies face a bewildering array of socioeconomic and political difficulties for which the military occupation cannot provide reliable solutions, and in fact may be the overt cause of many of these issues.

Since 2001, a plethora of political, ethical, and institutional challenges have complicated Washington's nation-building efforts, as has been painfully revealed by the U.S. military intervention and reconstruction of Afghanistan and Iraq. While the debate over counterterrorism measures remains unsettled, it is clear that efforts aimed at promoting sustainable methods of peaceful, democratic change have received more attention in the face of the 2011 Arab awakening in the Middle East and North Africa. The departure of Tunisia's and Egypt's long-ruling authoritarian presidents has exposed the long-term costs associated with supporting repressive yet pro-West regimes.

Some studies have shown that the means used to conduct the "global war on terrorism" threaten the core concept that they are supposedly defending liberal values. The pursuit of the global war on terrorism invariably generates profoundly difficult choices for societies espousing liberal values and identities. A choice must be made at the outset of the campaign between the approach to and the form of counterterrorism policies on the one hand, and the adherence to asserted values and practices of the liberal order on the other.[1] Many dilemmas arise out of the policy choices faced by liberal societies in responding to terrorism. The choice of insulation, repression, and the potential for creating egalitarian societies requires the fundamental compromising of liberal economic and political values. Can the United States defend its core values without resorting to the excesses and hysteria of securitization? Rethinking what is feasible and desirable in the Middle East has perpetually brought paradoxical and contradictory policies into the open. Despite the Arab revolts, U.S. foreign policy has followed the all-too-familiar and inconsistent pattern of supporting democratic change in one country (Egypt) while at the same time acquiescing to the status quo in another (Bahrain).

By invading Iraq on the pretext that the country's leaders had connections with al-Qaeda, followed by widespread prisoners abuses in Abu Ghraib and Guantanamo Bay, U.S. foreign-policy makers came face to face with the contradictions inherent in the asserted task of promoting democracy, security, and stability in the region. This chapter begins with an attempt to lay bare constraints and dilemmas of the Bush Doctrine. Its purpose is twofold: (1) to examine the ways in which counterterrorism measures undermine democracy promotion in the Middle East and North Africa; (2) to explain why military intervention and occupation are unjustifiable and ill-conceived methods of confronting terrorism and militancy in the region. U.S. foreign-policy makers must develop a better understanding of the nature of regional aspirations for peaceful, democratic change if they intend to play any constructive role in future events there. Except for cases of clear humanitarian motives like that of Libya, the United States must focus on enhancing basic rights rather than engaging in military incursions.

U.S. FOREIGN POLICY: TRADE-OFFS AND PARADOXES

Since the second half of the twentieth century, U.S. foreign policy toward the Middle East has centered on protecting the oil flow from the area, supporting Israel and the region's pro-Western governments, and maintaining political stability. Today, this list has been expanded to include other objectives such as combating terrorism, brokering a truce between the Palestinians and Israelis, as well as preventing the spread of nuclear weapons.

At present, the Middle East is home to some of the most repressive regimes, an oppressive Israeli occupation, religious persecution and intolerance, human rights abuses, economic disparities, unelected governments, and corrupt regimes. The Arab defeat in the wars with Israel and the failure of parliamentary democracy to make ruling elites and the military electorally accountable have precipitated a deepening sense of crisis in many Middle Eastern societies, playing an important role in prompting the resurgence of political Islam by the late 1970s.[2] The resurgence of Islam has come to be seen as a potent backlash against the failure of secular states and secular ideologies such as liberal nationalism and Arab socialism, and against secular processes and institutions.

Following the Soviet withdrawal from Afghanistan in 1988, the United States abandoned its support for the war-torn country. During the 1990s, the United States had no reconstruction program for post-Soviet Afghanistan. As a result, chaos and poverty prevailed throughout the country, providing a fertile ground for the Taliban to rule.[3] In the midst of Cold War thinking, the pretense for occupation was confronting and deterring communism; in the post–Cold War era, that fixation has been replaced with the Islamic threat. In the aftermath of the terrorist attacks of September 11, law enforcement's scrutiny of Muslims in America has in many ways rendered the war against terrorism as a war against Muslim populations. The U.S. foreign-policy makers have warned against such proverbial fault lines, as they have shifted their focus to the threats posed by radical Islamic movements. In the wake of this tragedy, two central questions arise: (1) how can global terrorism be explained? And (2) what is the best way to prevent global terrorism and ultimately eradicate it? In the sections that follow, we will attempt to explain how U.S. foreign policy is in disarray, in its attempt to balance its hegemonic and espoused ethical components in the age of terror.

WHY DID THE BUSH DOCTRINE FAIL?

A new doctrine of preemption, manifested in the invasion of Iraq, marked a drastic departure from the conventional U.S. foreign policy employed since the end of World War II—that is, containment and deterrence. This doctrine, generally known as "preemptive or anticipatory self-defense," was premised on a willingness to act unilaterally when/if necessary as well as an overriding sense that peace and stability require the United States to assert its primacy in world politics.[4]

The doctrinal basis for a new American unilateralism was intent on undermining the postwar consensus. The doctrine had two related parts: the unfettered use of American power abroad coupled with a radical exemptionalism of the United States from the international normative order and institutions.[5] Many experts did not support the idea of preemption. Most international lawyers argued that preemptive or anticipatory self-defense, if it was to be legitimized, must be strictly limited to cases involving an obvious and imminent attack that cannot be otherwise averted. Richard Falk argued that there was no plausible threat directed at the United States and no link to the al-Qaeda organization. Arguing that there was no factual plausibility based on imminence and necessity, Falk asserted that the war in Iraq violated international law, the UN Charter, and the moral and religious guidelines contained in the just war doctrine.[6] In sum, the Bush administration failed to show that Iraq had both the capability of harming the United States and a serious intent to do so. The abstract logical possibility that Saddam Hussein could have transferred weapons of mass destruction to stateless terrorists was not enough.[7]

Until the recent wave of uprisings in the region, feelings of impotence, humiliation, and frustration continue to pervade much of the Middle East, especially after the invasion and occupation of Iraq. This has been complicated by the region's authoritarian governments that practice widespread repression and give people little opportunity to participate in their own governance. The oft-repeated general point is that terrorism springs up in an atmosphere where opportunities for democratic participation are lacking and there is a broad sense of international and internal injustice. Countering terrorism entails attenuating the rage that it fuels, and hence the argument for democratic transformation of these societies.[8]

The Bush administration decided to support nation-building and democracy-promotion efforts in a region that has a dismal human rights record in the name of both fighting terrorism and pushing forth an American crafted "Freedom Agenda."[9] With almost 350 million people, the Arab states of the Middle East and North Africa included, prior to the 2011 Arab revolts, no "free" country. Free elections are not allowed in most of the Arab world. The region's nondemocratic regimes have proven to be shaky in the face of the 2011 Arab revolts. Some of these states have survived through dependency on either oil or security rents for their revenues and can thus be termed rentier states (Algeria, Bahrain, Iraq, Kuwait, Libya, Oman, Qatar, Saudi Arabia, Tunisia, and the United Arab Emirates). Others have relied on foreign aid (Egypt, Jordan, and Yemen). Clearly, oil revenues have had "an incredibly corrupting influence," rendering these states less accountable to public pressure and demands.[10]

An increasing body of evidence points to governance failures among the rentier states. These states are in fact the least advanced in observing civil liberties and political rights. Their citizens are among the least able—when compared to other transitional states of the former Soviet Union and Eastern Europe—to participate in the selection of their governments. Their media are not independent. Limited successes are largely confined to the rule of law and, to a lesser extent, control of corruption.[11] Although these countries control about half of the world's oil reserves, the region has higher unemployment and poverty than much of developing countries. Unemployment averages 15 percent and one out of five people live on less than $2 per day.[12]

The utilization of Arab women's capabilities through political and economic participation remains the lowest in the world as evidenced by the very low proportion of women in government both at the ministerial level and the number of seats in parliament held by women. Gender inequality in education and economic activity is widespread throughout the Middle East. It should be noted, however, that Arab countries have made great strides in girls' education. Female literacy rates have increased threefold since 1970, and female primary and secondary enrollment rates have more than doubled. Despite this progress, female enrollment rates are still lower than those for males.[13]

Moreover, Arab women remain marginalized and underutilized in all sectors of the economy and society, notably in terms of their economic, intellectual, and leadership potential.[14] Of the 25 percent of the unemployed, 82 percent are women. They are the most likely to be deprived of access to health and educational services because of financial pressures on families.[15] It is significant also to underscore the importance of the Middle Eastern region and why it figures prominently in the strategic calculation of the United States, the European Union (EU), and East Asia. The Persian Gulf region and the Caspian Basin together have by far the world's largest reserves of oil and natural gas. Since reliable access to reasonably priced energy is vitally significant to global powers, Zbigniew Brzezinski saw "strategic domination over the area, even if cloaked by cooperative arrangements" as "a globally decisive hegemonic asset."[16]

INDIGENOUS DEMOCRATIC TRANSITIONS: A NEW ERA FOR THE REGION AND U.S. FOREIGN POLICY?

The recent uprisings in North Africa and the Middle East constitute one of the most important global political developments since the fall of the Berlin Wall. These popular uprisings after decades of repression have shaken the Arab world and have the potential to drastically shape the politics of the region. While these uprisings, as Andrew J. Bacevich notes, have demonstrated that the people of the Middle East and North Africa have "an organic capacity to engineer change themselves,"[17] it is too early to know how far they will go in introducing fundamental changes in political structures and processes. Despite this uncertainty, the emergence of a new era for both the region and U.S. foreign policy in the Middle East is virtually undeniable.

Far from being called a social movement at this stage, these uprisings are largely street protests emblematic of frustration spontaneously fueled by failed economic and political systems. This moment in history is about the Arab street and the Arab world, which have become much more crowded and far more destitute than years past. Our analytical gaze thus must be focused on the causes of economic frustration and resentments toward Arab governments. One of the most inspiring characteristics of these uprisings has been the peaceful nature of their demand for democratic change that stands in stark contrast to the violent terrorist inclinations imagined by many in the United States.

The history of peaceful democratic change since the opening of the Berlin Wall points to mixed results. Experts have held that democratic changes can and must be initiated by civil society "from below" (as in the cases of Poland, Hungary, and former Czechoslovakia), or initiated by the state "from above" (as in the case of Argentina, Brazil, Uruguay, Chile, and Turkey since 1983). In some countries, internal bargaining, which involves a long-drawn-out process of give-and-take between competing political groups, has proven effective. The examples of the Philippines, Nicaragua, Mexico, Lebanon, and Iran fit this model of democratic transition. Clearly, we need to look at factors other than religion to fully comprehend the eruption of these uprisings.

It is important to examine the resurgence of multiple new, shifting identities among the youth of the Middle East and North Africa (MENA) as key contributions to the reconstruction of broader societal identities, as well as new demands on governments. Since the 1980s, young Muslims have struggled to come to grips with the massive changes in world politics—changes associated with globalization and the so-called third wave of democratization across Europe, Asia, and Latin America. Witnessing these movements, the Muslim youth have tried to find a way to reconcile their interests and values with modern moral orders and legal principles that are based on accountability, transparency, and participatory politics. Islamic feminists and secular feminists have also reasserted their identities and interests, as they have become further concerned with being in control of their own lifestyles as well as politics. Increasingly, youth and their organizations have insisted on a human rights framework that is both legally guaranteed and morally acceptable.

The Muslim world's social realities have resulted in a rising and vibrant forum for positive change. A combination of youth, readily accessible technology, and economic and political grievances has led to the emergence of a young and educated generation who could potentially cause further social turmoil and political instability. Some factors that contributed to the Tunisian uprisings—such as high unemployment rates, high prices of food, falling real wages, and police brutality—are widespread in the region, from oil-rich Libya to impoverished Yemen. On balance, however, Tunisians are better educated and more urbanized than their neighbors. With 7.2 percent of their GDP spent on education, Tunisians are steadily ranked among the most modernized countries in the Middle East and North Africa.[18] Ironically, but understandably, the question persists: Why did the revolution occur in Tunisia? While it is too early to authoritatively answer this question, it is clear that the answer is not because it took inspiration from American nation-building efforts in Iraq. The new Iraq, which was supposed to be a model for the transformation of political landscape in the Middle East, has proven to be a failure.

In fact, the role of outside powers that prefer stability over the uncertainty of democratization generally has had the opposite effect, serving as a barrier to political liberalization. In many situations, allied leaders' political survival trumps human rights. Leaders are typically caught between popular identity and structural constraints associated with external forces, making trade-offs among democracy promotion and other strategic goals. Concerned with stability over all else, U.S. foreign-policy makers have historically prioritized order above democracy and the realization of human rights. Convinced that the great nemesis of democracy is disorder, they have argued that forcing rapid political change in the Middle East would be difficult because it challenges entrenched power. While the Bush administration learned, however grudgingly, that democracy at gunpoint was unlikely to unleash a tsunami of democratic values throughout the Middle Eastern region, the real question that remains is for the Obama administration: Will the United States follow the lead of Arab youth and make support for indigenous democratization efforts a credible pillar of U.S. foreign policy for years to come?

U.S. HEGEMONY AND DEMOCRACY

Following U.S. interventions in Afghanistan and Iraq, many observers have raised the issue of whether U.S. actions taken in the name of the "war on terrorism" are indeed wars for empire. Although the Unites States quite arguably had a legitimate claim for self-defense in attacking al-Qaeda infrastructure in Afghanistan, the invasion of Iraq was more reminiscent of *imperium*.[19] Further it has been argued that U.S. interventions have never lived up to their pronounced intentions and that the politics of humanitarianism have rendered relief agencies and other NGOs subordinate to state interests and power in Kosovo, Afghanistan, and Iraq.[20] Key lessons that can be drawn from the United States' recent interventions in the Middle East include the premise that fighting terrorism, advancing hegemony, and promoting democracy are generally neither consistent nor morally justifiable. In the new era punctuated by recent Arab uprisings, it is no longer possible to rule over empires, as was historically the case, with absolute control and domination.

Appraising the role that youth spike played in 2011 uprisings in the Middle East and North Africa, one observer argues—regardless of ideological struggles—these rebellions were and to a significant degree are about jobs and the fact remains that youth without job equals social instability. U.S. foreign-policy priorities must, therefore, be accorded to supporting real economic development that stabilizes volatile states and enables democratic freedoms. Since countries with demographic youth bulge and no economic growth are becoming increasingly ungovernable, one of the most effective ways to minimize future global security risks is to target self-sustaining economic development on the ground, not laser-guided bombs from the air.[21]

The far more complicated question here is whether the United States is willing to forgo simultaneously pursuing goals of combating terrorism and promoting democracy. "No American government," Robert Jervis notes, "has been willing to sacrifice stability in order to further democracy in countries such as Algeria, Egypt, Saudi Arabia, and Pakistan, and at some point [President] Bush is likely to make the same choice."[22]

The Iraqi regime was advertised as a way to bring democracy and stability to the Middle East, discourage tyrants and energize reformers throughout the world, and demonstrate the American willingness to provide a high degree of what it considers world order, whether others like it or not, then, as part of a larger project.[23] The reality is that democracies in the Middle East will likely challenge U.S. policies (and what are understood in Washington as strategic interests) at key junctures, but the ability and self-determination to do this is precisely what may render the United States safer from terrorist attacks. This is because the wave of democratic and rights-based aspirations seizing the Middle East serves to marginalize and draw out terrorist or radical Islamist ideologies.

The fact remains that in the key Arab states of Jordan, Egypt, and Saudi Arabia, cooperation with the United States could not be sustained if the public had greater influence. Pointing to a key internal tension, Jervis elsewhere writes that "the Bush doctrine combines a war on terrorism with the strong assertion of American hegemony."[24] Protection from terror and asserting hegemony, Jervis continues, are contradictory goals. To reduce terror, the United States should seek a reduced role in world politics.

Despite considerable U.S. support to the Pakistani military, some experts observe, Washington holds relatively little leverage to influence events in Pakistan. Since 2001, the United States has given Pakistan more than $10 billion in assistance, channeled largely through the Pakistani military. And yet, the United States "has not made the necessary commitment to solidify the relationship for the long term."[25] Less than 10 percent of U.S. assistance goes toward development and humanitarian purposes. Only $64 million per year is earmarked for education of more than 55 million school-aged children. This amounts to $1.16 per child per year.[26] U.S. assistance has been the least concerned with the long-term domestic stability of the country. The seemingly unconditional nature of U.S. budget aid in the case of Pakistan demonstrates that economic goals have been largely subservient to broader U.S. political and military objectives.[27]

OUTSOURCING TORTURE AND PRIVATIZING WAR

A contemporary discussion of nation-building, human rights, and terrorism would not be complete without some mention of the human rights crisis presented by the post-9/11 era. During this era, grave human rights violations have been committed in the name of democracy promotion, human rights, and fighting terrorism. The Bush administration's war on terrorism has had a twofold effect. First, it has threatened the realm of civil rights, due process, and the right to privacy within the United States.

Second and perhaps more relevant to the current discussion, it has led to mass detentions, the use of military tribunals, and the use of torture. In the areas of investigation and prosecution, the federal government engaged in widespread practices that ran counter to liberal democratic values underlying the American political and judicial processes. Such acts were in clear violation of the civil rights and freedoms of noncitizens. These included, but were not limited to, applying extended detentions and interrogations, adopting expanded surveillance powers and tools, instituting financial strictures and rewards, altering the judicial system, and requiring greater information-sharing between agencies.[28] Along the same lines, shortly after September 11, 2001, the U.S. Congress adopted Public Law 107–56: "Uniting and Strengthening America by Providing Appropriate Tools Required to Intercept and Obstruct Terrorism," also known as the USA Patriot Act of 2001.

Extended detention and questioning interrupted due process of law, as many suspects were held incommunicado. Additionally, a Bureau of Prisoners (BOP) regulation authorized the BOP and the Department of Justice (DOJ) to monitor communications between the suspects and their attorneys. The application of this practice in certain cases amounted to harassment of an ethnic minority. By January 2002, of the more than 1,200 detainees, only a few were considered material witnesses, with others held on minor immigration violations. This amounted to a clear violation of equal protection under the law and a discriminatory practice based on religion and ethnicity.[29]

What made the issue of detainees particularly alarming was that the two options available to them were: (1) hold them indefinitely or (2) subject them to a military tribunal in which secret evidence and evidence obtained through coercive means such as torture could be used against them. The detainment camps at Guantanamo Bay have drawn strong criticism both inside and outside of the United States for detainment of prisoners without trial and widespread allegations of torture. The detainees held by the United States Army have been classified as "enemy combatants," who are not entitled to the protections of the Geneva Conventions. Some are subject to the practice of indefinite detention, others exposed to the flagrant and widespread abuse of their religious beliefs, including flushing the Qur'an down the toilet. Many detainees have filed petitions that the conditions under which they are being held are inhumane. The pervasive pattern and practice of abuse point to direct connections with official policies of the government.

The U.S. government argues that trial review of detainees has never been afforded to prisoners of war, and that it is reasonable for "enemy combatants" to be detained until the cessation of hostilities. Critics argue that the detainees' status as a potential or active terrorist have not been defined in any ratified treaties. The Bush administration has considered al-Qaeda and Taliban fighters as "unlawful enemy combatant"—not uniformed soldiers of a recognized government—and thus not deserving of being treated as soldiers. On June 29, 2006, the U.S. Supreme Court ruled against such an interpretation.

What is more, the growing security culture has overshadowed the human rights culture, bringing the United States in closer cooperation with the governments in China, Egypt, Pakistan, Russia, and Saudi Arabia, governments that are engaged in widespread and systematic repressive measures against their own populace. These countries have used the threat of global terrorism to weaken the fragile edifice of human rights law.[30] In many respects, the war against terrorism brought to light the myth of American human rights exceptionalism. The Bush administration, under the guise of counterterrorism, violated human rights by abusing prisoners as a matter of policy, by disappearing detainees into a network of secret prisons, and by abducting and sending suspects to be interrogated in countries that practice torture, such as Egypt, Syria, and Morocco. This outsourcing of torture, military detention, and security and intelligence operations has fueled serious human rights abuses across the globe.[31]

Amnesty International has found that more than 25 American companies may have transported men detained by the U.S. government to nations with a troubling record on human rights. These companies, too, may be complicit in the U.S. government's practice of outsourcing torture.[32] Similarly, the privatization of war by such companies as Blackwater USA (now known as Xe Services LLC) has fostered the growth and creation of other private companies who have benefited and stand to gain even further from an escalation of war.[33] This war contracting system has so invariably linked corporate profits to an escalation of war that these companies have no incentive to curtail their footprint in the war zone and every incentive to fuel it.

As such, the war outsourcing has facilitated impunity for private contractors and has undermined what remains of U.S. moral authority abroad. Consequently, many concerns have been raised about how to subject these private war contractors to transparency, accountability, and the rule of law. Private security companies have pressed the government to take over even more duties that are normally carried out by American soldiers.[34] According to the U.S. Department of Labor, at least 770 contractors had been killed in Iraq as of December 2006 along with at least 7,700 wounded. These casualties are not included in the official death toll that the U.S. government releases, helping to mask the human costs of the Iraqi war. More disturbing, however, is what this means for

U.S. democracy: the widespread use of private forces apparently accountable to no effective system of oversight or law.[35]

War outsourcing has created the corporate equivalent of Guantanamo Bay—a virtual rules-free zone in which perpetrators are unlikely to be held accountable for breaking the law. The U.S. criticisms of the governments of Uzbekistan, Colombia, and Russia for systematic human rights violations have been significantly muted. In the name of antiterrorism, counterinsurgency, or national security, private contractors, governments, and other perpetrators appear to have evaded the law. On June 29, 2006, the U.S. Supreme Court struck down the military commissions at the U.S. Naval Base at Guantanamo Bay, affirming the protections of common Article Three of the Geneva Conventions that ensures fair trial standards, and also prohibiting torture and other inhumane treatment. The Obama administration has also demonstrated concern that pursuing claims involving foreign government's human rights issues can potentially constrain the "war on terrorism."

CONCLUSION

The view that nation-building can be undertaken by military intervention and that it must be seen as a bulwark against terrorism has proven both untenable and costly. The advocates of the so-called war on terror have placed the commitment to human rights on the backburner, claiming that the strict observation of human rights is imprudent, given competing security interests. It has also become extremely difficult to set priorities and make sensible accommodations when faced with strategic choices, such as cutting foreign aid to Pakistan or continuing nation-building efforts in Afghanistan. It is safe to argue that U.S. policymakers are clueless as to how to pursue multiple, contradictory goals in the Middle East. The practical implications of a democracy-based approach to foreign policy are varied and many. Although there are palpable tensions between democratic changes and strategic considerations, it is clear that the old bargain with Arab autocracies has utterly failed since the 2011 Arab revolts. While some in Washington may regard the price of democratic transformation in the Middle East as substantial, the cost of preserving the status quo is tragically even greater in the long run.

Under such circumstances, the call for nation-building has come under closer scrutiny. The invasion of Iraq has exposed the flaws of the transformative tasks of the Bush administration, including the policies of preemptive strike and forcible regime change. The democracy promotion agenda has undermined the rule-bound international order of the post–Cold War era. A broad consensus holds that democratization is a complicated and difficult process that would illicit numerous uncertain consequences. In order for change to be sustainable, the pace of democratic transformation must be gradual, systematic, and directly linked to indigenous movements. Pressure for a higher standard of respect for basic human rights—including the rights of women, minorities, and children—in these countries must be pursued judiciously. There is now a rare opportunity for the United States to follow the lead of the people of the Middle East and North Africa who are directly involved in the looming battle for their freedom.

NOTES

1. Barry Buzan, "Will the 'Global War on Terrorism' be the New Cold War?" *International Relations*, Vol. 82, No. 6, November 2006, pp. 1101–1118; see especially 1115–1116.
2. John L. Esposito, *The Islamic Threat: Myth or Reality?* Third Edition, New York: Oxford University Press, 1999, p. 73.
3. For a stimulating analysis of U.S. foreign policy, see the opinions expressed by Melani McAlister, Stephen Baker, and Richard Ebeling in *Searching for Foreign Policy Lessons*, ed. Josh Burek, http://www. csmonitor.com, September 25, 2001. Last accessed on March 18, 2001.
4. Robert Jervis, "Understanding the Bush Doctrine," *Political Science Quarterly*, Vol. 118, No. 3, Fall 2003, pp. 551–583; see p. 551.
5. John Gerard Ruggie, "Doctrinal Unilateralism and Its Limits: American and Global Governance in the New Century," in *American Foreign Policy in a Globalized World*, ed. David P. Forsythe, Patrice C. McMahon, Andrew Wedeman, New York: Routledge, 2006, pp. 31–50; see p. 39.
6. Richard Falk, "War Prevention and the UN," *Counterpunch*, July 2, 2003, available at http://www.counterpunch.org/falk07022003 html. Last accessed on May 16, 2007.
7. Ibid.
8. Henry Munson, "Lifting the Veil: Understanding the Roots of Islamic Militancy," in *World Politics*, Annual Editions, Twenty-sixth Edition, ed. Helen E. Purkitt, Dubuque, IA: McGraw-Hill/Dushkin, 2006, pp. 179–181.
9. For a detailed discussion of this issue, see Mahmood Monshipouri, "The Bush Doctrine and Democracy Promotion in the Middle East," in *American Foreign Policy in a Globalized World*, ed. David P. Forsythe, Patrice C. McMahon, and Andrew Wedeman, New York: Routledge, 2006, pp. 313–334.
10. Stephen Krasner, director of the Center on Democracy, Development and the Rule of Law at Stanford University's Institute of International Studies, Palo Alto, California is quoted in Kenneth Jost and Benton Ives-Halperin, "Democracy in the Arab World," in The CQ Researchers, *Global Issues*, 2005 Edition, Washington, D.C.: CQ Press, 2005, pp. 181–206; see especially p. 187.

11. Robert Looney, "The Broader Middle East Initiative: Requirements for Success in the Gulf," *Strategic Insights*, Vol. III, No. 8, August 2004, pp. 1–11; see especially p. 7. Available at http://www. ccc.nps.navy.mil/ si/index.asp. Last accessed on June 7, 2005.

12. The CQ Research, *Global Issues*, 2005 Edition, Washington, D.C.: CQ Press, 2005, pp. 181–206; see especially p. 187.

13. The United Nations Development Programme, *The Arab Human Development Report 2002: Creating Opportunities for Future Generations*, NY: UNDP, 2002, p. 52. Also see UNDP, *Human Development Report 2004: Cultural Liberty in Today's Diverse World*, New York: UNDP, 2004; see especially pp. 225–237.

14. Ibid., p. 98.

15. See the report by the Canadian International Development Agency (CIDA), "Support to Gender Equality in the Middle East Region: Jordan, Lebanon, West Bank and Gaza, and Yemen," available at http://www. acdicida.gc.ca/cidaweb/webcountry.nsf/VLUDocEn/NorthAfrican andMiddleEast. Last accessed on June 6, 2005.

16. Zbigniew Brzezinski, "Hegemonic Quicksand," *The National Interest*, Vol. 74, Winter 2003–2004, pp. 5–16; see especially p. 13.

17. Andrew J. Bacevich, "Last Act in the Middle East," *Newsweek*, April 11, 2011, pp. 48–49; see especially p. 49.

18. Kristen Chick, "Why Tunisia? Why Now?" *The Christian Science Monitor*, January 31, 2011, pp. 8–10; see especially p. 10.

19. Peter J. Hoffman and Thomas G. Weiss, *Sword and Salve: Confronting New Wars and Humanitarian Crises*, Boulder, CO: Rowman & Littlefield Publishers, 2006, p. 158.

20. Ibid., p. 159.

21. Mark Lange, "Libya's Sharp Lesson for America's Foreign Priorities," *The Christian Science Monitor*, May 9, 2011, p. 34.

22. Robert Jervis, *American Foreign Policy in a New Era*, 2004: p. 84.

23. Ibid., p. 99.

24. Robert Jervis, *Political Science Quarterly*, 2005, p. 352.

25. Ibid., p. 9.

26. Ibid., p. 12.

27. Ibid., p. 14.

28. Laura K. Donohue, "Fear Itself: Counterterrorism, Individual Rights, and U.S. Foreign Relations Post 9–11," in *Terrorism and Counterterrorism: Understanding the New Security Environment, Readings and Interpretations*, ed. Russell D. Howard and Reid L. Sawyer, Guilford, CT: McGraw-Hill/Dushkin, 2002, pp. 313–338; see p. 319.

29. Ibid., p. 323.

30. Stephen J. Toope, "Human Rights and the Use of Force after September 11, 2001," in *Terror, Culture, and Politics: Rethinking 9/11*, ed. Daniel J. Sherman and Terry Nardin, Bloomington, IN: Indiana University Press, 2006, pp. 237–258; see p. 241.

31. See Annual Report of Amnesty International, Statement of Larry Cox, Executive Director, Amnesty International USA, May 23, 2006, available

at http://www.amnestyusa.org/annualreport/2006/statement.html. Last accessed on April 7, 2007.

32. Ibid.
33. Jeremy Scahill, "Outsourcing the War," *Nation*, available at http:/// www.thenation.com/doc/20070528/scahill. Posted on May 11, 2007.
34. Ibid.
35. Ibid.

British take Ottoman Emp.

Early Zionism - Secular non religious
- mostly culturally, homeland, Safety.
Bolshevik

·Nature' Karta

Amir Fayzal (King of
              Hejaz)

Changing religious/political ideas of migrant workers,
used as leverage, creating social crises upon
massive return.

CHAPTER 12

MIGRANT WORKERS AND THEIR RIGHTS IN THE UNITED ARAB EMIRATES

Mahmood Monshipouri and Ali Assareh

Migrant workers have lived in the Arabian Peninsula for more than two centuries. Starting in the 1970s, however, the dynamics of migration flows to the Persian Gulf region took a new twist with the rise in oil prices and the development boom in the region's newly independent countries. These changing dynamics were most notable in the United Arab Emirates (UAE).[1] In 1968, the population of the UAE was 180,000, of which two-thirds were nationals and one-third migrants.[2] By 2005, the UAE's population had risen to 4.1 million, of which about 80 percent were migrants.[3] The changing dynamics of migration flows to the region have triggered a debate over labor conditions and practices that violate the rights of migrant workers and subject them to modern day exploitation and abuse.

Three sets of problems facing migrant workers have become the subject of global media attention in recent years. The first set of problems relates to workplace conditions and the living environment of migrant workers. Problems of this sort include failure to pay workers' wages regularly and in a timely manner, and the prevalence of unsuitable working and living conditions, most notably unsanitary and poor safety conditions. The second set of problems is gender-related. The prevalence of sexual abuse among female migrant workers has become a major cause for concern, especially because the UAE Labor Law of 1980 or the Draft Labor Law of 2007 does not cover domestic maids or servants.[4] The third set of problems relates to the ability of workers to organize and demand the protection of their rights. In the UAE, workers are not allowed to protest, and those who do are typically punished in a harsh manner.[5] The UAE government has not allowed for trade unions to form despite its promise to do so in the past.[6] These problems are further compounded by global migration trends, which contain paradoxes and ambiguities related to underenforcement of laws and vagaries of the global market.

Some NGOs, such as the HRW, have recommended that the UAE establish an independent commission to publicly report on the condition of migrant workers, prohibit companies from doing business with exploitative recruitment agencies, aggressively investigate and prosecute employers that violate the UAE labor law, institute a minimum wage as mandated by existing UAE law, and permit the operation of independent human rights and workers rights organizations.[7] Despite recent improvements, deep structural and enforcement problems perpetuate the abuse of migrant workers' rights in the UAE. The existing networks of employment and recruitment networks for migrant workers are structured in a way that facilitates the abuse of the fundamental rights of migrant workers. Furthermore, there exists no powerful executive agency in the UAE to monitor or secure the rights of workers. The UAE government must assume a more active role in addressing a variety of serious structural and enforcement problems that often lead to substandard and undignified living conditions of migrant workers.

MIGRANT WORKERS DEFINED

Article 2 of the Convention on Migrant Workers (CMW) defines a "migrant worker" as "a person who is to be engaged, is engaged or has been engaged in a remunerated activity in a State of which he or she is not a national."[8] Although Article 5 of the CMW makes a distinction between documented and undocumented migrant workers, the distinction has been criticized in practice as "arbitrary," since "being documented does not afford an immigrant worker substantially more rights than undocumented workers."[9] The abuse of migrant workers' rights often is a problem of lackluster enforcement of existing legal protections. This is certainly the case in the UAE, where most migrant workers are documented, having entered the country through the recruitment network discussed in detail in Part V. The UAE, one commentator notes, "represents not only the document-independence of the workers' abuses, but also the irrelevance of having migrated legally."[10]

Under international human rights law and norms, migrant workers are entitled to certain economic, political, social and residence rights, although individual compacts afford them these rights to varying degrees. For example, several or all of the provisions of the Universal Declaration of Human Rights (UDHR), the International Convention of Civil and Political Rights (ICCPR), and the International Convention on the Elimination of All Forms of Racial Discrimination (ICERD) have been interpreted to be applicable to migrant workers. The International Covenant on Economic, Social and Cultural Rights (ICESCR), by comparison, affords less protection to migrant workers than the UDHR and the ICCPR.[11] Additionally, several regional compacts such as the European Convention for the Protection of Human Rights and Fundamental Freedoms and the American Convention on Human Rights protect the right of migrant workers. No such compacts, however, govern migrant workers' rights in the Persian Gulf.[12]

According to the United Nations' estimates, one out of every thirty-five people is a migrant worker, and approximately 175 million people work in a country other than their own.[13] In sharp contrast to previous eras, women now comprise approximately half of the global migrant population.[14] Although some observers expected massive returns of migrant workers to their countries of origin shortly after the emergence of the 2008 financial crisis, a 2009 study by the International Labor Organization (ILO) found that "to date, no mass returns of migrant workers have been observed."[15]

MIGRANT WORKERS IN THE UAE

The Persian Gulf region has a long history of hosting migrant labors through its association with international trade routes across the Indian Ocean, as well as economic activities connected with the annual Hajj pilgrimage.[16] The modern era of labor migration to the region, however, began with the discovery and production of oil in the region. In 1933, Bahrain became the first of the Persian Gulf states to successfully produce oil.[17] Saudi Arabia, Kuwait, and Qatar soon followed suit, with Abu Dhabi starting oil production later, in 1962. As oil production required high numbers of skilled and unskilled workers, both of which were scarce in the tiny kingdoms of the Persian Gulf, migrant workers from Iran, India, Pakistan and other Arab countries poured into the region.[18] The oil price explosion of the 1970s triggered an even more massive wave of labor migration to the Persian Gulf states. The migration trend was closely tied to the oil price boom in two important ways. On the one hand, it vastly increased the demand for labor in oil exporting countries, while on the other, it prompted countries with excess labor supply to provide every incentive to offset the crippling rise in oil import costs by encouraging their citizens to work abroad and remit as large a proportion of their wages as possible.[19]

In the UAE, the influx of migrant workers was further catalyzed by the country's emergence as a modern financial and economic powerhouse in the 1980s and 1990s. Successful efforts at economic diversification led to the rapid growth of non-oil economic sectors. In 1975, oil production accounted for more than two-thirds of the UAE's gross domestic product (GDP).[20] Today, oil and gas output comprises only a quarter of the UAE's GDP.[21] The decline in the share of oil in the UAE's GDP is largely attributable to the rapid growth of other economic sectors, such as real estate, manufacturing, and tourism. As these economic sectors involve labor-intensive activities, the UAE's demand for migrant workers has only increased over time. In fact, over the past five decades, the infusion of migrant labor into the UAE society has completely changed the face of the country. In 1968, the UAE's population stood at 180,425, of whom 63.5 percent were nationals and 36.5 percent were expatriates. Today, with its population reaching 5 million, migrants make up about 80 percent of the population and 95 percent of the private work force.[22] Table 12.1 reflects the massive infusion of migrant workers into the UAE society over the past five decades.

The size, characteristics, and nature of this massive migrant worker population have invited questions about not only the employment opportunities of migrant workers but also their rights. As a result, the labor laws of the UAE have come under closer scrutiny in recent years, especially after the release of the HRW's seminal 2006 report documenting widespread human rights abuses in the UAE in meticulous detail.[23] Largely in response to the international criticism generated from that report, the UAE Prime Minister, Sheikh Mohammad bin Rashid al Maktoum, ordered the minister of labor to enforce the country's labor laws by instituting a series of reforms based on the report's recommendations.[24] Recent reforms, however, have largely failed to bring about meaningful changes to the lives of millions of migrant workers currently residing in the UAE.

Table 12.1 Population of the United Arab Emirates[i]

Year	Total population	Nationals	%	Expatriates	%
1968	180,425	114,607	63.5	65,818	36.5
1975	557,887	201,544	36.1	356,343	63.9
1980	1,042,099	290,544	27.9	751,555	72.1
1985	1,379,303	396,114	28.7	983,189	71.3
1995	2,411,041	587,330	24.4	1,823,711	75.6
2005	4,104,695	824,921	20.1	3,279,774	79.9

[i] *Source*: Rima Sabban, "Migrant Women in the Untied Arab Emirates: The case of female domestic workers," GENPROM Working Paper No. 10; UAE Ministry of Economy, Economic & Statistics Reports, "Census 2005," available at http://www.economy.ae/Arabic/EconomicAndStatistic Reports/StatisticReports/Documents/census2005/Census%202005.pdf (Arabic).

THE UAE LABOR LAWS

Migrant workers in the UAE are covered by the Federal Law No. 8 of 1980 (the "Labor Law"). The Labor Law defines "worker" as "[a]ny male or female person who receives remuneration of any kind for work performed thereby in the services of an employer and under his management or control."[25] Significantly, however, the Labor Law exempts "[d]omestic servants working in Private residences and the like"[26] from its provision, which include chapters governing employment contracts, records and remuneration, working hours and leaves, safety and social security, employer disciplinary rules, contractual termination, indemnification, collective bargaining and labor inspections.[27] The Labor Law also prescribes penalties for violations ranging from fines to imprisonment.[28] Despite many of its relatively progressive provisions, the UAE labor law was designed in the 1970s, when policymakers "were not fully aware of the implications."[29]

Even more striking is the fact that the UAE has so far refused to implement one of the key provisions of the Labor Law mandating the establishment of a minimum wage. Article 63 of the Labor Law requires the Minister of Labor and Social Affairs to propose, to the Council of Ministers for the issuance of a Federal Decree, "minimum salary and the cost of living allowances" generally or for particular professions.[30] Despite the Labor Law's clear mandate and persistent calls by international human rights activists, this particular provision of the Labor Law has never been implemented. Noting that low wages are one of the "main grievances of construction workers" in the UAE, in July 2006 the HRW asked the then UAE Minister of Labor, Dr. Ali Abdulla Al Kaabi, why Article 63 of the Labor Law has never been implemented. Perhaps cynically, in its report later that year, the HRW wrote, "The September reply from the UAE government did not address this question."[31] Indeed, the government's failure to institute a minimum wage, despite the clear legal mandate, is emblematic of the larger problem of lackluster enforcement and weak oversight that has contributed greatly to the abuse of migrant workers' rights in the UAE.

The UAE's persistent refusal to extend the right to collective bargaining to migrant workers has in practice deprived them of the full enjoyment of the other rights enshrined in the ILO conventions. As a result, in its 2006 report, the HRW called on the UAE government to immediately ratify ILO Conventions 87 and 98 and incorporate them into the domestic labor laws.[32] In an effort to respond to widespread international criticism of its labor situation, the UAE government has attempted to implement safeguards to protect workers' rights. Recent reforms in the UAE laws have brought some changes. For example, workers have benefited from a recent change (effective January 2010) in the law that if a worker is not paid for two months, she/he can immediately file a complaint before the Ministry of Labor (MOL), as he or she is entitled to (a) file a complaint without prior notice to her/his employer, (b) she/he can claim for a cancellation of the contract, and (c) she/he can transfer the labor contract to another.[33] This would also enable the worker to avoid an absconder complaint that might be filed against him/her by the employer.[34]

More recently, in 2009, the MOL introduced a new electronic wage protection system (WPS) to address the issue of nonpayment of wages.[35] The WPS requires that the monthly staff salaries are paid directly to their bank accounts, eliminating the employers' control over delivering or withholding employee wages.[36] Approximately 80 banks and exchange stores have been authorized by the MOL to deliver this service. In case of a violation, the MOL will halt all transactions with the violator company by suspending its account on the ministry's website.[37]

The UAE government set a May 31, 2010, deadline for all employers to adopt the WPS, which would cover more than 4 million workers. As of August 2009, however, just 500,000 of the 4 million foreign workers were paid this way.[38] Furthermore, a new law announced by the MOL on May 24, 2010, has extended the summer midday working ban. The ban, which prevents laborers from working outside between the hours of 12:30 pm and 3 pm, will now be enforced from June 15 until September 15, extending the midday working ban period by one month compared to previous years, when this exemption ended in August.[39] Despite such improvements, deep structural and enforcement problems perpetuate the abuse of migrant workers' rights in the UAE.

EMPLOYMENT AND TERMINATION

As a structural matter, the existing networks of employment and recruitment networks for migrant workers are structured in a way that facilitates the abuse of migrant workers' right, not only in the period before they leave their country of origin and while in transit, but also during the entire period of their stay. Employment for noncitizens in the UAE is based on a sponsorship system involving nationals, expatriate labors, recruitment agencies, and employers. The recruitment agencies recruit labors in the country of origin and provide employers in destination countries with information regarding the employee pool's qualifications, size, and duration of occupation. These agencies carry out their functions in accordance with recruitment procedures approved by the UAE government. Also part of their own country's corporate business structure and politically well-connected, the recruitment agencies are primarily motivated by profit and often tend to take advantage of desperate migrant workers willing to pay huge sums of money for a chance to obtain employment in the UAE. Human rights organizations have argued that the labor supply companies must be held accountable for any breach of the local rules and regulations, while calling for stronger government control over them.

The UAE's sponsorship system of employment for noncitizens suffers from several flaws. First, this system links migrant workers to specific employers and precludes them from seeking alternative employment without the expressed approval of the original employer. In fact, recruitment agencies initially handle the distribution of labor to the various employers, a practice that has been likened to the gangmasters of the United Kingdom.[40] Second, this system of employment has in some cases led to the ill-treatment of migrant workers and the seizure of their passports, identity papers, or other documents. Because migrant workers often borrow money to pay recruitment agencies—a practice that is illegal under the UAE law—the majority of their subsequent wages goes toward repaying the initial debt.[41]

Law without Remedy

As an enforcement matter, quite simply there exists no powerful executive agency in the UAE to monitor or secure the rights of workers, as the existing agencies lack the necessary personnel and resources to perform the executive branch's supervisory or oversight functions. Migrant workers (whether temporary, seasonal, or circular contractual workers) face several obstacles in seeking available judicial remedies when their rights are violated. Aside from the language barrier and a general lack of knowledge about their rights, these workers are trapped in employment contracts that limit their social mobility and subject protections afforded to them to reciprocal agreements. Moreover, employers frequently withhold wages for months and confiscate passports as "security" to keep workers from quitting.[42]

Understandably, migrant workers are hesitant to challenge any of their employers' unlawful violation of their rights. An act of insubordination may subject a worker to a six-month ban or probation, which poses practical problems for the livelihood of the worker. Article 37 of Part III: Contracts of Employment, Records and Remuneration of the UAE's Labor Law reads:

> A worker may be engaged on probation for a period not exceeding six months, during which his services may be terminated by the employer without notice or severance pay, provided that a worker shall not be engaged on probation more than once in the service of any one employer. Where a worker successfully completes his period of probation and remains in his job, the said period shall be reckoned towards his period of service.[43]

Some foreign workers in Dubai have complained about unexpected termination and no gratuity paid for their services. One worker writes: "I worked in a company for more than two years. Six months ago, the company terminated me unexpectedly and did not give me my end-of-service gratuity as per law."[44] The trend toward increasing economic integration, communication and migration, however, has made it more difficult to exert absolute "social control" on migrant workers, who tend to come from countries in which labor is unionized and labor unions often resort to strikes if judicial remedies are not sufficiently or promptly provided. Given that no system is foolproof and aside from long-term structural issues of adjusting these workers to the laws of the host countries, issues of social control and the rights of migrant workers admit to no easy solution.[45]

SEX TRAFFICKING AND DOMESTIC WORKERS

Sex trafficking is a modern day form of slavery, in which a girl or woman is coerced or induced by monetary reward to provide sexual services to men. Many commentators argue that, globally, human trafficking has increased markedly since the 1990s. Some have linked the increase to globalization and the greater integration of global markets.[46] One commentator has identified four particular conditions of globalization that have worsened human trafficking in the recent years:

> First, globalization has increased and created great inequality among nations and within nations. . . . Second, globalization has accelerated the dismantling of borders to ease all trade, and exposed citizens to "unfamiliar and unpredictable forces. . . . Third, the rush to globalization encourages obsession with market goals and profit while overlooking the social and human goals. Fourth, nations are operating with antiquated institutions, struggling to deal with old problems that persist while being profoundly overwhelmed in trying to deal with new problems that have arisen.[47]

Other commentators have blamed the increase in human trafficking on the end of the Cold War. As one commentator has argued, with the end of the Cold War, "borders collapsed around the world. Countless displaced people were caught up in the fight for survival, and became easy targets for traffickers."[48] Other factors related to the Cold War, such as the financial disaster for the former states that comprised the Soviet Union,[49] the "promise" of the rich West, and the development of informal shadow markets of cross border trade in goods and labor.[50]

Lured by the promise of legitimate jobs and a brighter future, young girls and women have constituted the most visible wave of mass migrant workers in the UAE. Despite its illegality, prostitution is prevalent in the UAE. What explains its prevalence? Undoubtedly, globalization and the end of the Cold War have accelerated human trafficking in the UAE. After the fall of the former Soviet Union and the opening of China to tourism, many unscrupulous agents have become attracted to Dubai's wealth and find the easiest way to share in its spoils to be through the use of women. Today, one observer notes, "[t]he ability to buy sex so easily, while the government looks the other way, has certainly kept many of the tourist and businessmen who visit Dubai coming back."[51] The enactment of the Trafficking Victims Protection Act of 2000 (TVPA) has made sex trafficking a serious violation of Federal law in the UAE. Sex traffickers resort to both physical and psychological forms of coercion and bondage, including the use of threats of physical harm or restraint, against their victims.

The U.S. State Department 2009 Trafficking Persons Report stated that the UAE was a destination for men and women, predominantly from South and Southeast Asia, trafficked for the purposes of labor and commercial sexual exploitation. Migrant workers, who comprise more than 90 percent of the UAE's private sector workforce, are recruited from India, Bangladesh, Pakistan, Nepal, Sri Lanka, Indonesia, Ethiopia, Eritrea, China, and the Philippines. Women from some of these countries travel willingly to work as domestic servants or administrative staff, but some are subjected to conditions indicative of forced labor, including unlawful withholding of passports, restrictions on movement, nonpayment of wages, threats, or physical or sexual abuse.[52] Victims of sex trafficking can be women or men, girls or boys, but the migrant workers are overwhelmingly (90 percent) young males in their mid-20s.[53]

Trafficking of domestic workers is facilitated by the fact that the normal protections provided to workers under the UAE labor law do not apply to domestic workers,[54] leaving them more vulnerable to abuse. By the unique nature of their work in homes, domestic workers were generally isolated from the outside world making it difficult for them to access help. Restrictive sponsorship laws for foreign domestic workers often gave employers power to control their movements and left some of them vulnerable to exploitation. Some women from Eastern Europe, Southeast Asia, the Far East, East Africa, Iraq, Iran, and Morocco are reportedly trafficked to the UAE for commercial sexual exploitation. Some foreign women are also reportedly recruited for work as secretaries or hotel workers by third-country recruiters and coerced into prostitution or domestic servitude after arriving in the UAE.[55] Similarly, men from India, Sri Lanka, Bangladesh, and Pakistan are drawn to the UAE for work in the construction sector, but are often subjected to conditions of involuntary servitude and debt bondage—often by exploitative "agents" in the sending countries—as they struggle to pay off debts for recruitment fees that sometimes exceed the equivalent of two years' wages.

Currently, there is an average of one housemaid per two citizens in the UAE.[56] The vulnerability of women domestic workers in the UAE has been exacerbated by the popular attitudes that reinforce the legal imbalance resulting from exemption for the protection of domestic labor laws. Furthermore, because female domestic workers do not fall under the Labor Law, they are not legally entitled to its protections. As the 2010 Trafficking in Persons Report stated, "[t]he Government of the United Arab Emirates does not fully comply with the minimum standards for the elimination of trafficking; however, it is making significant efforts to do so."[57] The vulnerability of some migrant workers to trafficking likely increased toward the end of the reporting period as a global economic decline—noted particularly in the construction sector, the UAE's largest single employer of foreign workers—saw many laborers repatriated to their home countries where they still owed debts. Unpaid construction workers often were defrauded or forced to continue working without pay, as they faced threats that protests may destroy any chance of recovering wages owed to them.

Although the UAE government has demonstrated sustained efforts to prosecute and convict sex trafficking offenders in recent years and made modest progress to provide protections to female trafficking victims, no discernable anti-trafficking efforts have been made against the forced labor of temporary migrant workers and domestic servants. The UAE historically has not recognized people forced into labor as trafficking victims, particularly if they are over the age of 18 and entered the country voluntarily; therefore, the UAE is placed on Tier 2 Watch List.[58] In 2005, the UAE was dropped into Tier 3 in the State Department's anti-trafficking rankings.[59] In 2006, the emirate passed an anti-trafficking law that helped place it in the Tier 2 Watch List, where it remains, along with Mexico and Moldova.

One reporter noted, "I met women working as prostitutes who told me that they were doing so because they had chosen to." Sasha, for example, was trafficked from Siberia and serviced clients against her will. But then she managed to run away from her madam and decided to continue to work as a prostitute on her own. Her English was good, so I asked her why she didn't find a job as a salesperson in one of the many shopping malls in Dubai. She said she could earn more in one night as a prostitute than working a whole month in sales. And she wouldn't have to stand on her feet all day. Like many other girls I spoke with, Sasha charges $500 dirhams per hour (about US$140). She told me that the money she sends home to Siberia has allowed her family to build a house.[60]

In recent years, the law enforcement and MOL officials have attempted to apply strict laws targeting the recruiting agents and employers who are responsible for victims of trafficking and labor abuses. To improve protection of these groups the government intervention is imperative. So is collaboration with the NGOs and governments of countries from which labors flow in. The latter should be held accountable for confronting recruiting agencies that engage in trafficking. Without the cooperation and control of local recruiting agencies human trafficking cannot be significantly prevented. The UAE government must prosecute labor trafficking offenders. The UAE prohibits all forms of trafficking under its Federal Law Number 51 of 2006, which prescribes penalties ranging from one year's imprisonment to life imprisonment.

Conclusion

Migrant workers have figured prominently in all sectors of the UAE's economy, but more so in the construction industry where they have left an indelible mark on the country's infrastructure and urban development. Built over decades by migrant labors, Dubai stands out as a center of finance and reexport business of the Arabian Peninsula. Paradoxically, these workers are known as the human collateral damage of the global financial crisis that has crippled Dubai's booming housing and construction industry since 2008. When combined with food insecurity emanating from the 2008 global food crisis, the agony of migrant labor working in the UAE becomes apparent.

While some nationals have come to view migrant workers as a threat to the cultural integrity of their nation, others have cautioned against such skepticism, arguing that large-scale migration policies are needed to direct and strengthen the national economy. The UAE government needs to do a balancing job of determining the level of imported labors with that of its local needs within the context of its still emerging economy, while at the same time maintaining a reasonable capacity to defuse potential social unrest. The case for government intervention has never been more essential. The pervasive abuse of the rights of workers has led to a mounting pressure for direct government involvement. A proactive policy that seeks to improve standards and augment regulations is the best place to start. More federal control over markets is required if workers' rights are to be ensured.[61] The UAE labor department should suspend the license of an employer after proper hearing. The labor department must have a mechanism to provide for the most basic of amenities and living conditions.[62]

It is also essential to develop social support systems that protect and care for the victims of human and sexual trafficking. The UAE antihuman trafficking law (Federal Law 51, November 2006) is the first of its kind in the region.[63] A multilateral effort is needed to stem the tide of human trafficking. To prevent these abuses, there is a persistent need for a holistic approach that integrates legislation, enforcement, victim-support system, as well as bilateral and collaborative actions. This necessitates an attempt to combine domestic legislation with political and social frameworks by which new laws are implemented.

NOTES

1. The UAE is a federation of seven states, termed emirates: Abu Dhabi, Ajman, Al Fujayrah, Dubai, Ra's al Khayma, Sharjah, and Umm al Qaywayn.

2. According to the UAE's National Bureau of Statistics, the first population census in the UAE was conducted in 1968 by the Council of Developing Trucial States. http://www.uaestatistics.gov.ae. Last accessed on June 28, 2010. Even then a large percentage was expatriate Persian. See Frauke Heard-Bey, "The Gulf in the 20th Century," *Asian Affairs*, 33: 1, 3–17 (2002). See also Fred Hallliday, "Labor Migration in the Middle East," MERIP Reports, No. 59, pp. 3–17 (Aug., 1977); Frauke Heard-Bey, "The United Arab Emirates: Statehood and Nation-Building in a Traditional Society," *Middle East Journal*, Vol. 59, No. 3, Democratization and Civil Society, pp. 357–375 (Summer 2005); Onn Winckler, "The immigration policy of the Gulf Cooperation Council (GCC) states," *Middle Eastern Studies*, Vol. 33, No. 3, pp. 480–493 (1997).

3. "Preliminary Results of the General Census for Population, Housing and Establishments 2005," available on the official website of the 2005 UAE census, www.tedad.ae. Last accessed on June 28, 2010. The population for 2009 was estimated as hitting 6 million, of which more than 83 percent were migrants. Andy Sambidge, "UAE Population Hits 6m, Emiratis Make Up 16.5%," *Arabian Business Times*, June 28, 2010. The National Human Resources Development and Employment Authority expected the UAE population to rise further to 7.5 million by 2010. Andy Sambidge, "UAE Population Seen at 7.5m in 2010—study," *Arabian Business Times*, January 25, 2010. The 2010 UAE census was conducted from April 6–19, but the results have not been released yet.

4. Federal Law No. 8 on Regulation of Labour Relations, Part 2, Article 3, Section (c) states, "[d]omestic servants working in Private residences and the like" shall be exempt from the provisions of the Labor Law. *Al-Jarida al-Rasmiya*, 1980–04, No. 79, p. 26. English translation (as amended up to 2001), Abu Dhabi Chamber of Commerce and Industry, Government of the United Arab Emirates, United Arab Emirates, available at

http://www.ilo.org/dyn/natlex/docs/ELECTRONIC/11956/ 69376/F417089305/ARE11956.pdf. Last accessed on June 28, 2010. The Draft Labor Law of 2007 retains the exclusion of domestic workers from the protections afforded by the Labor Law. Instead, it proposes a new standard contract for domestic workers, which has been regarded by Human Rights Watch as "not a sufficient substitution for equal protection under the national labor laws." Human Rights Watch, "The UAE's Draft Labor Law: Human Rights Watch's Comments and Recommendations," No. 1 (March 2007), available at http://www.mafiwasta.com/hrw%20 draft%20labour%20law.pdf. Last accessed on June 28, 2010.

5. Federal Law No. 8 for 1980, Article 112 provides in part: "If the employee has been charged with premeditated crime, such as his involvement in a physical assault or robbery of property or other offenses such as the abuse of honesty, breach of trust or strikes, the said employee may be temporarily suspended from work" (emphasis added).

6. In fact, a recent ministerial resolution directed only at migrant workers banned them from employment in the country for at least one year in case of "an illegal strike or its instigation." Ministerial Resolution 707 of 2006 Regarding Rules and Regulations of Employment in the Country (UAE) for Non-Citizens, September 6, 2006, Article 13.

7. Human Rights Watch, "Building Towers, Cheating Workers: Exploitation of Migrant Construction Workers in the United Arab Emirates," November 11, 2006, available at http://www.hrw.org/en/reports/ 2006/11/11/building-towers-cheating-workers-0. Last accessed on January 4, 2009.

8. International Convention on the Protection of the Rights of All Migrant Workers and Members of Their Families, G.A. Res. 45/158, art. 2, U.N. Doc. A/45/49 (Dec.18, 1990).

9. John Lahad, "Dreaming a Common Dream, Living a Common Nightmare: Abuses and Rights of Immigrant Workers in the United States, the European Union, and the United Arab Emirates," *Houston Journal of International Law*, Vol. 31, p. 658 (2009).

10. Ibid., p. 675.

11. Ryszard Cholewinski, *Migrant Workers in International Human Rights Law: Their Protection in Countries of Employment.* Oxford: Clarendon Press, 1997, ch. 2.

12. The Human Rights Watch has called formally on the governments of India, Pakistan, Bangladesh and Sri Lanka, as well as the United States, the European Union, and Australia to formally address such issues with their counterparts in the UAE. See generally: Human Rights Watch, "Building Towers, Cheating Workers: Exploitation of Migrant Construction Workers in the United Arab Emirates," November 11, 2006, available at http://www.hrw.org/en/reports/2006/11/11/building-towers-cheating-workers-0. Last accessed on January 4, 2009.

13. Shari Garber Bax, Preface for the *Journal of the Institute for Justice and International Studies* (2005), p. vi.

14. Nisha Varia, "Sanctioned Abuses: The Case of Migrant Domestic Workers," *Human Rights Briefs*, Vol. 14, No. 3, p. 17 (2007).
15. Ibrahim Awad, "The Global Economic Crisis and Migrant Workers: Impact and Response," International Labour Organization, International Migration Programme, Geneva (2009), p. ix, available at http://www.ilo.org/public/english/protection/migrant/download/global_crisis.pdf. Last accessed on June 28, 2010.
16. United Nations Minority Rights Group, "Migrant Workers in the Gulf," Report No. 68, September 1985, p. 6.
17. John King, *Oil in the Middle East*, Heinemann-Raintree Library, 2005, p. 16.
18. United Nations Minority Rights Group, "Migrant Workers in the Gulf," Report No. 68, September 1985, p. 6.
19. Ibid.
20. Mohammad Shihab, "Economic Development in the UAE," in *United Arab Emirates: A New Perspective*, ed. Paula Vine and Ibrahim Al Abed, London: Trident Press (2001), p. 253.
21. Central Intelligence Agency, The World Factbook, United Arab Emirates Country Profile, available at https://www.cia.gov/library/publications/the-world-factbook/geos/ae.html. Last accessed on June 28, 2010.
22. David Keane and Nicholas McGeehan, "Enforcing Migrant Workers' Rights in the United Arab Emirates," *International Journal on Minority and Group Rights*, 15: 81–115 (2008).
23. Human Rights Watch, "Building Towers, Cheating Workers: Exploitation of Migrant Construction Workers in the United Arab Emirates," November 11, 2006, available at http://www.hrw.org/en/reports/2006/11/11/building-towers-cheating-workers-0. Last accessed on January 4, 2009.
24. Andrew Ross, "Away from Home: The Case of University Employees Overseas," *South Atlantic Quarterly*, 108:4, Duke University Press (2009), available at http://saq.dukejournals.org/cgi/reprint/108/4/765. Last accessed on December 30, 2010.
25. Federal Law No. 8 for 1980, On Regulation of Labor Relations, Art. 1.
26. Ibid., Art. 3(c).
27. Ibid.
28. Ibid., Art. 181 as amended by Federal Law No. 12 of 1986.
29. Rima Sabban, "Migrant Women in the Untied Arab Emirates: The Case of Female Domestic Workers," GENPROM Working Paper No. 10.
30. Federal Law No. 8 for 1980, On Regulation of Labor Relations, Art. 63.
31. Human Rights Watch, "Building Towers, Cheating Workers: Exploitation of Migrant Construction Workers in the United Arab Emirates," November 11, 2006, available at http://www.hrw.org/en/reports/2006/11/11/building-towers-cheating-workers-0. Last accessed on January 4, 2009.

32. Human Rights Watch, "Building Towers, Cheating Workers: Exploitation of Migrant Construction Workers in the United Arab Emirates," November 11, 2006, available at http://www.hrw.org/en/reports/2006/11/11/building-towers-cheating-workers-0. Last accessed on January 4, 2009.

33. This new law was mentioned to us during an interview in Sharjah, the UAE, by Aji Kuriakose, legal advisor, Al Roken and Bin Eid Advocates and Legal Consultants, Sharjah, on January 12, 2010.

34. Mohammad Al Shaiba responds to a worker whose employer has left the country and he has not received his salary for the past two months. See "Ask the Law," *Gulf News*, January 1, 2010, p. 6.

35. Ministerial Decree No. (788) of 2009 on Protection of Wages, available at http://rbsbank.ae/UAE/lp/doc/mol_degree_on_wps.pdf. Last accessed on December 26, 2010.

36. Ibid., Article 2.

37. Mohammad Ebrahim Al Shaiba, Ask the Law, "Rules on Worker Payments Must Be Strictly Followed," *Gulf News*, April 16, 2010, p. 5.

38. United States State Department, Bureau of Democracy, Human Rights and Labor, "2009 Human Rights Report: United Arab Emirates," March 11, 2010, available at http://www.state.gov/g/drl/rls/hrrpt/2009/nea/136082.htm. Last accessed on December 30, 2010.

39. See UAE Interact, available at http://www.uaeinteract.com/docs/UAE_Labour_Ministry_extends_midday_work_ban_by_one_month/41129.htm. Last accessed on May 25, 2010.

40. John Lahad, "Dreaming a Common Dream, Living a Common Nightmare: Abuses and Rights of Immigrant Workers in the United States, the European Union, and the United Arab Emirates," *Houston Journal of International Law*, Vol. 31, p. 670 (2009).

41. Ibid.

42. Human Rights Watch, "Building Towers, Cheating Workers: Exploitation of Migrant Construction Workers in the United Arab Emirates," November 11, 2006, available at http://www.hrw.org/en/reports/2006/11/11/building-towers-cheating-workers-0. Last accessed on January 4, 2009.

43. Jurists Association, UAE's Labor Law and the Ministerial Orders Implementing Federal Law No. 8 of the Year 1980. As Amended by Federal Law No. 8 of 2007, Part III: Contracts of Employment, Records and Remuneration, p. 32, Abu Dhabi, UAE Publications, 2007.

44. Dina Aboul Hosn, "Ask the Law," *Gulf News*, Friday, January 8, 2010, p. 5. In this section, Mohammad Ebrahim Al Shaiba of Al Bahar Advocates and Legal Consultants answers questions raised in a section called "Ask the Law."

45. We interviewed Dr. John T. Crist, Assistant Dean for Academic Affairs, Georgetown University, School of Foreign Service in Qatar, Doha, on January 7, 2010.

46. See, for example, Richard Poulin, "Globalization and the sex trade: trafficking and the commodification of women and children," *Canadian Women's Studies*, Vol. 22, Nos. 3, 4; Susanne Kappler, "The International Slave

Trade in Women, or Procurers, Pimps and Punters," *Law & Critique*, Vol. 1, p. 219, 235 (1990); Hilary Charlesworth et al., "Feminist Approaches to International Law," *American Journal of International Law*, Vol. 85, p. 613, 630 (1990); Ron Corben, "Asia-Rights: Open Borders Aid Sex Traffickers," *Inter Press Service*, Dec. 28, 1997.

47. Luz Estella Nagle, "Selling Souls: The Effect of Globalization on Human Trafficking and Forced Servitude," *Wisconsin International Law Journal*, Vol. 26, Spring 2008, pp. 152–155.

48. Ron Soodalter, Keynote Address, "The Commodification of Human Beings: Exploring the Reality and Future of Modern Day Slavery," *Connecticut Journal of International Law*, Vol. 25, Fall 1999, p. 40.

49. Ranee Khooshie Lal Panjabi, "Born Free Yet Everywhere in Chains: Global Slavery in the Twenty-First Century," *Denver Journal of International Law and Policy*, Vol. 37, Winter 2008, p. 2.

50. Janet Halley, Prabha Kotiswaran, Hila Shamir, and Chantal Thomas, "From the International to the Local in Feminist Legal Responses to Rape, Prostitutional Work, and Sex Trafficking: Four Students in Contemporary Governance Feminism," *Harvard Journal of Law and Gender*, Vol. 29, Summer 2006, p. 361.

51. Frank W. Hardy, "Prostitution in Dubai," available at http://sexual-abuse.suite101.com/article.cfm/prostitution_in_dubai. Last accessed on May 7, 2010.

52. U.S. State Department 2009 Trafficking in Persons Report, available at http://www.realcourage.org/2009/06/trafficking-in-persons-2009/. Pp. 292–294. Last accessed on May 7, 2010.

53. John Willoughby, " Ambivalent Anxieties of the South Asia-Gulf Arab Labor Exchange," in *Globalization and the Gulf*, ed. John W. Fox, Nada Mourtada-Sabbah, and Mohammed al-Mutawa. New York: Routledge, 2006, pp. 223–243; see especially p. 229.

54. Federal Law No. 8 for 1980, On Regulation of Labor Relations, Art. 3(c).

55. Ibid.

56. Staci Strobl, Policing Housemaids: The Criminalization of Domestic Workers in Bahrain, Cite as: 49 Brit. J. Criminology 165, *167 (2009).

57. United States Department of State, "Trafficking in Persons Report (2010)," p. 334, available at http://www.state.gov/documents/organization/142984.pdf. Last accessed on July 22, 2010.

58. United States Department of State, "Trafficking in Persons Report (2010)," available at http://www.state.gov/documents/organization/142984.pdf. Last accessed on July 22, 2010.

59. United States Department of State, "Trafficking in Persons Report (2005)," available at http://www.state.gov/documents/organization/47255.pdf. Last accessed on July 22, 2010.

60. PBS, "The Dark Side of Dubai," available at http://www.qatarliving.com/node/80024. Last accessed on May 7, 2010.

61. We interviewed Dr. Mohamed Abdulla Al Roken in Dubai on January 14, 2010. Dr. Al Roken represents Al Roken & Bin Eid, Advocates and Legal Consultants, Dubai, the UAE.
62. We interviewed Mr. Morison Menon, Chattered Accountants, Consulting Company, Dubai, the UAE on January 14, 2010.
63. The United Arab Emirates, National Committee to Combat Human Trafficking, available at http://www.nccht.gov.ae/En/Menu/index. aspx?MenuID=11&CatID=44&SubcatID=13&mnu=SubCat. Last accessed on May 25, 2010.

317,000,000 pop.

Chapter 13

Health and Human Rights in Palestine: The Siege and Invasion of Gaza and the Role of the Boycott, Divestment and Sanctions Movement

Jess Ghannam

Precis

The linkage between human rights and health rights has been well established and documented. A consensus position has emerged that insists on the inextricability between health promotion and the protection of human rights. Violations of basic health rights are now considered violations of human rights. Within the larger global context of human rights violations, the occupation and colonization of Palestine stand out as an egregious example of how the denial of health rights can lead to devastating consequences. This chapter will describe the current context of human rights violations in Palestine and the impact of these violations on health rights. Special emphasis will be afforded to the siege and invasion of Gaza and its aftermath.

A proposal for addressing the impunity of Israel and the failure of international entities—nation-states, NGOs, international judicial bodies—to hold Israel accountable for its human rights violations will be presented. The boycott, divestment and sanctions (BDS) paradigm will be presented as one strategy for establishing justice in Palestine and, in turn, for promoting health rights and an improvement in health-related quality of life for Palestinians. One component of the BDS paradigm is an international grassroots movement referred to as the academic and cultural boycott of Israeli (ACBI). The Government of Israel (GOI) deems the BDS movement a threat and has recently proposed a law that would punish Israeli academics who participated in the boycott movement. Additionally, some Israeli think-tanks have identified the BDS movement as "an existential threat" to Israel's legitimacy among nations.

Critical issues pertaining to academic freedom and freedom of education will be articulated in light of criticisms that have been offered as an argument against the boycott. Palestinian civil society has called on the international community, including all academic institutions, to engage in a comprehensive BDS project in order to end Israel's violations of human rights of the Palestinians, hold Israel accountable to international law, and end the occupation of Palestine. The academic and cultural boycott movement may represent one effective method to engage in social justice work within the larger global BDS movement.

THE CONTEXT OF HEALTH AND HUMAN RIGHTS

The right to health and wellness is considered to be among the most basic and essential human assets to be protected. Poor health can have dire consequences not only for individuals, but for families, extended families, communities, villages, cities, and nation-states. The World Health Organization (WHO) has stated that violations or the lack of attention to human rights can have serious health consequences.[1] The right to health is a fundamental part of any human right and the foundation of basic human dignity. According to the WHO, the right to enjoyment of the highest attainable standard of physical and mental health was first articulated in the 1946 Constitution of the WHO. The preamble states:

> Health is a state of complete physical, mental, and social well-being and not merely the absence of disease or infirmity. . . . Enjoyment of the highest attainable standard of health is one of the fundamental rights of every human being without distinction of race, religion, political belief, economic or social condition.[2]

This was articulated in 1946 as part of the preamble, but the 1948 Universal Declaration of Human Rights corroborates this and also mentions health as part of the right to an adequate standard of living. The right to health was again recognized as a human right in the 1966 International Covenant of Economic, Social, and Cultural Rights.[3]

Clearly, there is a long tradition within the international community and among a wide variety of human rights organizations and treaties to promote the right to health as essential to all states, nonstate actors, and developing communities. More recently, additional attention has been given by the WHO to promote the highest attainable standard of health and this has been further articulated by the Commission on Human Rights.[4]

In sum, it has been well established by the international community that health rights and human rights are inextricable and mutually dependent and that no state actor or even nonstate actor should be absolved from the protection and provision of adequate health rights as basic tenets of human rights.[5] Within this context we can better understand the implications of human rights violations carried out by the GOI and its military in the occupation of Palestine.

THE CONTEXT OF OCCUPATION IN PALESTINE

Given the well-established relationship between human and health rights, we can begin to understand the breadth and scope of human rights violations committed by the Israeli military and the GOI in Palestine as commencing even before the initial occupation in 1948 and the subsequent annexation of Gaza on the West Bank in 1967 which initiated. There began a slow, steady process of collective and individual violations of the Geneva Convention on the Palestinian civilian population. This chapter cannot comprehensively describe the scope and the magnitude of these violations and instead will be limited to a brief overview of some of these violations as they are currently manifested in the West Bank and more significantly in the Gaza Strip.

At a basic level, all occupations form the basis of human rights violations and violations of the Geneva Convention. The very fact that Israel extends its military presence throughout the West Bank in the form of checkpoints, bypass roads, and settlements means that every single aspect of Palestinian civil society is prone to the possibility of human rights violations on a daily basis. By some estimates, there are over 500 movable and immovable checkpoints dotted throughout the West Bank. These are military checkpoints staffed by the Israeli military and form the basis of the matrix of control that the Israeli military imposes on Palestinians. By doing so, Palestinians are separated from each other, from their families, from their ability to engage in gainful employment, for example, and their ability to tend to their farms.

Another element that can be construed as a human rights violation, as well as a violation of the Geneva Convention, is the separation wall, also called an apartheid wall, which Israel has erected. This apartheid wall, which is a concrete wall some twenty feet high and two to four feet thick with barbed wire in some areas, extends itself throughout the West Bank typically on the inside part of the green line. It snakes itself in such a way that it cuts deeply into the West Bank, often times bisecting Palestinian villages and cities, cutting off families and communities from one another, and making difficult, if not altogether preventing, employment. It also extends in such a way that it cuts off Palestinians from access to the Jordan Valley, one of the most fertile pieces of Palestinian land that could be used for Palestinians to sustain themselves. By virtue of the settlements, the bypass roads, and the apartheid wall, the amount of land that Palestinians on the West Bank are restricted to amounts to approximately 7 percent of original historic Palestine.

Among the most egregious of Israeli human rights violations is the widely used and accepted illegal use of torture on detained Palestinians, including women and children. Since 1967, over 650,000 Palestinians have been detained by Israel (either through civilian or military authorities).[6] Widely reported and condemned by international human rights organizations, Israel detention techniques routinely include torture on detainees and political prisoners. What is especially alarming is the use of cruel, inhuman, and humiliating techniques among Palestinian children by Israel. A recent report by the Defense for Children International (DCI) noted the widespread use of torture by Israel.[7]

According to DCI, nearly 700 Palestinian children in the West Bank alone are detained and imprisoned by Israel every year.[8] Furthermore, based on a survey in 2009 of 100 of these children, lawyers found that 69 percent were beaten and kicked, 49 percent were threatened, 14 percent were held in solitary confinement, 12 percent were threatened with sexual assault, including rape, and 32 percent were forced to sign confessions written in Hebrew, a language they do not understand.[9] Such institutionalized and systematic mistreatment is considered torture by the United Nations under international law and specifically contravenes the Convention on the Rights of the Child to which Israel is a signatory.

Gaza

Before the December 2008 invasion and the siege of Gaza, the health, economic, and basic services aspect of Palestinian life were already on the verge of collapse. According to a special focus report by the United Nations Office of the Coordination of Humanitarian Affairs, prior to the invasion, 80 percent of families in Gaza—that is, approximately 1.1 million people—had to rely on food aid compared to 63 percent prior to the siege.[10] In 2007, households were spending approximately 62 percent of their total income in food compared to 37 percent in 2004.[11] During the period of May to June 2007 alone, commodity prices for wheat flour, baby milk, rice, and flour rose some 34 percent,

30 percent, and 21 percent, respectively, according to the World Food Program (WFP).[12] During the period of June to September 2007, the number of households in Gaza earning less than 1.2 dollars per day soared from 55 percent to 70 percent, according to the WFP.[13]

Prior to the siege, the economy was also in a state of utter devastation. In September of 2000, some 24,000 Palestinians crossed in and out of Gaza every day to work in Israel, according to the World Bank.[14] Since the siege of Gaza, the figure for legal crossings into Gaza for work is zero.[15] Unemployment at the time prior to the invasion was close to 40 percent and was expected to rise, according to the Office for the Coordination of Humanitarian Affairs (OCHA) report of 2007.[16]

In the months leading up to the siege and blockade, around 250 trucks a day entered Gaza through the Sufa checkpoint with supplies, and today it remains less than a trickle of that amount.[17] Of Gaza's industrial operations, 95 percent were suspended due to the ban on raw materials and the blockade, according to the World Bank report of 2007.[18] These 95 percent of the industrial operations that were suspended occurred prior to the invasion. With respect to basic services, 40 to 50 million liters of sewage continued to pour into the sea on a daily basis, according to an OXFAM report of 2008.[19] As a result of fuel and electrical restrictions prior to the invasions, hospitals were on a regular basis experiencing power cuts lasting eight to twelve hours a day.[20] Prior to the invasion, there was a daily shortage of 60–70 percent of diesel required for hospital power generators.[21]

Regarding the specific health implications, according to the WHO report of 2007, 18.5 percent of patients seeking emergency treatment in hospitals outside of Gaza were refused permits to leave.[22] The proportion of patients given permits to exit Gaza for medical care decreased from 89.3 percent in January of 2007 to 64.3 percent in December, which at the time had been an unprecedented low. The WHO, during the period of October to December 2007, confirmed the deaths of at least 20 patients because of the denial of permits. This horrific situation represents the state of affairs in Gaza before the invasion and describes the basic state of affairs during the siege of Gaza. The siege was put in place after the Hamas government was installed in 2006, having won the elections that the international community had deemed to be fair and transparent. Israel, backed by the international community and with impunity, imposed a siege on Gaza, which amounted to collective punishment that is not only a violation of the Geneva Conventions, but also reflects a human rights violation as defined by the United Nations.

The Palestinian Center for Human Rights (PHCR) has compiled the causalities in a highly cited summary of the dead and wounded following the IDF offensive on the Gaza Strip and the following figures come from this report[23] (see exhibit 1 for a tabular summary of these findings).

By dividing Gaza into five provinces, the Northern Gaza section, the Gaza city province, the Central Gaza strip, the Khan Yunis area, and then the Southern tip in Rafah; we can begin to describe and understand the nature of the casualties and the breadth and the depth of the Israeli invasion. In the Northern Gaza District, for example, 26 bombs per square km were dropped, resulting in the deaths of 400 civilians, of these 125 children and 51 women.

In the Gaza City province, 313 civilians were killed, including 105 children and 41 women. In the Khan Younis District, 18 one- to two-ton bombs were dropped per square km, resulting in 61 civilian deaths, among these 16 children and 5 women. In the Rafah District area, 35 one to two-ton bombs were dropped per 1 square km area, resulting in 39 deaths to the civilian population, with 13 children and 1 woman among the killed. The magnitude of this assault on the civilian population of Gaza is unparalleled in this century (see Table 13.1).

When looking at the total number of dead and wounded, it was estimated that approximately 83 percent of the dead and the wounded represented civilian population, 21.8 percent were deaths among children, 8.6 percent were deaths among women, 26 percent of the wounded were children, and approximately 17 percent of the wounded were women. Many of the wounded men, women, and children subsequently perished as a result of the denial of access to medical care. As described above in the Geneva Conventions, health facilities should be protected during times of conflict.

Table 13.1 PHCR summary of deaths and injuries in Gaza during 23-day IOF offensive by province

	Total	Northern Gaza Strip	Gaza City	Central Gaza Strip	Khan Younis	Rafah
Total Number of Deaths	1,285	461	534	157	83	50
Civilian Deaths	895	400	314	81	61	39
Deaths among Children	281	125	106	21	16	13
Deaths among Women	111	54	41	10	5	1
Total Number Wounded	4,336	1,914	1,000	530	395	497
Wounded Children	1,133	591	200	140	100	102
Wounded Women	735	385	100	90	76	84

The previously cited report goes on to further describe the devastation of the attacks in other aspects of Palestinian daily life. There were upwards of 45,000 internally displaced civilians during this time, as Palestinians were not allowed to leave the Gaza Strip. Ten thousand buildings and homes were destroyed. Because a significant portion of civilian infrastructure was destroyed, including the sewage plant and the electrical grid, there were no completely functioning hospitals or clinics that could serve the dead or injured. Banned weapons were used, as will be further described below, including white phosphorus and dense inert metal explosives (DIME), and the civil infrastructure that was bombed included hospitals, schools, and UN buildings.[24] Medical providers were targeted and killed contrary to being protected by the Geneva Convention. For long periods of time during the two-week period, 800,000 people were without electricity or sanitation.[25] The WHO estimated that 95 percent of Palestinians at that time lived in extreme poverty, which amounts to less than one dollar a day, and hundreds of bodies remained unearthed for extensive periods of time. During that period Israel did not allow food, water, and medicine into the Gaza Strip, resulting in untold number of deaths and injuries. Acute medical care was delayed, prevented, or denied during that time too.

According to Physicians for Human Rights-Israel, there was evidence of damage to health facilities on January 13, 2009. This included a public health clinic destroyed by missiles and administrative buildings of the Red Crescent Society. According to a WHO publication describing the health situation in Gaza following the attacks, 48 percent of the 122 health facilities that were assessed were classified as damaged or destroyed, including 29 ambulances partially damaged or destroyed and 15 hospitals and 41 primary health care facilities damaged or destroyed.[26] Electricity and fuel supplies to health care facilities were severely curtailed, and the hospitals at this time were overwhelmed, frequently having to accommodate patients on the floor because of the lack of space.[27]

Internationally banned weapons were also used by the Israeli military against civilian populations and included the use of white phosphorus. This was clear and undeniable according to Amnesty International in their January 19, 2009, report.[28] When Amnesty International delegates visited Gaza, they found indisputable evidence of widespread use of white phosphorus. White phosphorus is a weapon intended to provide a smokescreen for troop movements in the battlefield at night. The Israeli military appeared to be using it as a weapon during daylight hours, and Amnesty International found evidence of white phosphorus wedges scattered all around residential buildings and evidence of white phosphorus burns on many of the wounded.

Furthermore, according to a report by Dr. Mads Gilbert, a member of the Norwegian triage medical team in Gaza, Israel had turned Gaza into a research laboratory to test out a new banned weapon.[29] According to Dr. Gilbert, the kinds of injuries that he had seen during the team's ten-day work in Gaza had proven that DIME was being used. DIME is believed to have strong biological effects, and Israeli planes attacked more than 50 targets in Gaza using this experimental weapon. This genotoxic 100 percent carcinogenic weapon, the Pentagon's alternative to depleted uranium-tipped bombs, kills within three months.

The Associated Press reported on January 16, 2009, that the medical system in Gaza was not only overwhelmed but was also close to collapse.[30] Health facilities numbering 16, including hospitals and primary health care services, had been damaged by the shelling and were not able to be fully functional. According to Tony Laurence, the head of the UN World Health Organization in Gaza, the attacks were "a grave violation of international humanitarian law."[31] The WHO went further to report 6 cases where the Israeli army shot at medical teams, and 12 medical personnel were killed and 17 were injured during the conflict. In 15 cases, the Israeli military attacked medical facilities and in most cases, because of lack of coordination, the wounded were left bleeding to death for anywhere from 2 to 10 hours. An open letter penned on January 14, 2009, by individuals from a number of organizations including the Israeli Information Center for Human Rights in the Occupied Territories, Center for Defense of the Individual, and Physicians for Human Rights-Israel, warned of a clear and present danger to the lives and well-being of tens of thousands of civilians in Gaza at the time, and reiterated and called upon the government of Israel and the military to honor the Geneva Convention.[32]

INTERNATIONAL ATTEMPTS TO BREAK THE SIEGE OF GAZA-THE FLOTILLA

According to a UN report issued after the Gaza invasion, the UN committee monitoring human rights abuses of Palestinians concluded that the situation in the Israeli-occupied territory of Gaza and in the West Bank was worse than it has ever been.[33] As part of the UN General Assembly international fact-finding mission, the culmination of which was a report detailing findings surrounding the Israeli attack of the flotilla of ships, there was a conference held on September 27, 2010. This conference was put together by the Office of the High Commissioner for Human Rights (OHCHR) and was based and prepared by the fact-finding mission established in June of 2010 that sought to understand the nature of the May 31, 2010, flotilla incident. That incident resulted in nine deaths and many injuries after Israeli forces intercepted and boarded a humanitarian aid flotilla, which was bound for Gaza. It would be impossible to understand the nature of the flotilla incident without having knowledge of the history of the Gaza blockade.

Since June 2007, humanitarian situation in Gaza has become a matter of increasing concern, and, in a 2010 statement by the President of the UN Security Council, the situation was described as unsustainable and the need for "sustained and regular flow of goods and people to Gaza as well unimpeded provision and distribution of humanitarian assistance through Gaza" was underscored.[34] The report depicted a dire scene where untreated sewage enters the environment on a daily basis and there are major health risks posed by dirty water supplies. The report also concluded and questioned the legality of the naval blockade in question, and this will be described in another section. The UN Commission is confident that the aid flotilla in no way posed any threat, and that the Israeli reaction was based on fears the flotilla activists would possibly gain a public relations victory. The UN mission also noted tension between the humanitarian goals of the flotilla and its political goals. There is evidence in fact that on May 30, 2010, leaders of the ship, the Mavi Marmara, decided to fight back against any attempt by Israel to board the ship, but there is little evidence of any unified command to defend the ship.

The report went on further to conclude that Israeli soldiers continued to shoot at wounded civilians as they were lying on the deck, and that the Israeli commandos used live and soft ammunition. Soldiers handcuffed detainees, dragging them by their hands and legs, and many flotilla passengers captured were not tended to medically and denied access to attorneys. Passengers were detained for 24 to 72 hours and were taken to an airport where the UN report describes that there was, "extreme and unprovoked violence," by uniformed Israeli personnel against the passengers. There is one report of an elderly passenger who was beaten as well as Irish and Turkish passengers who were physically assaulted, and scenarios in which individuals were attacked by soldiers with batons and beaten to the ground are described. One Turkish passenger recalled being taken away and kicked by a group of soldiers until police were forced to intervene.

Regarding injured passengers who were also treated in Israeli hospitals, some noted adequate care while others described that they were taunted and pressured to sign documents in Hebrew that they could not understand. A legal analysis on the treatment of the passengers within this report describes arbitrary illegal arrest and detention and, "torture and other cruel inhuman and degrading punishment," such as the perpetration of physical violence and abuse at the processing center. The mission considers these acts of torture and violence as defined in Article I of the Convention against Torture and against Article VII and X defined in the International Covenant on Civil and Political Rights.

Moreover, the passengers and crew who arrived at the prison were not technically prisoners of war but are described as being treated in a way that carries the hallmarks of a triumph of a captured prisoner. The detainees were also not allowed to contact their families. There were problems ensuring that the passengers understood the legal processes since many did not understand the nature of the proceedings given that the bulk of it were carried out in Hebrew, not a language that the majority of the passengers understood. The UN mission confirmed that a number of international laws were violated by Israel.

THE FUTURE OF ACCOUNTABILITY: BOYCOTT, DIVESTMENT, AND SANCTIONS

The end of apartheid stands as one of the crowning accomplishments of the past century, but we would not have succeeded without the help of international pressure—in particular the divestment movement of the 1980s. Over the past six months, a similar movement has taken shape, this time aiming at an end to the Israeli occupation.

Desmond Tutu

Given the vast and extensive nature of Israeli human rights violations and their consequent profound and significant impacts on the health conditions of civilian Palestinians, one conclusion that can be made is that Israeli impunity at committing these human rights violations remains unchallenged. Consistently, Israel maintains its occupation of civilian Palestinian territory as well as civilian populations and engages in activities as evidenced by the invasion in Gaza, the attacks on the flotilla, as well as the day-to-day occupation practices in the West Bank. These violations presently go unaccounted for within the international context and the various institutions that exist to hold nation-states accountable.

It can be established that nation-states, nongovernmental organizations, and judicial bodies have failed the people of Palestine. All attempts to hold Israel accountable for its actions, which include its occupation of Palestinian land, its siege of Gaza, its willful ability to engage in collective punishment, and its use of torture of Palestinians who have been held in detention, have failed and Israel continues to act with impunity.

The governing bodies that are used to hold nation-states accountable include the United Nations, the International Criminal Court, as well as the political will of various stakeholders and other nation-states. It would be easy to conclude at this time that these international entities and nation-states have failed to hold Israel to account and have failed Palestinians in their attempt to achieve a just solution. As a result, what we have witnessed is an attempt to hold Israel accountable through other methods, namely, the boycott, divestment, and sanctions (BDS) movement.

The BDS movement has been well established and described in many other contexts, especially in regard to the use of BDS in the dismantlement and delegitimization of apartheid in South Africa. In 2002, Palestinians civil society called for a global BDS movement to be engaged in to hold Israel to account for its war crimes and human rights violations. It is important to note that there have been many important BDS victories on the international stage and the following represents a small but growing international grassroots' attempt to begin to hold Israel to account and to hold it accountable for these human rights violations and what the Goldstone Report has concluded, action that amounts to crimes against humanity.

As part of the Palestinian civil society call to nonviolent resistance to the Israeli occupation of Palestine, a national Palestinian boycott divestment committee was established in 2005. The year 2010 marked the fifth anniversary of the Palestinian civil society's call for the BDS of Israel until it complies with international law and Palestinian rights. As articulated above, this movement was inspired by the South African struggle against apartheid and is rooted in a century-long tradition of the Palestinian civil and popular struggle for freedom, justice, and human rights.

The BDS call asserts the primacy of

the right to self-determination and addresses the fundamental right of three major components of the Palestinian people: 1) To live free from Israeli occupation in the Gaza Strip and the West Bank; 2) To end Israel's system of institutionalized racism and discrimination against the Palestinian citizens; and 3) For the Palestinian refugees and internally displaced great majority of Palestinian people to exercise their U.N. sanctioned right to return to their homes of origin and to receive reparations.[35]

This fundamental call for BDS is based on a progressive antiracist principle, and in the five years since this was initiated in 2005, it has been endorsed by a clear majority of Palestinian civil society. This has included consumer boycotts by a number of businesses including a number of major international retailers to review their sale of Israeli produce. This has included the Italian Supermarket Co-op, Nordiconad, and British supermarkets and Spencer & Company cooperative, which have all announced that they will cease to sell products from illegal Israeli settlements.

On March 30, 2010, campaigners from all over the world took part in the global day of BDS action of all aspects of the BDS movement.[36] The academic boycott is the most challenging form of boycott. In May 2010, the Congress of British University and College Union, the UCU, made history by voting to boycott the University Center of Ariel in Samaria, an Israeli illegal colony college in occupied Palestine. Additionally, university workers in the Canadian Union of Public Employees passed a motion calling for an academic boycott of Israel in February 2009.

THE PALESTINIAN ACADEMIC AND CULTURAL BOYCOTT OF ISRAEL

"We have to be careful not to over-exaggerate [*sic*] on this, but we also have to be careful not to ignore it," said Gerald Steinberg, a political science professor at Bar-Ilan University and cofounder of the International Advisory Board for Academic Freedom. "It is a festering wound and it needs to be countered, not ignored." "The danger is not these 15; the danger is if it (the USACBI) becomes 500" (Gerald Steinberg in the *New York Jewish Daily*, Wednesday, February 4, 2009.)

As a result of this, new ideas and analysis as to how to hold Israel accountable and put pressure on the State of Israel are emerging. One product of such ideas is the Palestinian campaign for the academic and culture boycott of Israel (PACBI). This campaign was a call from Palestinian civil society and was launched in Ramallah in April 2004 by a group of Palestinian academics. This was an additional call from a growing international BDS movement that built on the original campaign for a Palestinian call for a comprehensive economic, cultural, and academic boycott that was issued in August 2002. In July 2004, this campaign developed a statement of principles and addressed colleagues from all over the international community, urging them to "comprehensively and consistently boycott all Israeli academic and cultural institutions until Israel withdraws from lands occupied in 1967 including East Jerusalem, it removes all of its colonies on those lands, it agrees to United Nations resolutions relevant to the restriction of Palestinian refugee rights, and it dismantles the system of apartheid." This statement was met with consistent worldwide support, and it has been endorsed by at least 60 Palestinian academic, cultural, and other civil society institutions and includes unions, federations, and employees, essentially all sectors of Palestinian civil society.

Regarding the US manifestation of PACBI, US-ACBI was launched in 2009 by a group of 15 academics. Since that time, over 500 US-based academics have signed on to the call for an ACBI.[37] The ACBI is based on and formulated from the PACBI, which issued a worldwide call for the ACBI as a method for holding Israel to account for its illegal occupation of Palestine.

This Palestinian campaign for the academic and cultural boycott of Israel is inspired by and draws its inspiration from similar efforts to fight injustice in apartheid South Africa. Apartheid South Africa went through a similar BDS campaign that lasted for some 20 years, which many people believe led to the eventual dismantlement of the apartheid regime. Over the past number of years, various calls for divestment, sanctioning, and economic boycotts of Israeli products, as well as a consistent academic and cultural boycott of Israeli institutions, has resulted in a significant worldwide effort and crosses many international bodies from Europe to the United States, to Latin America, to Africa, and to Southeast Asia.

At its core, the academic and cultural boycott of Israel recognizes that "Israeli academic institutions that are mostly state-controlled and the vast majority of Israeli intellectuals and academics have either contributed directly to the Israeli occupation or at the very least have been complicit through their silence."[38] It should be noted that in Israel, contrary to the majority of other nation-states, it is required that all of its citizens except a small number participate in mandatory military conscription. Further, until the age of 45, all Israeli citizens, with the exception of those claiming religious exclusion, are required to maintain active participation in the Israeli military. Moreover, Israeli academic institutions and the Israeli military are in many ways coextensive, in that close partnerships and collaborations, inextricable if you will, exist at every level of the Israeli military and academic establishment.

In heeding the call for an academic and cultural boycott of Israel, dating back to April 2002, a number of British academics issued a call for a moratorium on European research and academic collaboration with Israeli institutions. France, in an appeal to the European Union, called for nonrenewal of its 1995 association agreement with Israel. Many other calls published in Italy and Australia were similarly articulated and, in the United States, student and faculty groups in universities from the East Coast to the West Coast were involved in the promotion of the academic and cultural boycott of Israel.

CAN BDS WORK?—ISRAEL'S CONCERN FOR BDS AND THE REUT REPORT

The international grassroots movement seeking to hold Israel to account for its violations of human rights and war crimes has grown in both breadth and depth, covering nearly every continent and sector of international social justice organizations. A recent article published in Counterpunch by James Marc Leas reviews a report from the Reut Institute, an Israeli think-tank.[39] The report was commissioned to address the viral-like growth of BDS projects and reflects the growing anxiety in Israel that it is becoming a pariah among nations. The conclusions are compelling and foreshadow the future of the Israeli response to this global phenomenon. The article

- validates two of the three demands of the rapidly growing Boycott, Divest, and Sanctions (BDS) campaign: for ending the occupation and for equal rights for all Arab-Palestinian citizens of Israel;
- admits the concern that Israel will become a pariah state if it fails to end the occupation and provide equal rights;
- asserts that "earnest and consistent commitment to ending occupation" and "to the equality and integration of its Arab citizens" are critical to combating delegitimization; and
- admits that the delegitimization crisis is "crippling" the Israeli government's freedom to launch such military attacks.

Among the more compelling conclusions is that many of the criticisms of Israel's actions can potentially harm the future integrity and viability of Israel. Clearly the potential of this mass international movement is far greater than anything initiated at the level of nation-state diplomacy or nonstate actors. The future of freedom and justice in Palestine seems to rest in the hands of this grassroots movement and not in the hands of the diplomats and NGOs. The international community of diplomats, nations, and NGOs may have failed the people of Palestine in its reluctance to take a firm stance against Israel for its human rights violations perpetrated, but grassroots international communities of individuals committed to social justice have decided to take action to bring about freedom and justice in Palestine. Only time will tell if these grassroots movements will have the power to bring justice and peace to Palestine.

NOTES

1. World Health Organization, "25 Questions and Answers on Health and Human Rights," July 2002 Health and Human Rights Publication Series, Issue No. 1.
2. Preamble to the Constitution of the World Health Organization as adopted by the International Health Conference, New York, June 19– July 22, 1946; signed on July 22, 1946, by the representatives of 61 States (Official Records of the World Health Organization, no. 2, p. 100) and entered into force on April 7, 1948. The definition has not been amended since 1948.
3. World Health Organization, "25 Questions and Answers on Health and Human Rights,". July 2002 Health and Human Rights Publication Series, Issue No. 1; See Art. 12 of ICESCR.
4. Ibid., Issue No. 1.
5. Ibid.

6. U.N. General Assembly, 12th Session. Agenda item 7. *Human Rights in Palestine and Other Occupied Arab Territories: Report of the U.N. Fact-Finding Mission on the Gaza Conflict.* Sept. 25, 2009 (A/HRC/12/48). Available at: http://www2.ohchr.org/english/bodies/hrcouncil/docs/12session/A-HRC-12-48.pdf , Sec. C.2.86. Accessed October 2010.
7. Defense for Children International. "Child Prisoners: The Systematic and Institutionalized Ill-Treatment and Torture of Palestinian Children by Israeli Authorities," June 2009. Available at http://www.dci-pal.org/english/publ/research/CPReport.pdf. Accessed October 2010.
8. Ibid.
9. Ibid., p. 11.
10. OCHA Special Focus. "The Closure of the Gaza Strip: The Economic and Humanitarian Consequences," December 2007.
11. Ibid.
12. WFP Food Security and Market Monitoring Report: Report 9, June 2007.
13. Joint agency report from Amnesty International UK, CARE International UK, Christian Aid, CAFOD, Medecins du Monde UK, Oxfam, Save the Children UK and Trocaire. "The Gaza Strip: A Humanitarian Implosion," March 2008. Available at http://www.oxfam.org.uk/resources/policy/conflict_disasters/downloads/gaza_implosion.pdf, p. 7. Accessed October 2010.
14. West Bank and Gaza Update, World Bank, Sept. 2006.
15. Joint agency report from Amnesty International UK, CARE International UK, Christian Aid, CAFOD, Medecins du Monde UK, Oxfam, Save the Children UK and Trocaire. "The Gaza Strip: A Humanitarian Implosion," March 2008. Available at http://www.oxfam.org.uk/resources/policy/conflict_disasters/downloads/gaza_implosion.pdf, p. 5. Accessed October 2010.
16. Ibid., p. 9.
17. OCHA Special Focus, "The Closure of the Gaza Strip: The Economic and Humanitarian Consequences," December 2007. Joint agency report from Amnesty International UK, CARE International UK, Christian Aid, CAFOD, Medecins du Monde UK, Oxfam, Save the Children UK and Trocaire. "The Gaza Strip: A Humanitarian Implosion," March 2008. Available at http://www.oxfam.org.uk/resources/policy/conflict_disasters/downloads/gaza_implosion.pdf, p. 4. Accessed October 2010.
18. PALTRADE Presentation to PSCC, July 2007.
19. Oxfam Jerusalem / CMWU Gaza February 2008. Cited in Joint agency report from Amnesty International UK, CARE International UK, Christian Aid, CAFOD, Medecins du Monde UK, Oxfam, Save the Children UK and Trocaire. "The Gaza Strip: A Humanitarian Implosion," March 2008. Available at http://www.oxfam.org.uk/resources/policy/conflict_disasters/downloads/gaza_implosion.pdf, p. 5. Accessed October 2010.
20. Ibid., p. 5.
21. Ibid., p. 5.

22. Ibid., p. 11.
23. *Weekly Report on Israeli Human Rights Violations in the Occupied Palestinian Territory.* March 2009. Available at http://www.pchrgaza. org/files/W_report/English/2008/pdf/weekly%20report%2003-09.pdf. Accessed October 2010.
24. U.N. General Assembly, 12th Session. Agenda item 7. *Human Rights in Palestine and Other Occupied Arab Territories: Report of the U.N. Fact-Finding Mission on the Gaza Conflict.* Sept. 25, 2009 (A/HRC/12/48). Available at http://www2.ohchr.org/english/bodies/hrcouncil/docs/ 12session/A-HRC-12-48.pdf. Accessed October 2010.
25. Ibid.
26. World Health Organization, UN Office for the Coordination of Humanitarian Affairs. "Health Situation in the Gaza Strip," Feb. 4, 2009. Archived from http://www.ochaopt.org/gazacrisis/admin/ output/files/ocha_opt_who_gazasituation_report_2009_02_04_english. pdf on 2009-02-13. http://www.webcitation.org/5eXoiYV1l. Accessed October 2010.
27. World Health Organization, "WHO Emergency Operational Plan: Gaza Crisis," Jan. 13, 2009. Available at http://www.emro.who.int/eha/ PDF/gaza_operation%20plan_13_1_09.pdf. Accessed October 2010.
28. "Israel Used White Phosphorus in Gaza Civilian Areas," *Amnesty International,* Jan. 19, 2009. Available at http://www.amnesty.org/ en/news-and-updates/news/israeli-armys-use-white-phosphorus-gaza-clear-undeniable-20090119. Accessed October 2010.
29. Cohn, Marjorie. "Israel's Collective Punishment of Gaza," *Huffington Post,* Jan. 6, 2009. Available at http://www.huffingtonpost.com/ marjorie-cohn/israels-collective-punish_b_155700.html. Accessed October 2010.
30. "Gazans Count Cost of War," *Al Jazeera,* Jan. 16, 2009. Available at http:// english.aljazeera.net/news/middleeast/2009/01/200911614413935 1463.html. Accessed October 2010.
31. Ibid.
32. F. El-Ajou, V. C. Barzilay, H. Yaakoby, et al. "A Clear and Present Danger: An Israeli Call for Urgent Humanitarian Action in Gaza," Jan. 14, 2009. Available at http://www.gisha.org/UserFiles/File/Press%20Materials/ HR%20Letter%20Gaza%20ENG%20Jan%2014-08.pdf. Accessed October 2010.
33. U.N. General Assembly, 13th Session. Agenda item 7. *Report of the Special Rapporteur on the situation of human rights in the Palestinian territories occupied since 1967, Richard Falk,* June 7, 2010. (A/HRC/ 13/53/Rev.1). Available at http://unispal.un.org/UNISPAL.NSF/0/ 33F2A0A73AB185DB8525773E00525D05. Accessed October 2010.
34. U.N. Security Council, 6326th meeting. June 1, 2010 (S/PRST/2010/9). Available at http://domino.un.org/unispal.nsf/0/e74146ac22d2d71f8 525773600528edb?OpenDocument. Accessed October 2010.
35. "Palestinian BDS National Committee Marks Five Years of Boycotts, Divestment and Sanctions," *Global BDS Movement,* Sept. 7, 2010.

Available at http://bdsmovement.net/?q=node/755. Accessed October 2010.

36. "Palestinian BDS National Committee Marks Five Years of Boycotts, Divestment and Sanctions," Palestinian Campaign for the Academic & Cultural Boycott of Israel, July 9, 2010. Available at. http://www.pacbi.org/etemplate.php?id=1305. Accessed October 2010.

37. "Press Release: USACBI Announces over 500 Academics Have Endorsed the Academic and Cultural Boycott of Israel," U.S. *Campaign for the Academic & Cultural Boycott of Israel.* USACBI, Sept. 28, 2010. Available at http://usacbi.wordpress.com/2010/09/20/press-release-usacbi-announces-over-500-academics-have-endorsed-the-academic-and-cultural-boycott-of-israel/. Accessed October 2010.

38. "About the Campaign." Palestinian Campaign for the Academic & Cultural Boycott of Israel, Dec. 21, 2008. Available at http://www.pacbi.org/etemplate.php?id=868. Accessed October 2010.

39. James Marc Leas, "Israeli Think Tank Calls for Sabotaging 'Delegitimizers' of Israel," *Counterpunch,* May 21, 2010. Available at http://www.counterpunch.org/leas05212010.html. Accessed October 2010.

LIST OF CONTRIBUTORS

Zehra F. Kabasakal Arat is Juanita and Joseph Leff Professor of Political Science and Chair of Political Science Program at Purchase College of the State University of New York. Her research focuses on democracy and human rights, with an emphasis on women's rights. Her publications include numerous journal articles and book chapters, as well as books such as *Democracy and Human Rights in Developing Countries* (1991) and *Deconstructing Images of "The Turkish Woman,"* (1998), *Non-state Actors in the Human Rights Universe* (2006); *Human Rights Worldwide* (2006); and *Human Rights in Turkey* (2007). She is the Founding President of the Human Rights Section of the American Political Science Association, Chair of the Human Rights Research Committee of the International Political Science Association, and Co-Chair of the Columbia University Human Rights Seminar.

Ali Assareh is pursuing a law degree at the New York University School of Law. His research focuses on the private sector in emerging democracies, human rights abuses in the Middle East, and Iran's economy and foreign policy.

Anthony Tirado Chase is Associate Professor of Diplomacy and World Affairs at Occidental College. His *Human Rights in the Arab World: Independent Voices* (coedited with Amr Hamzawy, University of Pennsylvania Press, June 2006) focuses on the Arab world's internal articulations of human rights and their intersections with, respectively, Islam, globalization, transnational advocacy, and the politics of key states such as Egypt, Morocco, and Yemen. He is author of a range of peer-reviewed articles dealing with human rights in Muslim societies in the context of free expression, economic development, and public health.

Lawrence Davidson is professor of History, West Chester University, PA. He is the author of *A Concise History of the Middle East* (Arthur Goldschmidt); *Foreign Policy, Inc.: Privatizing America's National Interest*; and *Islamic Fundamentalism: An Introduction*.

Manochehr Dorraj is a Professor of Political Science at Texas Christian University. He has published extensively on politics of the Middle East. Among his publications are: *From Zarathustra to Khomeini: Populism and Dissent in Iran (1990), The Changing Political Economy of the Third World (1995), Middle East at the Crossroads (1999)*, coeditor, *Iran Today: An Encyclopedia of Life in the Islamic Republic. 2 volumes (with Mehran Kamrava, 2008)*.

Nader Entessar is Professor and Chair of the Department of Political Science and Criminal Justice at the University of South Alabama. His areas of research have focused on Iran's foreign policy, ethnic issues in the Middle East, and North-South relations. His most recent book is *Kurdish Politics in the Middle East*, which will be released later this year by Rowman and Littlefield/Lexington Books.

Barbara Rieffer-Flanagan is an Associate Professor at Central Washington University in Washington State. Her research interests revolve around Human Rights and Humanitarian Politics and Religion and Politics. She has published a book and articles on Religious Nationalism, Human Rights in Iran and The International Committee of the Red Cross.

Jess Ghannam is Clinical Professor of Psychiatry and Global Health Sciences at the University of California, San Francisco, and Adjunct Professor of Ethnic Studies at San Francisco State University. He is a Psychoanalyst and practices in San Francisco and the East Bay. Dr. Ghannam specializes in working with chronic illness, including chronic pain and cancer. He also works and does research in the area of Global Health and Post Traumatic Stress Disorder. Dr. Ghannam is also a Qualified Medical Examiner (QME) for the State of California.

Bahey eldin Hassan has served as Director of the Cairo Institute for Human Rights since 1994. He is a Founding Member of the Egyptian Organization for Human Rights and served as its Secretary General from 1988 to 1993. He is also the recipient of the 1987 Annual Journalism Award of the Egyptian Press Syndicate for unique coverage of Lebanon war camps. Mr. Hassan is a lecturer and author on human rights issues and serves on the executive and advisory committee of various international human rights organizations.

Turan Kayaoğlu is an Associate Professor of International Relations at University of Washington, Tacoma. He is the author of *Legal Imperialism: Sovereignty and Extraterritoriality in Japan, the Ottoman Empire, and China* (Cambridge University Press, 2010). His current research focuses on religion and politics in international organizations, particularly Islamic politics in the United Nations.

Shadi Mokhtari is an Assistant Professor at the School of International Service at American University. She is the Editor in Chief of the *Muslim World Journal of Human Rights* and the author of *After Abu Ghraib: Exploring Human Rights in America and the Middle East* (Cambridge, 2009), which was selected as the cowinner of the 2010 American Political Science Association Human Rights Section Best Book Award.

Mahmood Monshipouri is an Associate Professor of International Relations at San Francisco State University. He specializes in human rights, globalization, and Middle Eastern Politics. He is the author of *Islamism, Secularism and Human Rights in the Middle East* (Lynne Rienner Publishers, 1998), coeditor of *Constructing Human Rights in the Age of Globalization* (M. E. Sharpe, 2003), and the author—most recently—of *Muslims in Global Politics: Identities, Interests, and Human Rights* (University of Pennsylvania Press, 2009). He is currently working on a book manuscript entitled, *Terrorism, Security, and Human Rights* (forthcoming).

Halim Rane is the Deputy Director of the Griffith Islamic Research Unit and a lecturer in the National Centre of Excellence in Islamic Studies at Griffith

University in Australia. He is the author of the highly praised book *Reconstructing Jihad amid Competing International Norms* (published by Palgrave Macmillan). His main areas of research and publication include the philosophy of Islamic law, jihad, Israel-Palestine, and political Islam. He is currently completing a forthcoming book entitled *Islam and Contemporary Civilization* (published by Melbourne University Press).

Jonathon Whooley is a Ph.D. candidate in the Department of Political Science at the University of Florida. He specializes in the Middle East and North Africa. He is currently working on issues of Pan-Arabism in the current uprisings in the Middle East as his dissertation topic.

INDEX